GENGHIS KHAN

www.**booksattransworld**.co.uk

Also by John Man

Gobi: Tracking the Desert
Atlas of the Year 1000
Alpha Beta
The Gutenberg Revolution

GENGHIS KHAN

Life, Death and Resurrection

JOHN MAN

BANTAM PRESS

LONDON • NEW YORK • TORONTO • SYDNEY • AUCKLAND

TRANSWORLD PUBLISHERS
61–63 Uxbridge Road, London W5 5SA
a division of The Random House Group Ltd

RANDOM HOUSE AUSTRALIA (PTY) LTD
20 Alfred Street, Milsons Point, Sydney,
New South Wales 2061, Australia

RANDOM HOUSE NEW ZEALAND LTD
18 Poland Road, Glenfield, Auckland 10, New Zealand

RANDOM HOUSE SOUTH AFRICA (PTY) LTD
Endulini, 5a Jubilee Road, Parktown 2193, South Africa

Published 2004 by Bantam Press
a division of Transworld Publishers

Copyright © John Man 2004

Maps by Hardlines

A catalogue record for this book is available from the British Library.
ISBN 0593 050444 (cased)
0593 053265 (tpb)

Typeset in 11½/14½pt Sabon by
Falcon Oast Graphic Art Ltd

Printed in Great Britain by
Mackays of Chatham plc, Chatham, Kent

1 3 5 7 9 10 8 6 4 2

Papers used by Transworld Publishers are natural, recyclable products made from
wood grown in sustainable forests. The manufacturing processes conform to the
environmental regulations of the country of origin.

Where is Genghis Khan? He is not dead. What happened was this:

There was a king in a far country with a daughter fair as the sun. Genghis Khan asked for the maiden. The king secretly said to his daughter: Here is a knife, very small and very sharp. Hide it in your clothes, and when the time comes you know what to do. As Holy Genghis lay with her, she took out the knife and castrated him. Genghis cried out when he felt the cut, and the people came in, but Genghis only said to them: Take this girl away; I wish to sleep.

He slept and from that sleep he has never awakened. But would not Holy Genghis heal himself? When he is healed, he will awake and save his people.

Mongol folk tale, adapted from
Owen Lattimore, *Mongol Journeys*

Genghis Khan is a spirit for all of us.

Sharaldai, theologian,
Mausoleum of Genghis Khan, Inner Mongolia

For Dushka, Will, Em,
Tom and Jonathan

CONTENTS

MAPS

ILLUSTRATIONS

Mongols Besieging a Citadel, thirteenth century, Persian School, MS 7926206 f. 149, Bibliothèque Nationale, Paris/Bridgeman Art Library, London; fragment of thirteenth-century lustreware found at Merv, the Mausoleum of Sultan Sanjar, Merv, and Little and Great Kiz Kala, all © Ancient Merv Project, Institute of Archaeology, University College London.

Mongol horsemen in combat from *Jami al-Tawarikh* by Rashid ad-Din, fourteenth-century Persian School, MS sup. pers. 1113 f. 231v, Bibliothèque Nationale, Paris.

Second section

Boys' horse race near Ulaanbaatar, James L. Stanfield/ National Geographic Image Collection.

Ch'ang-Ch'un Travels to Meet Genghis Khan, Chinese painting, © Ancient Art and Architecture Collection, London; *Genghis Khan as an Old Man*, painting on silk, National Palace Museum, Taipei, Taiwan/Bridgeman Art Library; Buddha, Xumi Shan, © John Man; colossal Buddha in Bamian, © Paul Almasy/Corbis.

Liupan Shan, all photos © John Man.

Funeral Cortège of Genghis Khan, Moghul miniature, *c*.1600, MS Or. 12988 f. 2a, British Library, London; contemporary Mongolian painting of the funeral cortège, photo © John Man.

Almsgiver's Wall, © John Man; reconstructions of a Mongol movable *ger*: line after Yule-Cordier; photo © John Man.

Main image: Karakorum, © Dean Conger/Corbis; *Battle of Leignitz*, manuscript illumination, © Ancient Art and Architecture Collection, London; memorial at Mohi, Hungary, © John Man; *Japanese Warriors Attacking a Mongol Boat*, by Nagataka Tosa, Tokyo National Museum. TNM Archives – http://TnmArchives.jp

Main image: Exterior of the mausoleum of Genghis Khan, © John Man; mobile shrine, 1936, photograph by Owen Lattimore, courtesy John Lattimore, from the Museum of Archaeology and Anthropology, Cambridge; Sainjirgal and interior of the mausoleum, © John Man.

On Holy Mountain, all photos © John Man.

Contemporary Mongolian strip cartoon; birthday celebrations for Genghis Khan, 1990, Ulaanbaatar, © Paul Harris.

A NOTE ON SPELLING

Genghis v. Chingis

In English the name has several spellings, the most common being Genghis, pronounced 'Djengis', with the first *g* soft as in *general*, the second *g* hard as in *guest*. Both spelling and pronunciation are faulty, a fault often compounded by English-speakers making the first *g* hard as well as the second. The soft first *g* of English (and French) derives from Persian and Arabic transliterations. There is no accepted national, let alone international norm. The old Mongol spelling of his name, still current in the vertical script of Inner Mongolia, transliterates as Chinggis, which is how some fastidious academics spell him. He is in fact pronounced Chingis (*ch* as in *church*; *g* as in *finger*, not as in *singer*), which is how he is spelled in modern Mongolian (and Russian). This usage is growing; but not, my publisher felt, fast enough to ensure universal recognition. The world, it seems, is not yet ready to abandon 'Genghis' – so thus he remains in this book.

For other Mongol names, I have mainly opted for a transliteration that best represents the modern Mongol.

Pinyin v. Wade–Giles

The two systems of transliterating Chinese still overlap. I have gone for whichever seems more appropriate in context, using pinyin mainly for modern names, Wade–Giles mainly for historical ones.

ACKNOWLEDGEMENTS

My thanks to the following for their help and guidance.

Overall, Charles Bawden, Emeritus Professor, and former Professor of Mongolian at the School of Oriental and African Studies, London, who planted the seed, and Bayarmandakh Gaunt, Mongolian and Inner Asian Studies Unit, Cambridge, who nurtured it; Igor de Rachewiltz, School of Pacific and Asian Studies, Australian National University, especially for sharing his experience of Burkhan Khaldun at a crucial moment; Chris Tyler-Smith, Department of Biochemistry, Oxford University, for his help on Genghis's genetic legacy.

On and in China, Sainjirgal, former Chief Researcher, Genghis Khan Mausoleum; Sharaldai, theologian, Genghis Khan Mausoleum; Driver Xiao and Driver Chog; Lars Laaman, History Department, School of Oriental and African Studies, London, for his help with Sharaldai (see Bibliography) and his translator, Geok Hoon Williams; Dr Moira Laidlaw, Teachers' College, Guyuan, Ningxia; the incomparable Jorigt, and Nasanbayar who introduced us, both of the Mongolian Language Institute, School of Mongolian Studies, Inner Mongolia University, Hohhot; Jorigt's brother-in-law Baatar in Zamyn Uud; Ruth Dunnell, Associate Professor of Asian History and Director of International Studies, Kenyon College, Gambier, Ohio, for sharing her expertise on Xi Xia; Nachug, Director, Institute for Genghis Khan Studies, Edsen Khoroo (Genghis Khan Mausoleum); Du Jian Lu, Xi Xia Institute, Ningxia

University; Chen Kun, Director and Yan Shi Zhong, Vice-Director, Guyuan Museum; Luo Feng, Director, Ningxia Archaeological Institute; Grace (Zhao Shu), Hohhot.

On and in Mongolia, Dalai, historian, Ulaanbaatar; Graham Taylor, Karakorum Expeditions, Ulaanbaatar; Erdenebaatar, Institute of Animal Husbandry, Ulaanbaatar; Professor Tsogt-Ochir Ishdorj, Head, Department of Historiography, History Institute, Mongolian Academy of Science; Luvsandamba Dashnyam, President, Mongolian Knowledge University; Baatamdash, philologist and historian; John Woods, Professor of Middle Eastern History, University of Chicago; my Mongol guides, Goyotsetseg Radnaabazar (Goyo) and Tumen; drivers Khishig and Erdenebaatar; Baatartsogt, Former Director, Khenti Museum, Öndörkhan; Gansukh, Zavia Tour Company, for advice on Burkhan Khaldun; Oyun Sanjaasuren, Member of the Great State Khural, leader of Citizens' Will-Republican Party, Head of Zorig Foundation.

On and in Central Asia and Europe, David Morgan, Professor of History, University of Wisconsin-Madison; Georgina Herrmann, Director, International Merv Project, Institute of Archaeology, University College, London; Andi Szegedi, for getting me to Mohi.

The quotations from *The Secret History* are for the most part directly from or adapted from Onon, with occasional reference to Cleaves.

This book would not have been possible without the unstinting support of Doug Young at Transworld and his team: Simon Thorogood, Gillian Somerscales, Sheila Lee, Fiona Andreanelli and Hardlines. Heartfelt thanks, finally, to Felicity Bryan for making it happen; and to my wife, Timberlake, for her support and encouragement.

John Man would be happy to hear from readers at: johngarnetman@ukonline.co.uk

INTRODUCTION:
ON DEATH AND HOW
TO SURVIVE IT

IN MARCH 2003 AN EXTRAORDINARY ARTICLE APPEARED IN THE *American Journal of Human Genetics*. A group of 23 geneticists had been studying the DNA from some 2,000 men across Eurasia. To their surprise, they found a pattern common to several dozen of their sample men, *irrespective of where they came from*. The same genetic pattern, with slight local variations, ran through sixteen population groups scattered across the whole territory, from the Caspian to the Pacific. If the proportion of men with this pattern (8 per cent of the sixteen groups) is extrapolated across the entire population of that area, the startling conclusion is that 16 million men are in effect part of one vast family.

How are we to explain this? The data came from a study of Y-chromosomes, which men possess and women do not. Each man has a pattern on his Y-chromosome that is his unique signature, but the signatures have similarities which allow geneticists to spot family relationships and represent them in family trees called 'star-clusters' (because they are drawn as star-bursts, not 'trees'). The first step was to analyse the star-clusters, and trace them back through time and space, pinpointing their 'most recent common ancestor'. Working with 34 generations and allowing 30 years for a generation, the team placed the common ancestor about 1,000 years ago, a median figure with a margin of error of up to 300 years either side (30 years per generation sounds a little high to me; reduce it to, say, 25, and the date of the most recent common ancestor comes down to 850 years ago). Moreover, most of the slightly different local variations were represented in just one of the selected areas – Mongolia.

This suggested a startling hypothesis: that one man living in Mongolia in the twelfth century had scattered his genetic material across half of Eurasia, with the result that it is now shared by one in 200 of all men living today.

Listen to Chris Tyler-Smith at Oxford's Department of Biochemistry on what happened next:

'We knew there was something extraordinary in the data as soon as Tatiana Zerjal, the D.Phil. student doing the analysis, drew the first network. The star-cluster stood out because of the high frequency, large numbers of neighbours, and distribution in many populations. We had never seen such a thing before. You can tell at a glance it represents a single extended family.

'Tatiana immediately said: "Genghis Khan!"

'At first it seemed like a joke, but as we accumulated more data and did the calculations to determine the most likely time and place of origin, this turned out to be the best explanation.'

Proof came when the researchers placed the 16 selected groups on a map of the empire created by Genghis in the early thirteenth century. The two made a perfect fit. Actually, one group, the Hazaras of Afghanistan, lay just outside the borders – but that fitted too, because Genghis was in Afghanistan for a year or so in 1223–4, before retreating back to Central Asia.

It is conceivable that the common ancestor of these 16 million males was one of Genghis's immediate forebears; his brothers may have shared the same pattern. In any event, though, it was Genghis who was responsible for scattering this genetic signature across northern China and Central Asia between 1209 and his death in 1227. Beautiful women were part of the booty in warfare, and it was a statement of leadership to demand the best of the bunch and be given them by subordinate officers. Genghis was a stickler for doing this correctly: it was a way not only of asserting his authority but also of displaying his generosity, since the girls could be handed on as gifts to his loyal generals. Genghis was no libertine, but he was certainly no ascetic either, and he had access to many hundreds of girls in the course of 40 years of empire-building. Let us conservatively grant him 20 children – it could have been hundreds – 10 of whom are boys, all inheriting the same pattern on their Y-chromosomes. Let us say that each son himself produces two sons. The consequences of doubling the number of Genghis's male descendants every generation for over 30 generations are so dramatic that the calculation escapes from the real world before its conclusion. After five generations – by about 1350 – he has a trivial 320 male descendants; but five generations later, in 1450–1500, he has 10,000; after 20 generations he has 10 *million*; and after 30, impossible billions.

To find 16 million descendants today, then, is well within the confines of reality. It sounds as if our progenitor's reproductive capacity must have been terrific to achieve this. It is tempting to attribute astonishing qualities to the mutation that threw up a man who achieved such power. We might posit a ruthlessness gene or super-stud performance. In fact, the particular genes this group of researchers studied are neutral; all they do is determine sex. So there must have been some other factor at work to ensure the survival of the Genghisid line. As Chris Tyler-Smith and his co-authors state, it can only be sheer political power with a vast geographical reach. Power did for Genghis and his close relatives what the fan-tail does for peacocks. The paper concludes: 'Our findings demonstrate a novel form of selection in human populations on the basis of social prestige.'[1] Sociologists and gossip columnists know about the sexual success of alpha males, but this is the first time it has been seen in action in evolutionary terms. Genghis was the most alpha of all alpha males.

It is fashionable these days to seek a genetic explanation of behaviour. Here, though, it is behaviour that lies behind the genetics, and it all goes back to a character – composed of strategic genius, drive, leadership skills, ruthlessness and many other traits – emerging on the Mongolian grasslands some eight and a half centuries ago.

This book is an attempt to realize an ambition conceived over three decades ago, when I wanted to travel somewhere really, really remote. Mongolia seemed as remote as I could hope for. In preparation, I started to learn Mongolian, and read something of Genghis Khan. Youth passed into middle age. Only then did the journeys start, in an attempt to understand the impact Genghis had on his world, and on ours.

Some impact, as it turned out. Genghis was driven – by poverty and humiliation (as we would say), by Heaven's command (as he claimed) – into a life of conquest, becoming the founder of the world's most extensive land empire, and also a sort of immortal, living on not only in the genes of his descendants but also in a world that was forever changed by the outrush of his nomadic warriors. So the quest involved journeys of two kinds: back in time, with the help of as many

[1] Tatiana Zerjal et al., 'The Genetic Legacy of the Mongols', *American Journal of Human Genetics*, 72, March 2003.

books as I could find; and across Inner Asia, from the mountains of Genghis's youth, to the scenes of many of his conquests, to a hidden valley where he may possibly have died, and finally to the sacred mountain which he regarded as the source of his divine inspiration and where, in all probability, he lies in a secret grave. But he does not lie quietly. His empire brought Mongolia and China together, with startling social and political consequences that rumbled down the centuries, and rumble on today. Everywhere the Mongols rode, the present is haunted by the shade of Genghis.

In December 1995 the *Washington Post* proclaimed Genghis 'the most important man of the last thousand years'. Why? Because 'the big story of the past millennium is that a single species fully exerted its will upon the earth.' Back in the year AD 1000, there were fewer than 300 million people in the whole world (some estimates claim as few as 50 million), and most of them didn't even know where they were in relation to other nations and other continents. No Eurasian people, except a few dozen Vikings, knew of America; and no-one from the northern hemisphere, except perhaps a few hardy Phoenicians, had travelled to sub-Saharan Africa. Polynesians, who had peopled the Pacific, knew nothing of Australia. Though Asians traded with the eastern remnants of the Roman empire, they knew virtually nothing of Europe. Overall, every culture lived confined by climate, geography and ignorance.

Now the world has become a village. How did this happen? Technology, economics, disease and many other vast, impersonal forces played their roles. So did countless individuals. Some leaders, inventors, explorers, thinkers and artists thrust peoples and technologies together more than others. This 'Mr Khan', as the *Post*'s researcher referred to him, certainly did.

Genghis's conquests forged new links between east and

west. He and his successors built or rebuilt the foundations of modern China, Russia, Iran, Afghanistan, Turkey, Syria, Tibet, the new countries of Central Asia, Ukraine, Hungary, Poland. The conquests realigned the world's major religions, influenced art, established new trade patterns. The effects remain as keystones in Eurasian history.

But in *world* history? Surely all this does not compare to the revolution initiated by the greatest leap forward in the formation of our global village – the European discovery of America (or rather its rediscovery, the link made by the Vikings around 1000 having vanished from memory)? If one has to choose a man of the millennium, does not Columbus take precedence over Genghis?

In a word: no. Columbus was far more an expression of his age than Genghis. If he hadn't opened up the New World, someone else would have done, because many others besides Columbus were being driven to explore. They and their backers were set on reaching China. Why China? Because its wealth, carried along the so-called Silk Road, had been legendary from Roman times until the rise of Islam in the seventh century limited trade; and because Marco Polo, on his travels there two centuries before Columbus's journey, had confirmed it to be the greatest source of wealth in the world, under the command of the great khan, Khubilai (or Kubla, as he is widely known in the English-speaking world). Signor Polo managed to get to China because by the thirteenth century the route across Eurasia was open again; and it was open because the Mongols were ruling from eastern Europe to China at the time, with Khubilai at their head; and Khubilai ruled because he had inherited his imperial role from his grandfather, Genghis.

When the Mongol empire splintered, Europeans were again barred from making the journey to China by land, blocked by newly revived Islamic cultures. Of course, trade flowed along the sea routes; but that journey was virtually impossible for

Europeans, because the routes were controlled by Arabs, Indians, south-east Asians and the Chinese themselves. It was Columbus's big idea to head round the world the other way, westward, over the unknown ocean, and short-circuit the route to China. America just happened to be in the way. Thus, by a series of coincidental knock-on effects down almost three centuries, Genghis's vision of empire made a crucial contribution to the rediscovery and colonization of the New World.

And it all so nearly came to nothing. In August 1227 Genghis had already conquered much of Central Asia, and was on the point of seizing his greatest prize, northern China, which would be the key to ever-wider conquests, when he died. The news might well have put new heart into the Mongols' enemies, and brought a quick end to Genghis's imperial dream. For a moment, all Eurasia, totally unaware, was balanced between two possible universes. As it happened, the death was kept secret, as he wished, and one of those possibilities popped out of potential existence. August 1227 marks one of the most significant and little-known turning-points in history.

Secrecy is an important theme in this book, and two great secrets still underpin Genghis's current stature: how and where he died; and how and where he was buried. The first secret allowed his heirs time to accommodate themselves to his death, and time to fulfil his dreams of conquest. The second secret explains in large measure his survival in the hearts and minds of ordinary people today.

The empire, brought to its high point by Genghis's successors, broke into separate entities – Chinese, Central Asian, Persian, Russian – and seeped away in a gradual process of transmutation and dissipation. To research the effects of the Mongol empire today is to become the historical equivalent of a radio astronomer, listening for the whispers of the Big Bang. One of those whispers has just been heard and magnified by Chris Tyler-Smith and his 22 associates. There are many others in the outlying regions of what was once the Mongol empire.

But in his heartland, Genghis's name sounds loud and clear, his brutalities forgotten or ignored in the rush of adulation. In Mongolia, after 70 years of Soviet-inspired suppression, people are free to parade his image, honour his birthday and name all manner of things after him – pop groups, beer, sports teams, institutes. In China, he is the revered founder of a dynasty, the Yuan.

And in both nations, Mongols worship him, in increasing numbers; for Genghis has become divine, the central figure in an ancient cult that now shows extraordinary signs of evolving into a new religion. Its heart lies in the Chinese province of Inner Mongolia, in a remarkable building known to Chinese as the Mausoleum of Genghis Khan. It is more accurately called the Lord's Enclosure, the name the Mongols gave it, for it is not a true mausoleum, having never contained a body. Here, Genghis's spirit is honoured in a combination of Buddhist and shamanistic rituals, as ancestor, dynastic founder and divinity. A 4-metre marble statue of Genghis, seated with hands on knees, is a focal point for numerous observances; worshippers burn incense-sticks and mutter prayers to 'relics'; murals portray Genghis as the genius who built a bridge between east and west, across which flow scholars, merchants and artists, lost in wonder, love and praise.

There are several curious things about the temple. It is modern; it is supported by China, in effect claiming the soul of Genghis as the founder of the Yuan dynasty; and, strangest of all to me, his cult has genuine religious aspirations, in which Genghis is emerging as a power through whom the true adept may make contact with the Mongols' overarching divinity, Eternal Heaven.

Genghis, reborn in spirit by the faith of his adherents, is more now than a help in ages past; he is a spiritual hope for years to come. It is a very strange transformation for a man born in obscurity, impotence and poverty.

I

ROOTS

1

SECRETS OF *THE SECRET HISTORY*

IT IS A HOT SUMMER'S DAY IN MID-JULY 1228 ON THE GRASSLANDS of central Mongolia. Most such days, a lone horseman would hear skylark song pouring from the clear blue sky, and the fizz of grasshoppers underfoot. Most such days, this apron of pasture, sloping down to a stream and a line of low hills beyond it, would be almost empty, save for a round tent or two, a herd of sheep, a few tethered horses. But on this day, other sounds drown the songs of skylarks and grasshoppers. The place is being transformed by a courtly gathering of epic proportions. Huge four-wheeled wagons rumble in, drawn by teams of a dozen or more oxen, 7-metre platforms bearing tents of felt and silk, some round in the Mongolian style, some square, each a mobile palace for a prince and his entourage. Commanders in chain-mail or armour of overlapping plates yell greetings. Family groups – most members on horses and camels, senior women in two-wheeled carts – accompany herds of sheep, goats, camels and horses, all spreading slowly over the steppe until they range out to the hills in their thousands, and downstream, southwards for several kilometres, to the banks of a broad and shallow river. From groaning camels and horse-drawn carts, Muslim and Chinese slaves unload the wall-lattices and rolls of felt needed to assemble smaller tents. Guards dressed in padded gowns and leather helmets keep order from horseback, short bows and a dozen different types of arrow slung at their waists. Herdsmen, dressed in wraparound ankle-length *deels*, slaughter sheep by the score for the feasting to come. Children gather dried dung for fuel and stack it in piles, while in the smoke-filled tents, blessedly free from the flies that pester on the steppe outside, women churn fermenting milk in leather bags to make milk-beer and milk-brandies.

There had been gatherings of this scale before, but never of this importance. The Mongols were now, after two decades of fighting, victors of campaigns in Central Asia, southern Russia and western China. Some of those meeting that summer in Mongolia came from Uzbekistan, some from Manchuria, from Xinjiang, from the newly conquered farm-lands of northern China. Their leader, Genghis, had died the previous year, having raised his people from insignificance, founded a nation and set both on the path to empire. His 40-year rule and its triumphs proved the force of his claim that he was the chosen one, under the protection of Eternal Heaven. His will had now to be done. The gathering was needed to confirm the succession of Genghis's chosen heir, his third son Ogedei.

It would also mark a new beginning, to fulfil the grand strategy sketched out by Genghis when he was on the verge of the greatest conquest yet: the seizure of all China, some-thing that no other 'barbarian' ruler from beyond the Great Wall had ever achieved. Yet even this was only a part of the vision inherited from him. Many of those gathering in 1228 had heard that westward, beyond Muslim lands, beyond the plains and forests of Russia, there were still other worlds to conquer: the grasslands of Hungary, and then perhaps even the ripe cities of western Europe. To achieve total victory, to fulfil their manifest destiny of world dominion, would demand a skill and ferocity to match those of their departed ruler, and utter subjection to his will. A new nation, a new empire was about to emerge as Eurasia's most powerful entity.

Why meet here? There is another element in this scene, an unlikely one for a culture of wandering herdsmen and far-ranging cavalry, but central to this particular gathering. It is a collection of stone buildings running in a rough line, like one side of a street, for about half a kilometre. The buildings are overlooked by a flattened mound, surmounted by pillars supporting an open-sided roof. Steppe-dwelling herdsmen have no need for buildings. Yet these sturdy structures have obviously been standing for many years. They are in fact the permanent core of a military headquarters, surrounded on occasion by arrays of tents and carts and men-at-arms and horses by the thousand. The pavilion on the mound does threefold duty as a reviewing stand, conference centre and shamanistic temple.

The place, originally named Aurag, was the Mongols' first fixed capital, founded when they began to dream of unity and conquest, some time in the twelfth century. It was chosen for its strategic position, guarding a route into the northern mountains that were the tribe's womb, yet also looking south-ward, the auspicious direction to which Mongols turn their tents. It also offered the benefits of healing waters from an ancient spring nearby – *aurag* is an old Mongol word mean-ing 'source'. To the south, for 600 kilometres beyond the river, lay open steppe giving way gradually to the gravelly expanses of the Gobi desert – one vast highway for those prepared to cross – and then the Yellow River, the final barrier before that source of wealth and danger: China. From Aurag, the Mongols could raid, gather reinforcements, conquer and, if necessary, flee to the protection of their mountain heartland.

Though Aurag has always been known to the Mongols themselves, few outsiders have ever heard of it. It has hardly rated a mention in history because it was abandoned shortly after this gathering occurred. Genghis had ordered a new capital further west, in a place better suited to dominate his growing empire. Soon, it would become famous as Karakorum, and its rise in the mid-thirteenth century would leave Aurag to collapse and vanish from history, if not from folk memory. Over the centuries, even its original name was lost. When the old Mongol word *aurag* fell from use, popular etymology seized upon something that sounded similar and had equally suitable connotations – Avraga, meaning both 'huge' and 'champion' (a term given to top-level wrestlers). Mongol orthography has its vaguenesses, so the central *ra* may be inverted. On maps, if it's there at all, you see it both ways: Avarga, Avraga. Neither properly represents its pronunciation, *avrag*, because the final *a* is an historical appendix. Let's go with 'Avraga'.

Over the centuries, Avraga's stones sank into the soil and it became a Mongolian Camelot, a place of legend with no material substance to it. But in 1992 a team of Japanese-backed archaeologists arrived with ground-penetrating radar. The Three Rivers Project, named after the three rivers that drain the Khenti mountains, aimed to find Genghis's grave. It failed; but its members made many important finds (and many claims, some of them pretty wild and contradictory, to which we shall return later in our story). Using their radar to survey Avraga's dozen enigmatic mounds, the Three Rivers team recorded echoes that suggested the presence of ditches and the remains of walls. Their report was superficial, and actual excavation amounted to no more than a single pit that revealed some undatable stonework. Still, this was the first hard evidence that Avraga had once been a reality.

*

The gathering in Avraga in 1228 marked more than a strategic and political turning-point; it was an inspiration. The Mongols knew they were in the midst of great events. They were already a greater people than they had ever been, greater than any they had yet encountered except the Chinese, and they had every intention of setting their bounds wider still and wider. How had this miraculous change come about? Many of those now meeting in Avraga had been with Genghis since the start of his conquests, and a few of the oldest had known him in his childhood, almost 60 years before. Together, as a collective memory, they could surely explain the transformation to themselves and to future generations.

And this was the perfect opportunity. For among the princes, officers, guards and family members there were those whose task it was to entertain assemblies with tales drawn from legend and history. Like all societies dependent for communication on word of mouth, the Mongols had bards, poets and storytellers who commuted between grassland camps and tent-palaces. They even became the subject of their own stories:

How Tales Originated among the Mongol People

Once upon a time, plague struck the Mongols. The healthy fled, leaving the sick, saying 'Let Fate decide whether they live or die.' Among the sick was a youth named Tarvaa. His spirit left his body and came to the place of death. The ruler of that place said to Tarvaa, 'Why have you left your body while it is still alive?' 'I did not wait for you to call me,' he replied, 'I just came.' Touched by his readiness to comply, the Khan of the Underworld said, 'Your time is not yet. You must return. But you may take anything from here you wish.' Tarvaa looked around, and saw all earthly joys and talents – wealth, happiness, laughter, luck, music, dance. 'Give me the art of storytelling,' he said, for he knew that stories can summon up all other joys. So he returned to his body, only to find that the crows had already pecked out its eyes. Since he could not disobey the Khan of the Underworld, he re-entered his body, and lived on, blind, but with the knowledge of all tales. For the rest of his life, he travelled across Mongolia telling tales and legends, and bringing people joy and wisdom.

If later traditions are anything to go by, the performances of bards, poets and storytellers brought more than joy and wisdom. They were crucial in moulding a sense of identity. Mixing legend and history, they explained traditions, re-collected origins and portrayed the deeds of heroes. The repertoire was huge, as was the range of instruments and styles. In some areas, it still is. Mongols have epics, 'long songs', 'short songs' and many in between; songs for every occasion, songs in praise of landscapes, battles, heroes and horses – especially horses. They have pipes, drums, jaw's harps and horse-head fiddles with as many sizes as western orchestral ones. Women may sing in powerful strident voices crammed with trills and turns, similar to Bulgarian and Greek styles familiar to fans of 'world music'. Men often adopt the same technique, but if they come from western Mongolia or the reindeer-herding areas to the north they also specialize in overtone singing, the astonishing two- or even three-tone technique that produces flute-like nasal notes floating like birdsong above a deep chesty drone. For epics, the men adopt a low-pitched guttural voice. And style and content alike vary from area to area. Some claim that song reflects landscape, pointing to west Mongolian tunes as contoured as their mountains, and to steppe melodies that flow like undulating grassland. And no performance should be under-taken lightly. Performance is – and surely always was – attended with ritual and formality, because music and song have powerful effects. Some songs can exorcise demons;

others invoke the spirits of forest and mountain and weather (it is bad form to whistle in a tent, because whistling calls up a wind-spirit, and there are too many spirits in tents already). Little that is current now can be dated back to the thirteenth century; but there is no reason to doubt the depth and variety of material from which later traditions evolved.

The bards gathering in Avraga in the summer of 1228 no doubt had a rich repertoire of traditional material in the form of legends about their people's origins. Now there was also a new subject to be explored – the rise of Genghis, the birth of the nation, the foundation of empire. But these were early days. The events and stories already being written into folklore were still part of living memory. Fact was in the process of being recast as poetry and legend, and perhaps distorted. Some of the older men and women at Avraga must have been muttering about the ignorance of young people. Yes, yes, it makes a good story, but it wasn't like that at all. We know. We were there.

The brightest and best of this Mongolian Camelot also commanded another novelty. Twenty years before his death, Genghis the nomad chief had emerged as Genghis the imperial ruler. He had realized that a realm that included cities and settled populations could not be administered by word of mouth alone. There had to be laws, and a system to administer them, and records. To produce these, the Mongols needed to write. For an illiterate chieftain it was a brilliant insight, since it meant admitting his own ignorance. That raised a question: what script should be adopted? The Chinese wrote, but their system took years to master; and anyway, no Mongol would willingly adopt the ways of a despised nation of farmers and urbanites, destined for conquest. Some neighbouring Turkish tribes also wrote, as their ancestors had; indeed, Genghis himself may well have seen one of their inscribed stone monuments. Luckily, one of Genghis's newly conquered Turkish-speaking vassal groups, the Naimans, had a script, which they had adopted from the

Uighurs of what is now western China. The script, written vertically, had a venerable ancestry, having been taken some 300 years before from Sogdian, a script and language that served as a lingua franca in Central Asia from about the fifth century. This in its turn had been adapted from Aramaic, itself an offshoot of old Hebrew. It thus had the advantages of being alphabetically based and easily learned. Genghis ordered his sons to adopt it for Mongolian, and to use it to form a bureaucracy. It is still used today in Inner Mongolia.

At Avraga in 1228, scribes and sources were present together. Someone saw that this was a perfect opportunity to capture legend and recent events in writing, with particular reference to the most momentous happening in Mongol history, the rise of Genghis. And so it was that Mongolia's first written work was commissioned: the book now known as *The Secret History of the Mongols*. It was completed, as its final paragraph records, 'at the time of the Great Assembly, in the Year of the Rat and the Month of the Roebuck, when the palaces were being set up at Seven Hills, Countryside Island on the Kherlen River'.

Kherlen, Khenti: these are not familiar names outside Mongolia. You can see both river and mountains on the flight from Beijing across the Gobi to Mongolia. If you glance out of a right-hand window a few minutes before touchdown in Ulaanbaatar, you will be looking north and east across an infinity of grassland marked only by the faint scribbles of car-tracks and the mushroom dot of a felt tent. In the distance the flanks darkened by fir forests and summits still whitened by snow are the Khenti mountains, the last outpost of the Siberian ranges that roll southward across the Russian frontier. This is a geographical borderland, where mountain gives way to grass, and rivers racing from high ground lose their force in gentle meanders.

One particular river runs due south from the mountains, sweeping round to head away north-east. This is the river, commonly spelled 'Kerulen' on western maps, which Mongols call the Kherlen, one of the three great rivers that drain their traditional heartland. The broad, 100-kilometre bend in the Kherlen cradles the southern tip of Countryside Island (Khödöö Aral), 4,000 square kilometres of tangled hills hemmed by the Kherlen and the Tsenkher, which flow parallel for 100 kilometres or so. Then the hills fall into grasslands, and the Kherlen swings east and north in the great bend I asked you to see in your mind's eye, and the two rivers meet around Avraga. From here a broad valley leads north-east into the heart of Genghis country. The mountains, the rivers, the valley and this particularly significant piece of pasture form the heartland of the Mongols, the region which, a little over 800 years ago, was the fount and origin of the tribe, of their greatest leader and of their nation – which was why, in the summer of 2002, I drove out to see it.

The vehicle of choice for Mongolian drivers is the Russian, or rather Ukrainian, UAZ (pronounced *wuzz*, to rhyme with *buzz*). The UAZ minibus or jeep – the basics are the same – is the workhorse for those without a horse, a quintessence of 4×4s. There was no power steering. Driving her was like wrestling an ox. But the driver, Khishig, a cheery character with bad burn-marks on his neck and arms, was her master, churning through mud, breasting rivers, climbing banks, riding fast over open steppeland.

Half a day's journey out of the capital of Mongolia, Ulaanbaatar, we struck south along the Kherlen, around foothills that are the outer flanks of the Khenti massif. It was late June, the best time of year, when horses are sleek and marmots are fat. It was best to keep on the move. If we stopped and got out, grasshoppers crackled beneath our feet like static, and the flies began to pester. On the move, we were at our happiest. Goyo[1], a soft-voiced English graduate, stocky and tough as a Mongolian pony, talked of her ambition to study abroad, and Baatar, a middle-aged museum director with an elfin face and studious spectacles, hummed folk tunes in a fine high tenor. A Buryat, from the subsection of Mongols who straddle the northern borders, he revelled in the songs of his people.

Avraga turned out to be two places. The first, the modern town, is a cluster of wooden houses – for this northerly transition-land shares Siberia's domestic architecture – apparently drawn loosely together on the universe of grass by their own gravity. In fact, the town owes its existence to a nearby mineral lake where Mongolians come to bathe in summer and smear themselves with sulphurous mud. Known only to a few adventurous outsiders, it is a pretty spot, with a broad sandy beach, lawn-like banks for sunbathing and a fence to keep cattle and horses clear. Nearby on the open plain was our base, a tourist camp of a dozen Mongolian tents – *gers*, as the big round yurts are known in Mongolia.

The second Avraga, our destination, lies over the steppe 10 kilometres to the south. There is nothing to see of the old capital itself, but the site is obvious enough. Just above the low mounds surveyed by the Three Rivers Project stands a square, white-fenced enclosure, like a huge parade-ground, 200 metres across. Statues of two spear-carrying soldiers, decked out with conical helmets, little round shields, curved swords and upturned boots, guard nine tents and half a dozen scattered monuments. But the real guard was at the entrance. 'Welcome to Genghis's palace,' proclaimed a notice board in Mongolian and English. 'This is its respected site. Here you

---

[1] Traditionally, Mongolians had one name, usually of two elements, commonly shortened to the first. Today, professional Mongolians usually add a patronymic, which comes second in English but first in Mongolian. Thus Goyo, used to English-speaking ways, was Goyotsetseg Radnaabazar; Baatar was Dorjiin Baatartsogt; the driver, Khishignyam.

can make contact with ancient Mongol history and culture. Please pay at reception.' It was a private operation, and sadly similar in spirit to many a 'heritage site' in the West. There was nothing authentic about these monuments, no evidence that a palace had ever stood here. The nine tents – nine being the number of most significance traditionally – held amateurish portraits of Genghis and his queens, with replicas of weapons and yak-tail standards. In each, visitors could offer prayers at shrines, lit by low butter candles and draped with lengths of the blue silk that is the traditional Buddhist offering.

It was all in honour of *The Secret History*'s 750th anniversary, which officially occurred in 1990. 'According to the last sentence of *The Secret History*,' said the site's guide, baldly, 'the book was finished in 1240.' But wait: my opening scenario had the date as 1228. The difference, the subject of much academic debate, is explained by *The Secret History*'s reference to the 'Year of the Rat', the first in the twelve-year cycle of animals that the Mongols adopted from the Chinese. Hence the twelve-year difference. But which might it be – one of these two, or some other, later rat-year? The argument centres on the fact that *The Secret History* covers the reign of Ogedei, but does not mention his death in 1241. So, if the text is taken at face value, it could only have been written in 1240. Other more technical arguments for later rat-years (1252, 1264) have also been made, but later records make no mention of any Great Assembly, and the immediacy of the writing, as we shall see, argues for a contemporary author. If we accept this, it leaves the problem of the twelve paragraphs on Ogedei's reign. In fact, scholars now widely agree that this is not really a problem: these paragraphs were a later interpolation, added just before Ogedei's death. The date we should go for is 1228.

For officialdom, however, 1240 represents an easy option, and a seductive one. During the communist years, Genghis –

the man whose heirs oppressed Russia for two centuries – was *persona non grata*. But from 1989 onwards, Mongolian governments have been eager to promote anything to do with their nation's founder. In 1990, when many scholars still favoured 1240 as the year of composition, the chance of celebrating the 750th anniversary was simply too good to miss – with the result that visitors are still asked to pay a few *tugriks* to enter a tawdry enclosure that celebrates a doubtful date with spurious monuments.

Memorials aside, this is a glorious site, and that summer evening offered the best of the glory. Above, dark clouds hung ominously, but the lowering sun sank to a clear horizon and spotlit the westward slopes. Glowing herdsmen at the feet of weirdly extended shadows rounded up glowing sheep, and a trainer yelled 'Pull back! Pull back!' to a ten-year-old boy galloping past in preparation for the National Day races two weeks hence. From the top of the rise behind, you could see across a plain made orange by the slanting light to the Seven Hills mentioned in *The Secret History*.

Ahead, down the slope, was the mound where the Three Rivers people had dug, now nothing but a shallow pit a few metres across. 'They found a few tiles, and a bit of a stone floor,' said Baatar, then stared into the middle distance, and back more than eight centuries. 'There were buildings all along here . . . Barracks . . . This was where families stayed when the men were off fighting. There was a palace . . .' His voice died, his vision faded, as Avraga itself had vanished into dream-time.

It was obviously a good place to build. In former times the Kherlen was much larger than it is now, and would occasionally have flooded and changed its course. But Avraga was well back from the river – 10 kilometres today – with its own water supply in the form of the little stream.

Down below us lay one of the reasons for building on this particular spot and the reason for its name. Across a water-meadow of tussocky grass, beyond the stream with its rickety metal footbridge, was a spring: the source, the original *aurag*, still producing the healing waters that drew Genghis's clan in the late twelfth century. It must have been old even then, having served predecessor clans and cultures for untold centuries. We filed down through a herd of horses, teetered from tussock to tussock to the footbridge, then up to the spring itself. Since nothing these days is off limits, it too had been privatized. A makeshift fence surrounded a little wooden shed topped by a Chinese-style roof. A notice proclaimed the spring's virtues and significance. Genghis drank here. The water was rich in this and that, and came from 100 metres beneath the surface. It was good for both body and soul. It cured twelve kinds of stomach condition, including cancer. It was also good for liver complaints and hangovers, and was therefore favoured by Ogedei, a notorious drinker (not favoured enough, apparently: he drank himself to death).

I wasn't at all sure about this miracle liquid. There were dark pools of it, covered with slime and bubbling slowly, releasing a smell that reminded me of something too remote to call to mind. Inside the shed, a plastic pipe led from a turnkey. Baatar hauled at it, and water gushed out in orgasmic jets, responding to some regular variation in pressure deep beneath us. I drank, and grimaced. Now the memories came: rotten eggs, sulphur, the smell of Norfolk marsh-mud at low tide. If you had a hangover like Ogedei's you wouldn't notice, but I had the impression I had just swallowed a lifetime dose of H_2S. This may have been what Genghis came for, but it seemed to me a good reason to commission a new capital.

Baatar suggested we visit a friend, the headmaster of the local school, who might know more about Avraga. Sunseltayar was a man in his forties, with a quiet authority rooted in pride that his school lay right beside the first Mongol capital. 'I tell the children they can go and dig and make important discoveries when they get older.' We were sitting in the long midsummer twilight outside his single-storey wooden house, nibbling hard curds brought by his teenage daughter. He knew more than most what made this place so attractive as a base. 'It's not just the mineral waters that drew people. This is an iron-rich area. You can see it in the red rocks. It's a good place to make weapons. And a good place to train horses, because the winters are mild and the pastures good. We are famous for our horses. Horses were brought here from all over Mongolia for cross-breeding. It's always been that way.'

'So Genghis's clan was not the first to come here?'

'People have been here since Hun times. Do you know about the cemetery?'

It turned out he was referring to an ancient burial-ground. It lay an hour or so away, in the foothills of the mountains. He would take us the next day.

So it came about that the next morning a new character entered this story: the marmot. An expedition like this is also an excuse for something else – for talk, or riding, or eating, or drinking, or as many of these things as possible. We would need lunch. The marmots were getting fat on grass-seed. All we needed was a hunter to see to our needs on our way to the burial-ground. The Headmaster knew a hunter, Enkhbat, who, prised from his house, turned out to be a wiry man with sunken cheeks, a lavatory-brush haircut and a toothy grin. Goyo thought he looked like a marmot, which was a good omen. But Enkhbat, the hunter, lacked a couple of essentials, namely a gun and ammunition. A friend of his had a gun. We headed out across the plain for a kilometre or two, to a tent, from which Enkhbat hurried with a .22 rifle. That just left the ammunition. Another dash back into town to another friend, and we were on our way.

Marmots have a special place in Mongolian culture, being a source of both food and danger. They and their fleas harbour the bacillus that causes bubonic plague, and some historians point to them as the ultimate source of the Black Death, carried into Europe by victorious Mongols along their trade routes in the early fourteenth century. The danger is still present, but well known, easily recognized and quickly handled, with injections given free in the local hospitals. Plague-ridden ones apart, marmots have always been part of Mongolian summer fare, with shoulder of marmot – known as 'human meat' – considered a delicacy.

Goyo told a story:

How the Marmot Got to Have Human Meat

Once there were seven suns in the sky. It was too hot. People found a good archer and asked him to shoot some of the suns. The archer was a daring man. He said, 'Tomorrow morning when the seven suns come out I'll shoot six of them with six arrows. If I fail, I'll be a marmot, cut off my thumb, drink blood instead of water, eat dry grass and live underground.' Well, he shot five. When he shot his last arrow, a sparrow flew in front of him. The arrow cut the sparrow's tail, which is why the sparrow has a forked tail. He did as he promised, and became a marmot. That's why the marmot has human meat on him.

Marmots are noted for their curiosity, a trait that has always allowed marmot-hunters to flourish. They are hypnotized by anything white. Waving a white cloth or feather makes them fall into a trance and turns them into easy prey. There are even special white marmot-hunting dogs which are trained to wave their tails, reducing the marmot to helplessness while the dogs creep close enough to pounce. This must all be true, because it was caught on camera in a TV documentary that, when shown in Japan, brought protests from outraged members of the main Japanese wildlife preservation society: Mongolian marmot-hunters were cheats! They took unfair advantage of poor, naïve Mongolian marmots! Marmot hunting should be banned!

Marmots are indeed charmingly naïve. Alarmed by a passing horse or van, they scamper off to their burrows, flapping over the ground like doormats in a high wind – and then, after a few minutes, when curiosity gets the better of them, they poke up their heads to see if all is clear. At this time of year, quite often it isn't. A Mongolian hunter is lying a few metres away, with a .22 resting on a support, cocked and ready. It's only a question of patience, and an ability to ignore the flies that gather like a veil on hood or hat. We left Enkhbat flattened on the steppe, surrounded by the electric clatter of grasshoppers, and bounced off to the hills.

Leaving the van in the shade of a grove beside a dried-up stream, we followed the Headmaster round the flank of a hill.

'It's known as the Mountain of Many People,' said the Headmaster.

I looked around. We were by a winter cattle-shed made of logs. Below us the plain, seemingly flat as desert in the midday glare, ran away into haze, broken only by a lake where a herd of horses stood haunch-deep, escaping flies and heat. A couple of *gers*, a squiggling car-track. In the far distance, 20 kilometres away, I could just make out the brown smear of Avraga's wooden houses. Not a soul in sight.

The Headmaster nodded. 'I think it means many *dead* people.'

There was certainly evidence of human presence, though no archaeologist had ever been here. We came upon a scattering of flat rocks, which formed a rough line if you looked from just the right direction. It was, perhaps, an ancient approach to something. We climbed on upwards, moving fast to leave the flies behind. The Headmaster beckoned me over to a small plant. He dug it up with his fingers and showed me the root: a garlic-like tuber which he called 'white potato'. He picked it clean, and offered it to me. It was crunchy as onion, but bland, actually quite like potato. I took his point – even this rocky wilderness had its food sources.

A shout from above summoned us to our destination, the cemetery. It was a rough collection of boulders, in eight groups, all intermixed with bushes and grass, set out in a rough 'h' shape. They could have been graves, I suppose. That apparently was what the locals believed, for the rocks were not overgrown. Someone, it seemed, kept them clear. There was nothing sophisticated about the piles, but each repre-sented an investment of time and energy. The Mountain of Many People: the site was enough to suggest that the name might have a basis in ancient burial practices. I looked down the rock-strewn hillside to the plain and imagined a funeral procession winding upwards: Genghis's forebears, perhaps, bringing their dead when they first came to Avraga.

In the woodland where the van was parked, Enkhbat had arrived with lunch: 5 kilos of fur and muscle, which he set about cooking in traditional fashion, with one or two more modern additions. For the most part his method would have been familiar to my imaginary twelfth-century families.

Casserole of Marmot

(To feed six. Time: approx. 1 hr)

You will need:
  1 marmot
  Good quantity of dried dung
  Assorted fist-sized stones
  1 knife
  String
  Wire
  1 pair pliers
  1 blow-torch

First, shoot your marmot. Using string, hang dead marmot from a branch. Skin it, peeling skin carefully downwards to keep skin in one piece. Discard entrails. Ignore flies. Remove and dice flesh. At the same time, arrange for visiting author to collect cow-pats, said author to ensure cow-pats are dried to texture of polystyrene. Make pile of dung. Use blow-torch to start slow dung-fire, arranging for smoke to drift over diced marmot flesh to discourage flies. Place stones in fire. Using wire and pliers, sew up limb-holes in marmot skin, binding holes tightly. Do not seal head-hole. Into your marmot-skin bag, insert meat and red-hot stones, using twigs to hold stones. Ignore attached dung, ashes etc. Bind up head-hole with wire, using pliers to secure. Apply blow-torch to skin, scraping off seared fur. Meanwhile, hot stones have begun to cook the meat from the inside out. Trapped air expands to form taut, round, sausage-like container. As fur is removed, blow-torch cooks meat from outside in. After an hour, cut open and serve meat with fingers. As stones cool, toss them about until you can hold them without too much pain: they are good for health and luck.

During the cooking, with the flies swarming and the blow-torch roaring, the driver Khishig explained about his burns. He had been doing exactly this, blasting the fur off a marmot, when the blow-torch sprang a leak and exploded, spraying burning petrol over him. As part of his treatment he had come here, to Avraga's lake, to benefit from its health-giving muds. It was not the mud exactly that would benefit him, but its fauna: microscopic creatures referred to locally as its 'natural doctors'. Apparently, they have a taste for scabrous flesh. Immersed in the sulphurous water, he allowed his scar tissue to be nibbled off. It hurt, but it helped. I backed away as he blasted the last bits of fur and Baatar scraped at the oozing fat.

The result, when Baatar sliced open what now looked like

a sweaty football with odd appendages, was a casserole of paradoxes. The juice from a marmot cooked by dung-fire and blow-torch is nectar: rich, dark, addictive. The meat *tastes* pretty good. But its texture, to a soft westerner, leaves a good deal to be desired. Marmots live by tunnelling and scampering for their lives. They are all muscle, and more than a match for the jaws of those who dine in restaurants and eat processed food. For others, with the strong white teeth that seem to be a feature of country-bred Mongolians, the experience was unadulterated joy, especially as we had some Genghis Khan vodka with us. The Headmaster picked out a grape-like object, the gall-bladder, and swallowed it with a happy smile. While I hauled shreds from my teeth, the rest of the marmot vanished, skin and all, in a haze of vodka and dung-smoke.

As we settled back into the oven-hot, fly-infested van, Baatar cleared his throat and began a Buryat folk song in his clear, high tenor. With the windows open, and wind blowing the flies away, he sang us back to Avraga: 'The cuckoo is calling me, and I am coming to you, my lover, among my homeland, my rivers, my mountains.'

How *The Secret History* was lost and found again makes a curious story. The original possibly became 'secret' – that is, known to and guarded by only a few privileged officials – soon after the Mongols completed the conquest of China in 1271 and commissioned a more formal history. After the Mongol dynasty fell to the Ming in 1368 Ming officials, eager to preserve access to a language spoken by so many of their subjects, developed a strange system of recording Mongol so that they could train interpreters. They used bilingual scholars to transliterate – or rather trans-syllabarize – Mongolian into Chinese, with each Mongolian syllable matched by the Chinese sign that sounded most similar. This was, and remains, a standard way of writing foreign names and phrases in Chinese.

But Chinese has its limitations: each sign and syllable has to begin with a consonant and end with either a vowel or an *n*. In transliterations, the result is a gross pastiche of the original. The capital of Inner Mongolia, Hohhot, which is formed from two Mongol words (*khökh khot*) meaning Blue City, becomes a series of syllables, Hu-He-Hao-Te, each of which has its own meaning, but which together make nonsense, which tells Chinese readers that the name is foreign. America comes out as Mei-Guo, Los Angeles as Lo San Ge, Paris as Pa Li. Genghis Khan becomes Ch'eng Chi Ssu Han.

You can get a flavour of what happens to Mongolian in the sinified version of *The Secret History* by recasting a well-known soliloquy syllable by syllable into nonsensical French.

> Tu bille orne hôte tu bille, sa tisseur qu' ouest y un.
> Ou est serre tisse noble air insère m'Indes tu sous phare . . .

A Chinese reading the transliteration of *The Secret History* would sound as if he were speaking Mongolian with a terrible Chinese accent. Since it made no sense in Chinese, a rough guide to the meaning was added beside each vertical line.

Eventually, as Mongol influence declined, the Chinese lost interest in preserving the original Mongol version of the text and kept only the Chinese phonetic versions, together with the gloss. Several copies lay unrecognized until rediscovered one by one in the late nineteenth and early twentieth centuries. Thereafter, scholars worked to restore the original Mongolian. Easy enough if you know the original, and if both languages are closely related and living, as in the example above; but tricky if you are working from fourteenth-century Chinese to restore thirteenth-century Mongol, neither of which anyone knows how to pronounce, both of which belong to separate language groups. This painstaking work has been done and redone several times, the most recent version being published in the 1980s. Though linguistic and geographical problems still remain to be solved – for no original Mongolian version has ever surfaced – *The Secret History* is now available in several languages.

Scholars debate the balance between fact and fiction, but agree that much of *The Secret History* is rooted in actual events, for its coverage seems to have chimed with that of another contemporary – and equally secret – work known as the *Altan Debter* ('Golden Notebook'). This vanished, but some of it is summarized in Persian and Chinese histories. In terms of primary sources for Genghis's time, that's about it. Many other works are known to have existed, but all have vanished or been destroyed (some quite recently: one medieval chronicle was burned by a Chinese warlord in 1927). A seventeenth-century work, *Altan Tobchi* ('Golden Summary'), draws on *The Secret History* and later legends, but encrusts them with Buddhist theology. A fourth source is the official history of the Yuan (Mongol) dynasty, compiled by the Mongols' successors, following the customary practice when one set of rulers replaced another; but by comparison with *The Secret History* these notes are brief, lacklustre and clerkish.

The Secret History remains prime. It is an intriguing and frustrating creation. Because it claims to explain Mongol origins, it invites comparison with other great 'foundation' works – the Bible, the *Iliad*, the Norse sagas, the *Nibelungenlied*, the *Mahabharata*. But it lacks their scope – it contains only 282 paragraphs, amounting to 60,000 words, one-third the length of the *Iliad*. And although it shares some elements of the 'foundation epic' – myth and legend grading into anecdote and what seems like history – it lacks both epic grandeur and historical rigour.

As an aspiring epic, *The Secret History* has strong roots in the Mongol tradition of narrative verse. It shares with the *Iliad* and the *Odyssey* the rare distinction of being an oral work captured in writing. Clearly, by definition, there can be no *written* evidence for an *oral* tradition, but in Homer's case scholars have suggested a theory that could offer a model for the creation of *The Secret History*. After the War of Troy in about 1250 BC, Greek bards, travelling from court to court and marketplace to marketplace, spun stories about the heroes and events which portrayed the origins of Greek society, telling them who they were and what made them tick. After this storytelling had been going on for about 500 years, Homer welded some of these tales into an artistic whole just at the time when the Greeks adopted Phoenician writing. Once written, the stories were frozen, as it were, in flight. An oral medley became two unified works of literature.

The process by which song is captured in script is not entirely conjectural. A bardic tradition in the Balkans survived for another two millennia, into the 1930s, when the anthropologist and ethno-musicologist Milman Parry recorded them in the coffee-houses of Serbia, Bosnia and Hercegovina. As his pupil Albert Lord relates in *The Singer of Tales*, Parry discovered that bards, passing songs from generation to generation, had astonishing abilities. It was not a question of memorizing vast chunks of text for recitation, but of turning every performance into an improvisation. In performance, a bard based each song on traditional themes and formulae, which accounted for 25–50 per cent of the 'text'; the rest arose from his own recombining, trimming and extending in response to the feel of the audience, while always fitting the song into the same verse form.

Something like this may have happened in Mongolia and China in the years leading up to the writing of *The Secret History*. It seems likely that in the early middle ages Mongolian bards, like pre-Homeric singers, acted as national memory banks, working incidents and characters into traditional verse forms, singing their songs to some simple stringed instrument, the ancestral form of today's horse-head fiddle. In the 1220s, when the Mongol empire was still on the rise, these poet–historians would already have begun the unplanned task of capturing what had happened – what was still happening – in verse. Given time, they would, perhaps, have spun a poetic fabric as rich as the traditions on which Homer drew, and some Mongolian Homer might have worked an equal magic.

But the process of creation, assuming it had started, was short-circuited by the introduction of writing. In Homer's case, writing captured mature oral verse. In the case of *The Secret History*, we are left with the raw material of poetry. Signs of orality exist in plenty, for much of the text is in verse, with the first words of lines echoing each other in the Mongolian equivalent of rhyme. There are numerous catch-phrases, a common device in oral traditions to anchor the narrative. Children destined for fame have 'fire in their eyes', people who are killed 'blow in the wind, like ashes'. The anecdotes are as vivid as anything in the *Odyssey*.

The Secret History never made the leap to great epic poetry because it is also, in part, a prose history. But it doesn't work as history either, for two reasons. First, it was written too soon after the events it records; and second, Mongolia, lacking a literary tradition, also lacked historians. Immediacy does not necessarily inhibit good historical writing – Thucydides wrote his history of the Peloponnesian War as it was happening; but Greece in the fifth century BC could already look back on three centuries of writing and an extensive literary tradition. The Mongols in 1228 had had hardly more than 20 years of literacy, and it was limited to a few experts. So the *History* stops short of 'real' history, as Thucydides and Macaulay and modern historians would understand it, because it contains few details of how Genghis made his mark on the world. Two decades of campaigning in

Central Asia and China, years that saw the destruction of cities by the dozen and the deaths of millions, are dismissed in a few paragraphs. Perhaps at the time of writing the history of imperial expansion was already in the domain of official records, now lost; perhaps these events had not yet been worked into the repertoire of the storytellers; perhaps no bards went along on the campaigns. For whatever reason, we are left with the equivalent of an album of family snaps – the story of Mongol origins, Genghis's rise, the unification of the Mongol tribes and the beginnings of empire.

If this is neither a great epic nor great history, what are its virtues? There are two: vividness and selectivity. It is as if a senior editor has drawn on a range of available sources – poets and contemporary verbal accounts – under strict instructions to include only what is most relevant, and above all no whitewash. This is not hagiography. It rings true because it portrays the bad along with the good. Genghis was, it appears, frightened of dogs. He murders a brother, and is chastised by his mother. He almost causes a military disaster, and is rebuked by his childhood friend.

Who was responsible for this mixture of the heroic and the human? It has been suggested that the author was Genghis's adopted brother, Shigi, who had been found abandoned in a Tatar camp. He was obviously high-born, since he was wearing golden earrings, a nose-ring and a sable-lined satin waistcoat. Raised by Genghis's mother as her sixth son, and the youngest by a good 20 years, the boy became both a general and a judge. Shigi may well have had the literary and writing skills – but if he was the sole author, with time on his hands, he would surely not have been content to skimp on the details of campaigning, administration and legal matters.

Who laid down the agenda? The obvious choice is the newly elected heir, Ogedei. Only he would have had the authority to approve the selection of material. And he would have derived his authority from his late father. Genghis himself would have heard the legends and incidents included in *The Secret History*. Indeed, so much relates to him that many of the incidents must have come from him in the first place. He was a realist. He knew his rise to power had depended on the choices he had made, in politics, in friendships, in strategy. In old age he could see the mistakes of his youth, and would have been concerned to point them out, telling stories against himself to underscore his growing maturity, and emphasize his themes. Divine protection, yes; but the Mongol god, Eternal Heaven, only helps those who help themselves. Success is the hard-won product of suffering and failure. What we have in *The Secret History* is something wonderful, a psychological profile of what it took for a down-and-out to become a hero and an emperor.

I imagine a scholar–administrator, Shigi perhaps, now approaching 40, being given the task of compilation by his lord and kinsman Ogedei, and getting down to work with some bright young assistant, versed in the Uighur script and able to take dictation. Together they summon eye-witnesses, do the rounds of tents, and gather stories, verses and accounts from those who were there. Time is short. Soon summer will be over, and everyone will ride off to their bases and family tents for the winter. They leave out most of the military details – after all, some of the most senior generals are still on battle stations abroad. What seems good and appropriate of the verses they keep. The rest they tie together as best they can in prose, focusing on the most vivid anecdotes and the most revered of the legends.

It was a perfect time – perhaps the only possible time – to gather the material that would allow a new nation to understand its own origins.

2

THE COMING OF THE MONGOLS

NORTH-EAST OF AVRAGA, A FIELD THE SIZE OF A SMALL COUNTRY runs alongside the Khenti massif to the birthplace of Genghis Khan, and of the Mongol nation. The earth and grass, packed firm by high summer, rolled as empty as the open sea. We were the point of our own dusty wake, with nothing to slow us. Heat had reduced the Tsenkher, Countryside Island's frontier, to a trickle; a road heading east from the capital, marked on the map as a highway, was a track too faint to see when we crossed it.

We stopped only once, to honour a rare occurrence: the appearance of another vehicle, a UAZ van like ours. Such occasions offer a chance for gossip and cigarettes, and for the relief of bladders; a time of brief contemplation that Mongolians call 'seeing to one's horses'. The other van contained a couple surprising in their youth, beauty and internationalism. He was a Mongolian with designer-stubble hair, she a slim, blonde waif from Estonia who smoked her cigarette squatting on her haunches. They had met while both were living in Tokyo, fallen in love, got engaged. Coming from opposite ends of the ex-Soviet empire, they both had Russian as their main second language, but spoke to each other in English. His father was professor of history in the military academy in UB, he said, blowing smoke through pursed lips. Perhaps I should meet him. But he was not impressed enough with me to force the point, as if English writers were two a *tugrik* on the road from Avraga.

These lands were part of Mongolia's prehistory. We swung down from a low ridge on to a flood plain created by a sluggish little river, the Khorkh, which at one point formed a small, shallow lake. Baatar directed us up towards a rocky outcrop on another ridge, from which the past lay spread out like a map. There was not a *ger* to be seen, but I was standing on a place once crowded by Mongolian standards. Millennia ago, the river below spread out for miles, creating a lush area that attracted a stone age community. The ridge on which we were parked had once been a lakeside rise, and the outcrop of rock, with its overhangs and shallow caves, a factory. Petroglyphs of human and animal shapes were dimly visible on the walls. Strolling down the slope, Baatar stooped, and beckoned. He held a handful of different-coloured stones, all flaked from artefacts – arrowheads, spearheads, knives – that must have been used and traded across Mongolia. It was in this broad, much-used valley and the one ahead, made by the Onon, that the Mongols first settled around AD 800.

The junction of the Onon and Khorkh looks today much as it would have looked then, if you ignore the little town of Binder, with its dark-wood houses and rutted tracks. The Mongols would still feel at ease with the savannah of scattered firs and maples, the valley of gentle hummocks and riverside foothills, the Onon burbling softly over shallows. Today, new arrivals don't need to set up tents. On a slope overlooking the river stood a summer camp of holiday *gers*, in neat rows behind a freshly painted fence. It was deserted;

no guests, no staff. But there followed the usual Mongolian sequence of random events by which problems become pleasures. Our arrival had been noted in town. A car hove into view, bringing two young women in sky-blue *deels*, the elegant, ankle-length traditional gowns. They tried to start a generator to power the electric lights and the restaurant's cooker. There was no fuel. Khishig ran them to and from the town, and the camp sprang to life, with light, food and good news: Binder's post office had a black-and-white TV. It was Sunday, 30 June. After supper we drove into town, crammed into the wooden shack that served as a post office and, through a haze of static and Genghis Khan vodka, watched Brazil beat Germany 2–0 in the final of the World Cup.

That band of Mongols approaching the Khenti around AD 800 must have seen the river junction much as I saw it the following morning: a forest opposite tinged by the rising sun; the soft ground aerated by field-mouse burrows and covered by a dozen species of grasses, white and yellow flowers, and dwarf bushes. A skylark's song tumbled from a heaven of utter purity. Distant hills were as crisp in the crystal air as the *gers* below. It was wilder then, of course. Today, Binder is a dark-brown smear of timber buildings a few kilometres away, and there are fewer animals. Back then, there would have been white-tailed gazelle skittering away, scuffing up little puffs of dust; now the gazelle are relegated to remoter parts of the Gobi. It was a good spot for the migrants. The grass was rich, their animals would breed. Upriver, the forested foothills of the Khenti offered game, and sanctuary in war for those who could follow the deer-trails into the steep-sided valleys and the austere uplands.

Centuries later, their legends would claim that these people were the descendants of a wolf and a doe. Perhaps, back then, they knew better – that their two ancestral clans were named Wolf and Doe. And perhaps their folk tales also recorded their origins, in the mountains north of the great Siberian lake, Baikal, or in Manchuria. By the time their surviving legends were recorded in *The Secret History*, half a millennium on, folk memory had dimmed, leaving only shadowy references to animal ancestors and a 'sea-crossing'. Apparently, this migrant group already called themselves Mongols, or something like it, a name the Chinese picked up and distorted into Meng-ku or Meng-wu. What it meant, if anything, no-one knows.

This borderland, where the mountains and forests of the north meet southern grassland, was the crucible that turned forest-dwelling hunters into plains-dwelling herdsmen, making them experts in a way of life quite different from the systems that have dominated most of humanity's social evolution.

In AD 800 that expertise, when seen in the wider context of history and prehistory, was something relatively new. For 90 per cent of their 100,000 years on Earth humans had been hunter-gatherers, making the best of seasonal variations, the habits of animals and nature's bounty. About 10,000 years ago, as the last great ice sheets withdrew, social evolution accelerated. Change became measurable not in aeons but in millennia. Two other systems arose in quick succession. One was agriculture. By 5000 BC agricultural communities dotted the continental fringes, spreading along the great rivers of Egypt, Mesopotamia, India and China. From this revolution cascaded the changes that came to define today's world – population growth, wealth, leisure, cities, art, literature, industry, large-scale war, government: most of everything that static, urban societies equate with civilization.

The third system (after hunter-gathering and agriculture), which the first Mongols were already beginning to exploit, was one of herds and wandering herders – pastoral nomadism, as it is called. A century ago, it was the fashion for prehistorians to see a neat progression taking us from wandering barbarism to settled civilization, like this:

Hunter-gathering > Pastoral nomadism > Agriculture > Urban living

Not so, according to current thinking. Now, the consensus is that agriculture came second, providing a resource of tractable domestic animals with which herders were free to develop pastoral nomadism. This gives rise to a different sequence:

Pastoral nomadism
↗
Hunter-gathering > Agriculture + herding
↘
Urban living

In other words, pastoral nomadism is not a 'primitive' lifestyle, but one that is as sophisticated as farming. When this change occurred – around 4000 BC, in southern Russia and western Siberia – a new world beckoned: the sea of grass, or *steppe* (English has adopted the Russian term), which spans Eurasia for over 6,000 kilometres from Manchuria to Hungary.

To hunter-gatherers and farmers, the steppes were un-promising. Flowing across the Eurasian heartland between tundra and desert, forest and mountain, the grasslands of Inner Asia are high, exposed and badly watered. From the Urals to the Pacific, there is little to provide a focus for settlement. Large rivers, which elsewhere are civilization's arteries, flow north, into Arctic wastes, or debouch uselessly into inland seas. The Amur, into which the Onon flows, runs eastward for 4,300 kilometres, but is frozen for six months of the year. Beyond the moderating effects of any ocean, temperatures reach over 40°C (104°F) in summer, while a winter gale can freeze exposed flesh in minutes (and does: to preserve your meat through the winter in town or country, you simply leave it outside).

In this ocean of green Mongolia's grasslands form a lagoon, 1,600 kilometres long and 500 kilometres wide, linked to the further steppes beyond through mountain corridors that run westward between the Altai and Tien Shan ranges, and eastward along the valley of the Amur into Manchuria. Bracketed to the north by the mountains and forests of Siberia, and to the south by the Gobi's gravelly wastes, this is a challenging environment for humans. Even 'lowlands' lie at some 1,200 metres above sea level. In the Gobi, in high summer, daytime temperatures of over 40°C plunge to leave a rime of frost on tents overnight. From November to April, country-dwellers still harvest water as blocks of ice and melt them on fires.

Farmers found they could make a living only on the shores of the grassy ocean, where it rolls into deciduous woodlands and savannahs of scattered trees, or in rare oases and fertile river valleys. Those living on the edges of these habitable regions had a tougher time, and more of an incentive to seek something better out in that universe of grass which, when properly used, would provide for food, mounts, increased populations, armies and, eventually, empires. No such ends were in sight, of course, for the unrecorded experimenters who first dipped their toes into the sea of green. Progress out onto the grasslands must have been the result of countless trials, errors, dead-ends and retreats, as animals that were once prey were captured, then penned, bred, eaten, tamed and, at last, ridden. Several species proved amenable: reindeer on the borderlands of Siberia and Mongolia, yaks in Tibet, camels in the semi-deserts. But one in particular became the key that unlocked the wealth of the grasslands: the horse.

In Asia the domestication of horses was under way by 4000 BC, the date of an archaeological site on the lower Don.

At first – as their piled-up bones here reveal – horses were raised for food; then, immeasurably slowly, a revolution occurred. A knife dating from around 2000 BC, found on the upper Ob river, shows a man holding a tethered horse. By then, it seems, people were breeding the wildness out of these flighty creatures, using bronze bits to impose their will, turning a prey into a partner, breeding and adapting the horse for tractability, strength and endurance. After a further thousand years of enforced evolution, this new subspecies still looked wild – stocky, thick-necked and shaggy – but its character was very different. Mongolian horses are much the same today as they were then. To European eyes they are not pretty creatures, but they are as tough as ever, living out through the winter, scraping away snow to get at the grass beneath. Only the grimmest weather – like an ice-storm, which seals the pasture in an impenetrable carapace – can kill them. Most years, they survive to breed in numbers far beyond the needs of the inhabitants. By 1000 BC the Central Asian horse was the prime means of transport, an aid for tending herds, invaluable in hunting, essential in war: the mainstay of the grassland economy.

The spirit of Mongolian horses is truly astonishing. On 11 July, National Day – Naadam – every region has a series of horse races. The riders are children, typically aged around ten, and they ride bareback; yet the event is held to test not the jockeys but the horses, which run over 20 kilometres in several age categories. The best of them race outside the capital, Ulaanbaatar. In 2002 I was at the finishing post to watch the five-year-olds come in past an ecstatic crowd, many on horseback themselves, jostling those on foot in front of them, waiting for the horses to appear over the rolling grassland. When they began to straggle in, strung out across several kilometres, some of the horses were close to total exhaustion. One stopped on trembling legs 2 metres from the line. The ten-year-old jockey lashed and kicked to no avail.

He got off and hauled at the reins. No reaction. The crowd was going wild, as horse after horse cantered by in a haze of dust and sweat. Eventually, three men hurried forward and pulled, pushed and cajoled the horse forward. Seeming to know what it had to achieve, it took a few unsteady paces, crossed the line, stopped again for a few seconds, and only then toppled onto its side. More men crowded round. They took it in turns to kick-start the animal, literally, by booting it in the heart: all-out, full-power, penalty-style kicks. It's the usual technique in such cases, and sometimes works. This time, it was no use. More men gathered round and hauled it onto its feet, only to see it collapse again. It was a corpse. While the young rider squatted in tears beside his beloved mount, a fork-lift arrived to cart it off. It was all rather up-setting for western tourists. But such deaths happen every year, and in many races, all over the country. The fork-lift had been busy with similar cases further down the track, and would no doubt be busy again. This was evolution in action. Only the strongest survive to breed. The result is a creature not only tough enough to live through grim winters, but also with the sheer inbred guts to drive itself to death if asked – a useful trait when carrying warriors across all Eurasia.

The other types of nomadism, based on reindeer and yaks, have endured; but the horse – the fastest and most adaptable of mounts – confers a special sense of superiority. This equestrian expertise is reflected in language and in attitude. Mongolians will tell you that they have over 100, or 300, or some other vast number of horse-terms. One number at least can be quantified. It is 169, based on the significance of the number 13 in Mongol folklore. According to this arcane classification system, there are 13 main horse colours (from light bay to grey), each with 13 subdivisions (one of the 'light bay' subdivisions is 'elegant-while-running-from-a-far-place light bay'). Thus a horse can be identified by colour, general physique, minor attributes (like mane or tail), ability and character, and any combination of these qualities.

As the Mongols already knew when they moved up the Onon valley, a herdsman is free to roam the grasslands and exploit them by raising the other four types of domestic animal – sheep, goats, camels and cattle (with yaks replacing camels in the mountains). From them come meat, hair, skins, dung for fuel, felt for clothing and tents, and 150 different types of milk product, including the herdsman's main drink, a mildly fermented mare's-milk beer. In much of Central Asia it is known by the Turkish term *kumiss*; in Mongolian it is *airag*. 'As long as one is drinking, it bites the tongue like vinegar,' wrote Friar William of Rubrouck in north-eastern France, one of the first Europeans to visit the Mongol court in the thirteenth century. 'When one stops, it leaves on the tongue the taste of milk of almonds and greatly delights the inner man.' *Airag* – indeed, the milk of any of the 'five animals' – can be further distilled into a spirit that resembles vodka, but with the smoothness of a good wine. This too greatly delights the inner man.

On this foundation, pastoral nomadism evolved into a highly specialized life that could, in theory, be utterly self-contained. But it wasn't. Its connections with other cultures and environments were always vital, both for trade and for access to essential materials.

Take, for example, the Mongolian *ger* (pronounced with a hard *g*, and to rhyme with 'bear', 'dare'). Domed and circular to shoulder the strong winds without needing guy-ropes, a *ger* is made today, as it always was, by stretching one or two layers of thick woollen felt over roof-spokes and trellises. Those who like to romanticize the demanding and specialized lifestyle of the nomad often praise the *ger* as an ideal, as if it sprang from the steppes themselves. It didn't. It evolved from forest origins. Its lattice walls and roof-spokes are made of wood, and wood is rare on the steppe. The prototype *ger* was a forest tent, an arched tepee-like structure which today's hunters occasionally make as an overnight shelter. As pastoral nomadism matured, herders found they could use horses and carts to carry more gear, and make life more comfortable. One luxury was to turn a low tepee into a roomy house by adding walls, raising the tepee to form a roof. But the wood for *gers* and carts still had to come from the forest. Though the steppe nomads *could* be self-sufficient, the existence of *gers* and carts acts as a reminder that in order to live well these sailors on the ocean of grass needed their forest ports.

Our group of Mongols already possessed another tool vital for peace and war: the composite, or recurved bow. The composite bow, similar in design across all Eurasia, was very different from the English longbow, and altogether less impressive at first glance. A modern unstrung composite bow looks like nothing but a 3-foot claw of drab plastic. But to flex one against your thigh and feel its latent power is to understand why this little object ranks with the Roman sword and the machine-gun as a weapon that changed the world.

The 'composite' elements – horn, wood, sinew, glue – were all readily available. The trick was to combine them correctly. This must have occurred as the result of a series of chance discoveries in an unrecorded dream-time three or four thousand years ago. Imagine a forest-dweller, an Everyman with a basic wooden bow, which he breaks. He discovers that a piece of deer-horn – or cow-horn, if he has cattle – is as whippy as wood. He whittles a short strip to use as a splice. He also finds uses for other parts of animals. Any hunter cooking the remains of an animal will be left with tendons, which after several days of slow boiling produce a powerful glue. (Alternatively, glue can be made from particular parts of fish: fish-glue was a prized item of trade across Asia.) Pulverizing a tendon with stones reduces it to individual threads, which prove useful as binding. He notices that the wooden bow, now combined with horn and sinew, actually works better. Horn resists compression, and forms the bow's inside face. Sinews of the right kind – the Achilles tendon is best – resist extension, and are laid along the outside. This is just a hint of the basics of the bowyer's art. It takes years to master the materials – the widths, the lengths, the thicknesses, the taperings, the temperatures, the time to set the shape, the countless minor adjustments. When this expertise is applied correctly with skill and patience – it takes up to a year to make a composite bow – the result is an object of remarkable qualities.

Composite bows, in use by the first millennium BC, evolved into weapons that bear comparison with guns. When forced out of their reverse curve and strung, a powerful bow feels as unyielding as a car-spring. To pull a really 'heavy' one, you need to exert a force equivalent to a one-arm pull-up with just three fingers. Later, Turkish archers used a thumb-ring to draw the bow, but Mongol mounted archers, firing at a gallop, relied on nothing but fingers toughened by use.

The power that can be stored in this yard of horn, wood and sinew is truly astonishing. In the eighteenth century, English archery experts became fascinated by the composite bows used by the Turks. They were amazed to discover that the Turkish bow – essentially the same as the Mongol weapon – far outperformed the English longbow. Longbows rarely shoot further than 350 yards (the world record is 479 yards). Yet on 9 July 1794, in a field behind Bedford Square in London, the Turkish ambassador's secretary, Mahmoud, using a composite bow, shot 415 yards against the wind, and 482 yards with it. Mahmoud modestly said this was nothing: his master, the sultan in Istanbul, was an even more powerful bowman. And indeed, in 1798 the sultan supposedly lived up to his reputation, firing an arrow 972 yards, well over half a mile, the distance allegedly being measured in the presence of the English ambassador to the Ottoman empire, Sir Robert Ainslie. Modern archers simply don't believe this. Today, with modern materials and specially designed carbon arrows, hand-held composite bows fire almost three-quarters of a mile; wooden arrows, though, carry little more than 600 yards. But perhaps the sultan's claim should not be dismissed out of hand. The world record for a bow drawn purely by muscle power is over a mile; it was achieved in 1971 by an American, Harry Drake, with a 300-pound bow which he fired lying on his back, pulling with both hands and the bow braced by his feet, despatching a carbon arrow as thin as a knitting-needle. It carried 2,028 yards (1,854 metres).

Shooting for distance – 'flight archery' – is a specialized activity, and the tough little needle-arrows are not aimed at targets. Distance does not combine easily with accuracy. Yet Mongol archers worked at both, as one of the very first inscriptions in Mongol reveals. It was carved on a metre-high stone, probably in the mid-1220s. Found in 1818 on the lower Onon near present-day Nerchinsk on the Trans-Siberian railway, it is now in the Hermitage, St Petersburg. It was carved when Genghis had just returned from campaigning in Turkestan, on his way to his last campaign in China. Arriving home in triumph, he ordered a celebration with the traditional sports: wrestling, horse racing and archery. Genghis's nephew, the prince and general Yesunge, decided to display his legendary strength and skill. The astonishing result was deemed worthy of this monument, which reads in part: 'While Genghis Khan was holding an assembly of Mongolian dignitaries . . . Yesunge shot a target at 335 *alds*.' An *ald* was the distance between a man's outstretched arms – let's say 1.6 metres, about 5 feet 5 inches. So here was a man who set a mark of some unspecified kind at a distance of over 500 metres – and then, in view of his khan and assembled bigwigs, hit it. Perhaps it was a big target, like a *ger*; perhaps he took several shots; but he would surely never have tried without being confident of success.

At that distance, of course, an arrow on a high, curving flight loses a good deal of its force. At close range, say

50–100 metres, arrows from a 'heavy' bow have more penetration power than many types of bullet. They leave the bow at over 300 k.p.h. – a quarter the speed of a bullet, but since they are many times heavier they pack an equivalent punch. At 100 metres, the right sort of arrow with the right sort of head (of which there were dozens) can slam through a couple of centimetres of wood. Armour was not much of a defence.

Mongolian archery today is not what it was, having been robbed of its power by three centuries of Chinese rule. Though archery is still one of the three 'manly sports', today's bows are sloppy things, with a pathetic range and arrows tipped by fat pads that are fired at, would you believe, nothing more than rows of wickerwork baskets a few dozen metres away. The bows I have tried send their arrows wobbling like a reed in a gale for not much more than 50 metres. I have not yet heard of anyone in Mongolia making bows in the old style, or of anyone backing a revival of old-style archery.

There remained a final stage in the evolution of the warrior nomad. To be truly effective, a bowman needs a delivery system. In the first millennium BC there were two possibilities. The first, obviously, was the horse. But it was hard to ride bareback and fire at once, so a number of ancient Inner Asian peoples, notably the Scythians, developed the second sort of vehicle, the two-wheeled chariot. These fast and manoeuvrable firing platforms, however, were available only to well-organized, semi-urbanized people who had access to wood and carpenters, mines and skilled metalworkers. True nomads had to await the arrival of the stirrup, an invention as in-fluential as the composite bow in the development of warfare. Perhaps because expert horsemen can manage without them, perhaps because chariots provided a partial solution to the problem of wielding a bow, stirrups developed surprisingly late and spread surprisingly slowly. They were first recorded in India in the second century BC, as supports for the big toe. The idea was carried to China, where proper iron foot-stirrups emerged in the fifth century AD. From there they spread westward, perhaps reaching Europe with the Huns in the fifth century in leather form, the first iron ones dating from the sixth century.

By about AD 500, therefore, the pastoral nomads of Inner Asia had an advantage over settled societies. With stirrups added to saddle, bridle and bit, horsemen could out-manoeuvre chariots, fire arrows, wield spears or use the lasso while at full gallop.

There remained the problem of raising and controlling armies – and here again the solution was embedded in the culture of pastoral nomadism. Horse riding was a key to three overlapping skills: herding, hunting and warfare, with hunting as the central element linking the other two. The hunt could control predators (particularly wolves, the bane of the herdsman's existence) and provide furs for clothing and trade. As the Mongols increased in numbers, hunting also became an exercise in co-operation and a vital preparation for war. In autumn (not in spring or summer when the animals were breeding), clans combined to practise hunting manoeuvres in exercises lasting many days. Scouts would spy out the ground; bands of hunters would gather, making a line many miles across, and then, over several days, sweep slowly forward, with express riders tearing back and forth keeping commanders informed of progress, while the army urged wolves, gazelles, even the occasional snow leopard into an ever-decreasing area where the animals would be killed. Like warfare, hunting demanded diplomacy to bring together disparate groups, leadership, strategic skill and effective long-distance communication, all underpinned by terrific horse-manship, endurance and marksmanship. Groups that could hunt together could fight together.

That is, if they could stay together. But in this unforgiving world, little could be relied on. Despite complex rules governing access to pastures, disputes were endemic, violence common. War was not something separate from peace – old Mongol had no word for either 'soldier' or 'civilian', for a herder was both. Fighting demanded no huge investment in equipment, no need to abandon one way of life and adopt another. Hunting and herding readily stretched to cattle-raiding, kidnapping rival chiefs or their wives, taking revenge for wrongs and outright warfare. Every man and woman, every family, had their bonds, but all had to reach out on occasion – for pastures, trade goods, marriage partners – and test the dangerous borders where the bonds of family and friendship came up against enemy territory. A young man might pledge himself to a leader; friends might swear eternal brotherhood; but it could all evaporate. A chief who could no longer guarantee protection and booty would see his dis-gruntled power-base vanish in a cloud of dust across the steppe. Today, as ever, Mongolians are individualistic in ways that charm and infuriate outsiders in equal measure. No wonder that to Genghis loyalty was the moral equivalent of gold: rare, hard-won, easily lost.

Though sophisticated in their pastoral–nomadic way of life, the Mongols would have lacked other refinements. Missionaries spreading Buddhism and Christianity among nearby Turkic tribes made no impact on them. They were shamanists, retaining an ancient belief in the sanctity of natural events and objects. Rivers, springs, thunder, fire, sun, wind, rain, snow – such things were invested with significance, identified as the domains of spirits, while the supreme power, Blue Heaven, Khökh Tenger, watched over events below with a remote benevolence. *Tenger* means both 'sky' and 'heaven', as the equivalent does in many languages, a distinction made later by a shift of emphasis, with 'Blue' increasingly replaced by 'Eternal'. Tenger could be sensed dimly by ordinary people if they climbed the highest peaks, or by shamans when they read the ominous cracks in the scorched shoulder-bones of sheep. This faith was common to all Central Asian peoples. Tenger (also spelled Tngri, Tangra or Tengri) was the god of the sixth-century Turkic tribes that migrated westward and eventually became Bulgarians. He, or it, gets a mention in a Greek inscription on an eighth-century bas-relief known as the Madara Horseman in eastern Bulgaria.

From the start, the ancestral Mongols would have felt their new-found homeland was blessed. Exploring their new territory, venturing out on to the grasslands with their herds, returning to the forest for game and wood, they would have climbed its bulky central peak, the one that is now known as Khan Khenti, the King of the Khenti. It is not a hard climb. Khan Khenti's 2,452-metre summit would go unnoticed in the Alps or Rockies. Its snow does not last the summer, and there is no glacier. From the bald and windy plateau at its highest point, the Mongols would have checked the lie of the mountains, the way great rivers flowed from the heights – Onon to the east, Kherlen to the south, Tula to the west. As they prospered, they came to see this mountain as the spiritual centre of their world. Here, they felt closest to the benign spirit that had led them here, and would guide them to power and prosperity. They called the peak Sacred Kaldun – Burkhan Khaldun. Their survival as decades turned to centuries justified their faith. If Khenti was the heartland of the Mongols, Burkhan Khaldun was their Olympus.

So it remains today. Although some historians are sceptical that Burkhan Khaldun and Khan Khenti are one and the same, the two have been equated at least since the late thirteenth century, when Genghis's great-grandson Kamala built a temple there. On Khan Khenti's bald pate stand hundreds of those little pyramids of stone – ovoos – that Mongolians make on high places. Stuck with slender poles which flutter with ribbons and silks, many are strewn with offerings – coins, tins, bottles, cigarette cartons – that honour the spirit of the place and the spirit of the man who forged the nation and its empire.

Such were the tools, skills and beliefs possessed by the descendants of the Mongols who set up camp in the Onon valley in AD 800. For almost 400 years thereafter they lived in obscurity, until Genghis came along. Lucky for them he did: the late twelfth century was the last moment at which a conqueror could have emerged. A few decades later, advances in gunpowder technology made the nomads' traditional fighting skills obsolete. As it was, Genghis was just in time to gather the Mongols' inherent forces, like an archer drawing a recurved bow, and release them with devastating effect.

3

A FALSE DAWN FOR A
NEW NATION

GENGHIS WAS DESTINED FOR GREATNESS BY HEAVEN, SAYS *THE*
Secret History with all the advantage of hindsight. Certainly
he had the right background – a lineage of three ambitious
khans who took the Mongols to the brink of empire. But
there was nothing inevitable about his rise. At the time
of Genghis's birth, it looked as if the Mongols had had
their day.

Around 1140 Genghis's great-grandfather, Kabul, became
the first chief to 'rule over all the Mongols', and the first
to take the title of khan. Unity under his authority drew the
tribe into the wider world of Asian politics (whose major
players are outlined overleaf). The Mongols' main rival was
another up-and-coming power to the south, a kingdom
usually referred to as Jin (Golden) after the dynastic title
assumed by its rulers the Jürchen, a Manchurian tribe who
had occupied northern China in a fast and brilliant campaign
a decade before. With their eyes on two other rival neighbours, the Jin needed security on their northern frontier.
Kabul and his Mongols were a threat. The Jin emperor,

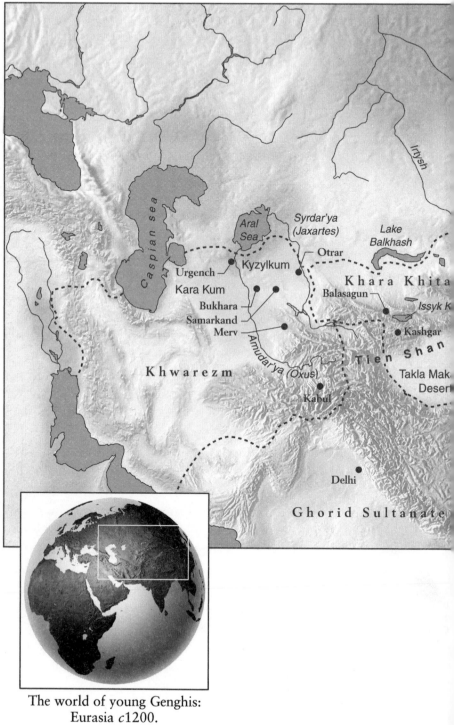

The world of young Genghis:
Eurasia c1200.

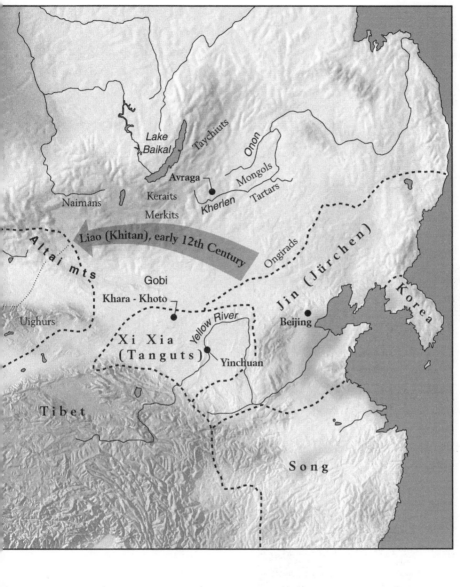

Lake
Baikal

Taychiuts

Onon

Avraga

Mongols

Keraits

Kherlen

Tartars

Naimans

Merkits

Altai mts

Liao (Khitan), early 12th Century

Ongirads

Jin (Jürchen)

Korea

Gobi

Khara - Khoto

Yellow River

Beijing

Uighurs

Xi Xia
(Tanguts)

Yinchuan

Tibet

Song

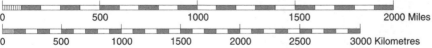

0	500	1000	1500	2000 Miles

0	500	1000	1500	2000	2500	3000 Kilometres

Ho-lo-ma, approached Kabul, proposing a deal. Kabul risked a journey to Beijing – Zhong-du (Middle Capital), as the Jin called it – to talk terms. There was, inevitably, much *airag* consumed. Towards the end of the celebrations, Kabul felt sufficiently at ease to lean across and tweak the emperor's beard. Ho-lo-ma's courtiers were appalled at such a liberty. No deal ensued. Kabul, as an official guest, was allowed to leave in peace, laden with gifts, but the emperor's generals thought better of allowing this drunken and unreliable chief to prosper. A force was sent off to ambush him. He escaped back across the Gobi, but neither side forgave or forgot. The Jin would remember Kabul's affront and their own failure to capture him until the opportunity came to deal with these insolent nomads.

Thus for the first time a Mongol leader stumbled up against the issue that defined Central Asian politics over the course of almost 2,000 years – the tortuous relationship between the settled and the unsettled, the nomad and the farmer, the world of the Inner Asian steppes and that of Asia's socio-political bedrock, China. Since the rise of the first nomad empire around 300 BC the two had been locked into a night-mare of a marriage, bound by need, divided by hatred, each side regarding itself as superior, the other with contempt.

To nomads, their way of life was a glorious freedom, and the farmers mere earth-grubbers, of less value than horses. China's worth lay not in its culture but in its material assets: its metals, silks, weapons and tea (which became a part of the nomad way of life in the tenth century, and remains so today). If trade produced the goods, fine; if not, they could easily be seized. But in acquisition lay danger. The nomad soul was secure when clothed in the armour of traditional life, but vulnerable to the corrupting luxuries on offer beyond the Gobi.

The Chinese, from emperor to mandarin, merchant, scholar and serf, saw their own ancient and sophisticated ways as the basis of true culture, the nomads as mere barbarians, the embodiments of greed and destructive lust. Similar epithets were used by historians for almost 2,000 years: the nomads were ravenous wolves, grasping, insatiable, avaricious, exacting, brutal, untrustworthy. A first-century writer summarized the Chinese opinion of the barbarians: 'Sage rulers consider them beasts, neither establishing contacts nor subjugating them . . . Their land is impossible to cultivate and it is impossible to rule them as subjects. Therefore they are always to be considered as outsiders and never as intimates . . . Punish them when they come and guard against them when they retreat.' One had to trade with these degraded creatures, of course, if only to acquire the horses with which to fight them off. But the relationship was not to be defined by any term so civilized as 'trade'. Nomads offered 'tribute', Chinese graciously conferred 'gifts'. Any connection between the two was an illusion.

For centuries, the leaders of China's shifting kingdoms and empires had wrestled with the 'nomad question' and the problems of the unstable northern border, in particular the Ordos, the scrub-and-desert region within the loop of the Yellow River. How was it best to limit aggression: by appeasement, negotiation, confrontation or invasion? There was no single solution, for in the end the nomads would always have an advantage if they chose to press it. Agricultural societies could be laid waste, but nomad societies could not. Their armies dissipated like smoke over the plains, only to re-form and return when it suited them.

One theoretical possibility was to bar entry. From about 300 BC many walls were built between rival Chinese states, mud-brick embankments that were among the most elaborate defensive structures in the world. On several occasions the emperor of some new and larger kingdom would link up different little walls into a great one. The remains of several 'great walls' can still be traced. One of the oldest runs through the southern Gobi, where its hard-packed earth core is used as a road, and on through Inner Mongolia past the town of Pao-t'ou. Another, built by the Jin themselves, straggles across north-eastern Mongolia. Both are marked on many maps as the 'Wall of Genghis Khan', though they long pre-date him. You come across bits of these walls scattered across northern China, running through desert or dividing wheatfields, mostly worn down to stumps that seem part of the earth, all abandoned and eroded – except for today's Great Wall, built of stone in the sixteenth century, the last and grandest manifestation of an ancient urge. Yet this urge, surprisingly, was not the practical one of keeping nomads at bay. The Great Wall's magnificent progress over peak and valley reveals its redundancy as a defensive structure. Nomad armies do not gallop over hills; the Great Wall was never stormed in war and never stopped an invasion. But it served many other purposes: as a raised road for troops and observers, as a frontier marker to keep peasants in their place and extort taxes, and as proof of a ruler's ability to raise a vast labour force and engage in large-scale projects. The Great Wall and its predecessors were symbols of power and prestige, much as fighter planes and palaces are for modern dictators.

They were also symbols of an age-old prejudice, of a mental Great Wall that marked the frontier of civilization. In the words of the second-century BC historian Ssu-Ma Ch'ien, inside the Wall 'are those who don the cap and girdle, outside are the Barbarians'. The nomads – the antithesis of all virtue and reason, the fearful and evil-smelling opposite of culture – were literally 'beyond the pale', civilization's palisade. To combat the barbarian was a ruler's destiny, the proof of ability, the justification of power; and a wall was an outward and visible sign of his commitment.

It was an unending struggle, for no policy worked for long. Eventually, nomadic clans or leaders would arise who ignored treaties and galloped round walls, pushing the cultivators

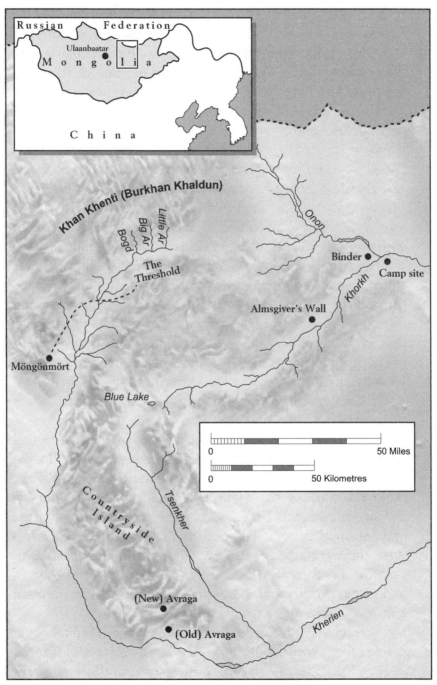

The Mongol Heartland.

away from newly colonized areas back into their own agricultural heartlands. Even here nomads would penetrate, taking cities, sometimes overthrowing dynasties and establishing their own (as the Jürchen had done), until, corrupted and urbanized by the civilization they envied, they in their turn became as obsessed as their predecessors by the 'nomad problem'.

What, then, became of the demon when he crossed the Wall? A magical transformation took place. Once inside, the demon was a demon no longer, but a Chinese ruler. His presence within the Wall became proof not of nomad military power but of the power of China to civilize even the most demonic of external forces. Genghis himself would suffer the very transformation he feared, emerging (in Chinese eyes) from his barbarian chrysalis into panoplied grandeur as the founder of a Chinese dynasty. It was this transformation that the Jin emperor Ho-lo-ma had already undergone when Kabul came calling in the 1140s. That was why his generals took such offence at Kabul's presumptuous gesture, and why they awaited so eagerly the day they could take revenge.

That vengeance fell on Kabul's successor, Ambakai, after he was captured by Tatars, vassals of Jin. He might in other circumstances have been ransomed back to his people; but the Tatars seized this chance to please their Jin overlords, and delivered Ambakai to them. He was executed in a bizarre and grisly fashion, being crucified on a frame known as a 'wooden donkey'. His last message, relayed back to the Mongols just after his capture, acted as a rallying cry to his heirs: 'Until the nails of your five fingers splinter, until your ten fingers drop off, strive to take vengeance for me!'

Kutula, Genghis's great-uncle, responded, launching a series of raids on the Tatars and Jin, earning himself a reputation as a Mongol Hercules. Stories conferred on him a voice like thunder and hands like bear-paws. He ate a sheep at every meal and could snap the strongest man like an arrow.

But strength did not guarantee victory. In about 1160, in unspecified circumstances, the Jin defeated the Mongols. Their clans once again became leaderless. They were a nation no longer.

For a few years the Mongols collapsed back into anarchy. It was the worst of times. Two generations later, according to *The Secret History*, a sage eager to make Genghis's achievements shine the brighter recalled for his khan these dark years, when

> The surface of the earth
> Turned on itself
> And the whole nation was in strife.

In this chaotic, poverty-stricken world, one of the small-time chieftains was the future father of Genghis Khan, a man named Yesugei. Not even *The Secret History*, usually keen to confer stature on Genghis's family, calls him a khan. But he was the grandson of Kabul, the khan who had tweaked the Jin emperor's beard, and was a leading figure among his own clan, the Borjigins.[1] Since clans – in effect, extended families – evolved and split as generation followed generation, few clans retained an identity for long, but the Borjigins were a proud group which looked back 150 years to that vague time between memory and legend when they were one of just five clans. By now, the Borjigins had spun off eighteen other clans, yet preserved their own identity as a sort of royal house (people still boast of being a Borjigin, more so than ever since the collapse of communism). Yesugei would have been well known among the people who ranged the steppe and hunted in the forested mountains to the north, along today's Siberian border.

---

[1] Borjigin is the singular, Borjigid the plural. It seems fair to anglicize, in line with 'Mongols'.

As a young man Yesugei made the best of his dire circumstances, weaving patterns in the texture of nomad life that would prove to be of immense significance. A prime aim was to create and cement alliances. One potential ally was a Turkish tribe, the Keraits, neighbours to the west, whose obscure history laps into a couple of odd backwaters.

By 1180 the Keraits had been nominally Christians for almost two centuries. Two Kerait chiefs, father and son, even bore the same Graeco-Latin Christian names: Marcus Kyriakos. They owed their Christianity to a sect not much remembered nowadays, named after the fifth-century patriarch Nestorius, who was anathematized for asserting the equality of Christ's two natures as God and man. In effect, this meant opposing the cult of the Virgin as Theotokos ('God-bearer'), which Nestorius said compromised Christ's humanity. Formal condemnation did not end Nestorius's heresy. His followers fled to Persia and thrived, spreading eastward to China and into Central Asia, where they converted several tribes, including the Keraits: the Metropolitan of Merv claimed that 200,000 of them were baptized in 1009. This unlikely news, with its vastly exaggerated figure, was in part responsible for starting an astonishing and enduring rumour in the Christian world that there lived in Central Asia a Christian king referred to in Europe as 'Prester John' ('Prester' being a contraction of 'presbyter' or 'priest'). In the words of the German bishop who first recorded the rumour in 1145, Prester John, a descendant of the Three Wise Men, would gallop to the aid of western Christians in case of need. Later, this garbled account of a heretical Christian sect and its obscure Central Asian converts would loom large in Europe, when Christian crusaders in the Holy Land were assailed by Muslims and hoped against hope that the armies marauding westward belonged to Prester John coming to save Jerusalem. They were, of course, the Mongols, under Genghis.

The Keraits' current leader was Toghrul ('Falcon' in

Turkish). He had had a colourful career, having been abducted and ransomed twice in childhood, before slaying several uncles to secure the throne. Then, probably in the 1160s, he had been forced to flee by a vengeful relative. Yesugei had helped Toghrul regain the leadership of his tribe. We are not told how this was achieved, but it must have involved raising an army, an indication of Yesugei's authority. After that Toghrul and Yesugei became 'sworn brothers', an alliance which would later prove of peculiar importance in the re-emergence of the Mongols.

A chance meeting changed the course of Yesugei's life, and the world's. One day he was out hawking on the banks of the Onon when he came across a man riding beside a little black two-wheeled cart pulled by a camel, a form of transport reserved for carrying wealthy wives. Perhaps Yesugei recognized him – it was Chiledu, the younger brother of the chief of another neighbouring tribe, the Merkits, who lived in the forests to the north-west. *The Secret History* says it was the glimpse of a girl under the cart's cover that inspired him – Yesugei had no wife, and she was a beauty. Moreover, her clothing showed she was of a clan traditionally linked to the Borjigins by marriage, the Ongirads, who lived on the eastern plains over towards Tatar country. He galloped home, fetched his two brothers and with them overtook the slow-moving little procession. Chiledu fled round the flank of a hill, with the three Mongols in pursuit. But he was not ready to abandon his bride. Circling the hill, he returned to save her. With seconds to spare, she knew escape for them both was impossible. Hadn't he seen their faces? she asked. 'They want your life!' Leave me, she urged, save yourself, find another wife – 'As long as you live, there will be girls on the front seats of carts!' As the three brothers galloped into sight, she tore off her shirt and threw it to him, crying: 'While you live, remember my fragrance!'

Chiledu slapped his horse into a gallop, chased by the

brothers until they realized they could not catch him. Then they returned, grabbed the camel's tether and set off slowly across the grassland, with the young woman, Hoelun, bewailing her fate, throwing herself back and forth, plaits flying, in an agony of grief.

Later sources omitted this incident, as if the authors saw something discreditable about the kidnapping of a woman who was so obviously in love with her current man and so unwilling to become the bride of the 'hero' Yesugei. But *The Secret History* displays a Homeric feel for both narrative and realism: wife-snatching was common, tribes had traditional marriage partners, the Merkits were fair game, and Yesugei's action provides essential motivation for a conflict with the Merkits later in the story.

One of the brothers, riding beside the cart, told Hoelun to shut up and forget Chiledu:

> The one who embraced you
> Has crossed many ridges;
> The one you cry for
> Has crossed many waters.
> Even if you cry out,
> Even if he looks back, he will not see you.

So Hoelun had little option but to accept Yesugei as her new husband and protector in their life of herding and wandering, of raiding and being raided.

Six months later, when Yesugei returned to his camp on the Onon after a springtime raid on the Tatars, Hoelun greeted her husband with the news that she was pregnant.

4

THE ROOTS OF AMBITION

PRACTICES RECORDED IN THE NINETEENTH CENTURY SUGGEST that at the time of Genghis's birth Hoelun's *ger*, protected from evil by a bow and arrows hung up over the door, would have been off limits to all but the immediate family and a female shaman to act as midwife. The shaman would have looked closely at the baby for some omen. It would not have taken much imagination for her to read a suitable sign in the blood on the new-born son of a powerful chief. *The Secret History* reports that the baby emerged with a clot of blood in his right hand, which was naturally later interpreted as a sign of strength. The baby would have been anointed with butter-oil, wrapped in lamb's wool, and placed in a wooden cradle with bore-holes along its sides so that it could be strapped onto Hoelun's back as she rode.

Then came the matter of the name. Yesugei had returned from his raid with a captive, a Tatar chief. Following tradition, he named the boy after his captured foe (of whom we hear no more; perhaps he was returned to his people in exchange for a ransom), and the future Genghis Khan entered life with a Tatar name: Temujin.

Given Temujin's later success, many have been tempted to read significance into the name. It is sometimes said to derive from *tömör*, 'iron', the first element in *tömör dzam*, literally 'iron road', i.e. railway, and in *tömörchin*, 'blacksmith'. This notion seems to have come originally from the thirteenth-century Flemish traveller, Friar William of Rubrouck, who referred to Genghis as a blacksmith by origin, without further comment. Where did he get this odd idea? It sounds like a detail that he might have picked up from his interpreter, the adopted son of a Parisian goldsmith who had been working for the Mongols. Perhaps he asked what 'Temujin' meant, as any aspiring anthropologist would, and received a casual reply: 'Oh, well, it sort of sounds like "man of iron" . . .' The friar's account of his adventures is a prime source of information on the Mongol empire as it approached its peak, but on this point he was wrong. Since the name was that of a Tatar chieftain, it was the *captured* Temujin that would have been the blacksmith, if anyone. In fact, he wasn't. The name has no *r* sound in Mongol. But somehow the mistake endured, as false etymologies will. In Persian, an alternative spelling crept in, Temur̄jin, with that spurious *r*. As the result of an error repeated in two languages, the false derivation became so firmly entrenched that it has appeared in many books. It would be suitable if the world conqueror and destroyer of nations were the Man of Iron, as Josef Djugashvili became 'Stalin', the Man of Steel, but it was not so.

When exactly all this occurred is of passionate concern to Mongols. The generally accepted date of Genghis's birth is around 1162, and this is the year on which officialdom still insists. At the National Day celebrations in 2002, banners proclaimed the year was another special one – the 840th anniversary of Genghis's birth. At this rate, every year ending with a '2' will be another excuse for celebration. But other historians, swayed by the probable date of the Jin victory over the Mongols in about 1160 or working from estimates of Genghis's age at his death, opt for anything between 1155 and 1167. At present it is impossible to be certain; 1162 is as good as any.

If experts argue about when, they also dispute where exactly Genghis was born. *The Secret History* says it was on the Onon, near a place named Deluun Boldog. The name means 'Spleen Hillock'. Your average outsider would not see much likeness between hillocks and spleens, yet two Spleen Hillocks contend for the honour of marking the hero's birthplace.

One is near Dadal, close to where the Onon meets a tributary, the Balj, 80 kilometres north-east of the singularly neat *ger* camp near Binder. This site, complete with 10-metre statue, was officially selected as Genghis's birthplace at the time of the supposed 800th anniversary of his birth in 1962, which was also celebrated with an issue of stamps and an Academy of Sciences symposium. These were all authorized soon after the completion of the Genghis Khan Mausoleum in Inner Mongolia, and it was not hard to interpret the celebrations and the statue as a counter to China's attempt to capture Mongol nationalist sentiment. It was a decision several came to regret, because it fell foul of Soviet ideology. Genghis being a villain in Soviet eyes, and Mongolia being a vassal, it was risky to recast him as a hero. But it seemed a risk worth taking. The Soviet Union had just broken with China, and a show of strength north of the Gobi should not have been out of place. As it happened, things went the other way, perhaps because the statue's sponsor, Central Committee member Tömör-Ochir, had dared criticize Mongolia's Stalinist president, Tsedenbal. In an ideological crackdown, Tömör-Ochir was fired for 'inflaming nationalist sentiment' and heading an 'anti-Party group'. He was exiled to a museum job in a grim little northern industrial town, under

KGB supervision, returning to public awareness only when he was murdered in unexplained circumstances in 1985. The statue itself, however, was allowed to stand, suggesting some tacit high-level support. Today, it is the main tourist attraction in a lakeside resort.

The other contender is the place I could see in front of me that summer morning, standing on a rise above Binder's *ger* camp, with the effects of the previous night's World Cup vodka fading fast. I was by a little rock-pile, made by someone honouring the spirit of this hill. The Onon's fast-flowing shallows, still shadowed from the sun rising behind me, rippled over stones. Beneath a divine sky of the purest blue a skylark and two cuckoos called, the only sounds rising from the sweep of forest and river, the grasslands, a lake, and the hill that was the key to this historical conundrum.

We had driven right over this Spleen Hillock the day before. It looked like any other wave in the ocean of grass, but it was memorable because along its base ran a fearful mess. A couple of generations ago, Binder lay at the base of the hill. Communist authorities ordained a move. The whole town shifted a few kilometres sideways, leaving the brick foundations and heaps of tin sheeting, where they remain to this day. I could still see the old town's faint shadow from my hill some 4 kilometres away. Conservationists would call it an eyesore; but the steppe has its own rules. The grasslands are vast, there are no roads, herds can wander freely and there's no hint of pollution. Why bother to clear it up?

This is the more recent claimant to be Genghis's real birthplace. It is coming up fast, for sound historical reasons, summarized in a pamphlet on sale at the *ger* camp – by Professor Sukhbaatar of Genghis Khan University in Ulaanbaatar – and in words I had heard the day before from a man of equal eminence.

We had been driving over a slowly rising expanse, hills on the horizon, nothing of interest in view, until in the distance appeared a little house of dark wood. It was like something out of a fairytale, with a porch and a single room. This miniature Siberian *dacha* was, apparently, the summer residence of one of Baatar's many friends. To Baatar's question, a wizened lady pointed further along the faint track. A light rain was falling by now. Ahead through the spattered windscreen was a strange figure, which, as we swung around beside him, turned out to be a remarkably handsome man in his seventies, dressed in a tattered shirt and pulling a small, four-wheeled trolley, with some sort of black-and-white sheepdog by his side. This was Badamdash, philologist, historian and professor at the Mongolian National University for thirty years until his retirement, hauling a metal churn full of water, which he had just collected from a nearby spring. Accepting Baatar's sudden arrival with no comment, he crowded into the van, with the damp dog on his lap. Baatar loaded the water-churn and trolley. I stroked the dog, which licked my hand and whined pathetically. This was a total novelty. The main purpose of dogs in the steppe is to scare off wolves and thieves, so most are monstrous and vicious, making no distinction between wolves, criminals and well-intentioned strangers. Mongolian dogs are by nature man-eaters. Some try to eat passing cars. The first thing you do as you approach a *ger* is to shout, from a safe distance: 'Keep down your dogs!' Never before out here had I come across a dog smaller than a pony, certainly not a friendly, nervous one.

Back in the one-room *dacha*, Baatamdash told me of his researches into Genghis's birthplace. He was familiar with *The Secret History* from childhood, of course, and knew Genghis was born 'on the Onon'.

'When I went to Dadal, I believed Genghis must have been born in such beautiful country, such wide open spaces. But now I've changed my mind.' He had been up and down both sides of the Onon on horseback several times. *The Secret History* says that Genghis caught fish in the Onon as a child, so the camp must have been near the river. The site near Dadal is 20 kilometres from the river; but the one near Binder a mere 5 kilometres away. Besides, Dadal is more enclosed. There's not so much space for troops to gather, and Genghis's father had raised armies. No doubt in Baatamdash's mind: the junction of the Onon and the Khorkh, the plain I saw from my hillside viewpoint that summer morning, the hill that rimmed it – this was Genghis's birthplace.

When the boy was eight, Yesugei set out to arrange a marriage for Temujin with Hoelun's relatives. On his way eastwards across the grasslands, before he reached Hoelun's immediate family, he came across a couple from her clan, the Ongirads. They had a daughter, Börte, a year older than Temujin, and were keen for a match. Yesugei and Dei-Tsetsen – Dei 'the Wise' – agreed, in a stock phrase, that both their children had 'fire in their eyes and light in their faces' – meaning they were destined for fame. To seal the bond, Yesugei left his son with his future in-laws, perhaps so that they could be sure of his character, perhaps so that the boy could work off the cost of Börte's future dowry (a lavish one, as we shall see). On leaving he told Dei to look after Temujin, and make sure to keep control of the dogs, because 'my son is afraid of dogs. My kinsman, don't let my boy be frightened by dogs!'

Westerners may raise an eyebrow. The future ruler of all Eurasia afraid of *dogs*? In fact, it could simply be a reflection of the general truth I mentioned earlier. Mongolian dogs were *always* notorious. I'll bet Genghis himself included this wry detail, which must have struck the author of *The Secret History* as a nice human touch. You see? The mighty Genghis was an ordinary man at heart, with ordinary fears.

During the journey home Yesugei came across a group of Tatars feasting; in accordance with the rules of hospitality on the steppe, he was offered food and drink. By the time he reached home three days later he was sick, indeed dying. Later, looking for an explanation for his illness, his descendants fixed on the Tatars. Obviously, the band *must* have included people who had been the victims in one of Yesugei's raids. He had not recognized them – so this rationalization ran – but they must have recognized him, and seized the chance to take revenge by mixing poison into his drink. Or perhaps he just fell ill. In any event, just before he died, he summoned Temujin back from Dei's tent.

Hoelun was left without a protector, and with six children aged between three and nine: four of her own and two by an unnamed 'minor wife'. The family – even Yesugei's brothers, who should have supported their sister-in-law – were no help. Their world, their hopes for success in war, their insurance against catastrophe had suddenly vanished. They abandoned the widow, leaving her destitute.

But she was a woman of spirit. With no herds to call her own, she became a hunter-gatherer. *The Secret History* depicts her, skirts hoisted, noblewoman's hat firmly on her head, grubbing with a sharpened juniper stick in the forested flanks of Burkhan Khaldun and along the banks of the Onon for fruits and roots. The boys learned to make hooks and use nets to catch fish.

> With wild onions and garlic
> The sons of the noble mother were nourished
> Until they became rulers.
> The sons of the patient noble mother
> Were reared on elm-seeds,
> And became wise men and lawgivers. (tr. Onon)

No doubt the stories overdid Hoelun's mother-of-god nobility, but the point is clear. For three or four crucial years, Temujin knew what it was like to be at the bottom of the heap, to be without the protective network of family, companions and close friends, without enough animals to provide meat, milk or felt for a new *ger* covering. He may well have grown up feeling trapped in the brutal hand-to-mouth existence of down-and-out hunter-gatherers, longing for the relative wealth and freedom of the steppe.

During this harsh time Temujin found a best friend, a boy named Jamukha. At the age of ten, the two exchanged gifts. In winter, swaddled in furs against the cold, they swapped animal dice made from sheep's ankle-bones, which they rolled on the frozen Onon. Children and adults still play with ankle-bone dice today, naming the six sides, each knobbly in its own way, after animals. In the spring, as the grass grew sweet through the melting snow, Jamukha made Temujin a whistling arrowhead in exchange for an arrow tipped with horn. (Whistling arrows are useful in deer-hunting: they startle the deer into lifting their heads to listen, motionless, thus turning them into perfect targets.) Twice the boys swore they would be the equivalent of blood brothers – *anda*.

This was a family under stress – a single woman raising four of her own children and two stepchildren. It was hardly surprising if the two eldest boys, Temujin and his half-brother Begter, felt a growing sense of rivalry. One autumn, when Temujin was thirteen, the two quarrelled over a lark and a minnow Temujin had caught. When Temujin complained to his mother, Hoelun reproached him. How could he say such things at a time when

> Apart from our shadows we have no friends
> Apart from our horse-tails we have no whips.

Why couldn't they get along better? Temujin slunk away, seething, taking his younger brother Kasar, aged eleven, with him. Then, bows at the ready, they crept up on Begter, who was on a rise watching over some pale-bay geldings, and killed him, in cold blood.

Other later sources omit this foolish and cowardly act, presumably because it reflects badly on the future emperor. Why would Genghis, or the bards, or *The Secret History*'s editor, or all of them, include it? Perhaps because it makes two points. First, even as a child the future world conqueror showed the ruthlessness necessary to win and keep leadership. More importantly, it reveals just how much this headstrong boy had to learn.

There was only one person who could teach him the error of his ways. When Hoelun discovered the crime, she was distraught. In words that had been turned into poetry by the time *The Secret History* was written, she delivered a scathing condemnation. 'You destroyers!' she yelled,

> Like a wild dog
> Eating its own afterbirth . . .
> So you have destroyed!

Resorting to one of its many catchphrases, *The Secret History* has her 'citing old sayings, quoting the words of old men', then asking again how they could do this at a time when 'apart from our shadows we have no friends'? Later, it was said that Temujin never lost respect for his mother, who had in such searing terms instilled the need to balance the urge for vengeance with the need for co-operation and loyalty. The lesson was well learned. Temujin never expressed a flicker of regret for killing Begter; but the family stayed together, and Kasar would later become a close aide to his elder brother.

No friends apart from shadows; and now more enemies. Not long after this, perhaps the following April, the Taychiuts, relatives of the Borjigins, launched a raid on Hoelun's camp. Motives are obscure; possibly their chief was jealous, already seeing the bright, assertive Temujin as a future rival. If so, Begter's murder gave him an excuse to seek Temujin out as a criminal. When they came, though, Temujin and two of his brothers escaped across the melting snow into a narrow valley, where they remained, trapped. 'Send out Temujin!' called the attackers. 'We don't want the rest of you!' Temujin fled alone through the forest and hid for nine days, until hunger drove him out into the arms of the Taychiuts. He was led away, a captive.

This episode and the adventure that followed are power-fully told in *The Secret History*, partly no doubt because they make a good story, and partly because they contain a number of insights about life on the steppe and Genghis's character. He himself must have told the tale many times, and approved its retelling as a way of showing his growing strength, maturity and Heaven-sent good fortune.

For a week or two, Temujin was held prisoner by the Taychiut chief, Kiriltuk, a man of such bulk that *The Secret History* refers to him by his nickname, 'Fatty'. He preferred not to ride a horse, being taken about in a cart. Under 'Fatty' Kiriltuk's orders, Temujin was passed from camp to camp each day. He was not bound, but made to wear a heavy wooden collar knotted round his neck and wrists. Known as a cangue, this portable pillory was the usual method of restraining a criminal all across Mongolia and China until recently. It had a chain or rope attached, which was used to lead the prisoner and tie him up.

His prospects could hardly have been worse; but character and chance were about to come to his aid. One night Temujin found himself billeted with a man named Sorkan-shira, a member of one of the Taychiuts' subject tribes, and not as loyal to their fat leader as he might have been. He allowed his two sons to loosen Temujin's cangue to allow him to sleep more comfortably. Here was a tiny foundation for friendship, which could be built upon if and when the time came.

The next night was a full moon: Red Circle Day, as the Mongols call it. The Taychiuts had gathered for a celebration. Imagine the broad valley of the Onon, scattered trees overlooked by ridges, horses and sheep grazing the pastures, dozens of round tents, smoke curling from the smoke-holes, horses tethered outside each tent, hundreds of people from the surrounding encampments, an air of rejoicing. Among the gathering crowds that afternoon is the captive Temujin, in his cangue, guarded by a 'puny youth' who has been given the task of holding the prisoner's rope, leading him through the crowd, accepting the rounds of *airag*, proud of the attention.

As the long summer twilight dwindles, the people – most of them the worse for drink – head for their tents under the full moon. Temujin seizes the moment. He jerks the rope out of his guard's fingers, swings his wooden collar, clouts the poor boy on the head and flees into the woods. Behind him he hears a plaintive yell – 'I've lost the hostage!' – and knows they will be after him. No time to linger, not with that moon. But here is the River Onon. He runs to the bank, finds a backwater, staggers in, and lies down, his head raised clear of the chilly water by the wooden cangue.

His pursuers stick to the woods, all except one, who is on his way home downriver. It is Sorkan-shira, taking no real part in the hunt. He spots Temujin. Astonished, he mutters, 'No wonder they say there's fire in your eyes and light in your face! No wonder they're jealous of you! You just lie there, and I won't say a thing.'

Then, seeing the pursuers in the distance, he turns towards them. Learning they are about to extend the search, Sorkan-shira delays things with a suggestion that everyone should first look again where they have searched already, just to make sure. Off they go, leaving Sorkan-shira to whisper to Temujin that his captors are sharpening their teeth, so he'd better lie low and keep quiet.

Again the pursuers search, and again Sorkan-shira accosts

them, making fun of their failure, urging them to look once more before calling off the search until the morning. As the forest and nearby pastures fall silent, Sorkan-shira tells Temujin to wait until the coast is clear, then go off to his mother's – and 'If you are seen by anyone, don't say you saw me.'

Temujin, though, has a better idea. He is in a dire state. His hands are fixed in the cumbersome cangue, which has rubbed his neck and wrists raw. He could not ride even if he had a horse. To flee on foot would make him obvious. He is in sodden woollen clothes, shivering in the icy water. The night air is near freezing. Flight would mean at worst death by exposure, at best recapture. So he totters after Sorkan-shira downstream, looking out for the tent where he passed the previous night, pausing now and then in the moonlight to listen for the slop-slop of paddles in leather buckets as women churn mare's milk late into the night to make *airag*.

He hears the noise, finds the tent and enters. At the sight of the shivering and dripping fugitive, Sorkan-shira is horrified, imagining his fate if the searchers come by. He's keen for Temujin to be off at once, whatever the risk. His family, though – his wife, his two sons, his daughter – are as sympathetic as before. They untie the cangue and burn it. They dry Temujin's clothes, feed him and hide him in a cart of sheep's wool. He sleeps.

The next day is hot. The Taychiuts continue their hunt, turning from the forest to the tents, and come at last to Sorkan-shira's. They poke about, looking under the beds, and then in the cart, with its pile of wool. They are just on the point of revealing Temujin's foot – a detail surely included by some bard seizing a chance to increase the tension – when Sorkan-shira can stand it no longer.

'In this kind of heat,' he says, 'how could anyone bear it under that wool?'

Feeling foolish, the searchers leave.

Sorkan-shira sighs with relief. 'You almost had me blowing in the wind like ashes,' he says, and tells Temujin to get out. There's talk, perhaps an argument, about what is right and best. In the end, Sorkan-shira makes sure Temujin has a good chance of escape, giving him food and drink, and a horse. But he does not provide a saddle, or tinder, or a bow. Temujin must have nothing that can be traced back to him, nor be tempted to light a fire or risk a fight. Temujin rides upstream, picks his way safely past the sleeping Taychiuts, follows in his mother's tracks to her place of refuge on the upper Onon, and finally rejoins his family.

Though the details vary in other sources, *The Secret History*'s version has the ring of truth, for it portrays the experiences and reveals the reactions that form Temujin's character. He knows what it is like to be poor and outcast. He knows the crucial importance of family. He sees when to act, and acts decisively, but he has steady nerves, and can contain himself. Crucially, he can spot a potential ally, and understands how to build loyalty (Temujin would remember the crucial kindness of Sorkan-shira's boys, and would make one of them a general). By the time he arrived back at his mother's tent, he might have been eager for revenge, but overriding that impulse must have been a clear commitment to rebuild what had been lost. Revenge would be sweet, but only if it served the most fundamental need: security.

To achieve that, he needed more than bravery, more than a warrior's skills. He needed the social and political skills of the true leader – in a word, charisma. By the age of fifteen, he was well on the way.

The Secret History continues with another epic incident. A year passes. The family has herds, and nine horses: enough for their needs, but not enough to count as wealth. One day, when Temujin's surviving half-brother Belgutei is out hunting marmots on the best horse, a chestnut, thieves steal the other eight. Temujin and the others can only watch in helpless rage.

Towards evening, when Belgutei returns, the boys argue briefly about who will take up the pursuit. Temujin, the eldest, insists it must be he, and gallops off on the one remaining horse, tracking the thieves across the grass for the next two days.

On the third morning he comes across a tent, and a large herd of horses being tended by a teenager, a 'strong and handsome youth' named Boorchu. Yes, he saw Temujin's light-bay geldings being driven past earlier. Insisting that Temujin leave his own exhausted horse and take a new one, a black-backed grey, Boorchu shows Temujin the tracks. By now Boorchu has seen how drained Temujin is by the ride. Besides, horse theft is a crime and deserves punishment. Boorchu takes a sudden decision. 'All men's sufferings are common,' he says. 'I will accompany you.' He doesn't bother to return to his tent to tell his father what is happening. Off they go together.

Another three days later, the two catch up with the robbers and their herds, including the stolen horses. The two companions act instantly, riding into the herd, cutting out their own horses and galloping off. A lone horseman follows, only to fall back when Temujin shoots an arrow at him.

Approaching Boorchu's father's camp, Temujin makes a generous gesture. 'My friend, without you, how could I have recovered the horses? Let us divide them. You must tell me how many you want.'

No, no, Boorchu replies. He wouldn't think of it. His father is rich and Boorchu is an only son. He has all he needs. Besides, he acted in friendship. He couldn't possibly take a reward, as if the horses were mere booty.

When the pair arrive back at Boorchu's tent, there is an emotional reunion between the boy and his father, who has been devastated by the disappearance and presumed death of his son. Boorchu, the typical teenager, is unrepentant. He's back, so what's the problem? After the scolding and the tears of relief, father and son give Temujin food, and the father,

Naku, seals the bond between the two boys: 'You two are young men. Look after each other. From now on, do not abandon each other.' Temujin will remember Boorchu's selfless nobility, and Boorchu will later become one of the greatest of Mongol generals.

There remained a promise to be fulfilled and a ready-made ally to be rediscovered. Temujin, now sixteen, returned to Dei-Tsetsen's tent to marry his betrothed, Börte, as arranged by his father some seven years previously. Börte was seventeen, quite ready for marriage, and her parents were delighted. Dei had heard what had happened and feared the worst. Now there was a cause for celebration.

The Secret History says nothing of the wedding, probably because its ritual would have been familiar to its listeners and readers. It would have been quite an event, for Dei was not poor. A shaman would have declared a propitious day, on which the couple would 'bow to Heaven'. Marriage ceremonies changed after Buddhism became the dominant religion in Mongolia in the sixteenth century, but enough of the ancient rituals endured until recently to imagine the scene: the groom in smart *deel*, carrying his bow and arrows; a formal meeting of the family groups; a poetic recitation of genealogies to assert status and prove the bride and groom were from different clans; a grand entry into Dei's tent; the presentation of new clothes and a new bow and arrows to Temujin; an exchange of good wishes; a feast, with the eating of a particularly tough piece of mutton to symbolize the strength of the marriage-bond; and the farewell, preceded by ritual banter – the groom insisting on staying with his new wife in her family's tent, the bride's family driving them off with mock abuse, throwing dried animal dung at them ('the nomadic equivalent of confetti'); and the departure, the bride bearing her clothing – in this case, her dowry, a black sable gown. It must have been a magnificent object: jet-black, sleek as oil, with sleeves long enough to cover the hands in cold weather and a hem reaching down to mid-calf.

It's fair to assume that by now Temujin's ambition matched his aristocratic ancestry. He lost no time in capitalizing on his increased status as a married man and head of the family. He sent off Belgutei, his compliant younger half-brother, to find Boorchu to be his right-hand man. He could already count on his own family, two 'sworn brothers' and another Mongol clan, Börte's and Hoelun's people, the Ongirads. He could do with more help, though, and knew where to look for it. Before his birth, his father had sworn brotherhood with Toghrul, the Kerait leader, who was now powerful enough to command two 'ten thousands', that is, two divisions. His sway stretched from central Mongolia – his headquarters was actually on the Tula river, on the outskirts of Ulaanbaatar, today's capital – to the Chinese border south of the Gobi. Here was a man with real clout.

Telling himself that his father's sworn brother was 'almost like my father', Temujin took his brother Kasar and half-brother Belgutei off to win himself a new ally. But what if Toghrul didn't agree? Temujin had something that might be persuasive: Börte's dowry, the black sable gown.

Temujin guessed right. Toghrul didn't respond when Temujin reminded him of the connection with his father. But the gift did the trick. 'In return for the sable jacket,' Toghrul said, 'I will unite your scattered people.'

Soon after this, probably in 1184, when Temujin was around 20, came another reverse, and another success. News of Temujin's rise had reached the forest-dwelling Merkits. Temujin's mother, Hoelun, had been stolen from their chief's brother, Chiledu, who had since died. Now was a good time to take revenge, before Temujin became too powerful. This would demand a large-scale operation that would take the men away from their flocks for two to three weeks, for the Merkits were based over 300 kilometres to the north on the Selenga river, over the border that divides present-day Russia and Mongolia.

The raid comes soon after dawn, when Temujin's family are camping in a broad valley near the headwaters of the Kherlen – the only valley that leads towards Burkhan Khaldun, the valley that slopes down from forest across pasture to riverside willow bushes; the valley that anyone has to follow if they wish to visit the mountain today. An old serving woman, woken by the beat of galloping hooves, yells a warning. Hoelun snatches up the five-year-old girl, Temulun, and joins the young men fleeing upriver, over a ridge between two hills, and along the forested flanks of Khaldun. The ridge, known as the Threshold, is not considered worth mention in *The Secret History*, because it is easy to cross with horses, though not with wagons (or cars, as you will see in chapter 17). Only Börte and the old servant, Koagchin, are left without mounts. Koagchin thrusts Börte into an enclosed ox-drawn carriage, perhaps aiming for the Threshold, when Merkits gallop up, demanding Temujin. There's his tent, she says, but as for Temujin, she has no idea. Anyway, she's only there to help with sheep-shearing, and now she's off home. She might have got away, but the rough ground snaps the cart's wooden axle. The Merkits gather again, wondering what's in the cart. Sheep wool? Not likely. Take a look, boys. Young men dismount, open the door, and see a prize, 'someone who seemed to be a lady sitting there'. Two men order her out, haul her up onto one of their horses' rumps, and join in the search for Temujin on Burkhan Khaldun's forbidding flanks, squelching through muddy flood plains and forests thick enough to stop a bear. At last, they withdraw with their captives. 'We have taken our revenge,' they tell each other, and begin the week-long haul back home. Once there, Börte is handed over to Chiledu's younger brother, Chilger.

Temujin, meanwhile, has been lying low, following

deer-trails he has known since childhood, sleeping rough for three nights beneath shelters of branches torn from the willow bushes that cover the lower slopes.

When the coast is clear on the morning of the fourth day, Temujin emerges from cover, and is overcome with gratitude for his survival. At least, that is how he presented the experience in later life. He was free to do so, for there was no-one else with him at the time to tell the story differently.

> On Sacred Khaldun
> I was a louse
> But I escaped,
> And my life was spared.
> With a single horse,
> Following elk-trails,
> Making a tent of bark,
> I climbed Khaldun.
> On Sacred Khaldun
> I was a swallow
> But I was protected.[1]

Though all mountains are sacred, this mountain of all mountains surely deserves special reverence. He vows he will honour it always as the place of his deliverance by remembering it in his prayers every morning: 'The seed of my seed shall observe this.' Facing the rising sun, he drapes his belt around his neck, removes his hat in reverence, beats his

---

[1] My version, with a hint of the problems for translators in the penultimate line. Onon and Damdinsuren have 'swallow', Cleaves has 'grasshopper'. In Mongol, they are similar: *kharaatsaa/tsartsaa*. 'Grasshopper', an insect-image like the earlier 'louse', seemed right, for isn't a swallow a free spirit, and a poor metaphor? No: for Mongolians (Goyo pointed out), the swallow is a prey for hawks, and a victim. With help, I checked the original. The first character in the Chinese is not a *ts* but a *kh*, to rhyme with Khaldun, which begins the previous line. 'Swallow' it is.

chest, and makes a ritual ninefold obeisance towards the sun, kneeling to anoint the ground with animal fat and *airag*.

Perhaps nothing like this occurred. Perhaps after he founded his empire Genghis chose to dramatize his survival and emphasize the divine right by which he ruled, as Chinese emperors claimed to rule by the 'Mandate of Heaven'. But the mandate normally became apparent only *after a dynasty had come to power*. Genghis goes one better, claiming that Heaven had always been with him, *in advance of* any success, when he was still a louse on the side of a mountain. He could not have chosen a better setting for his claim. The mountain had always been the Mongols' cathedral. It was only natural that Genghis, as ruler, would wish to be seen as its high priest, and to cast his younger self in that role.

This was no mere political stance. I think he believed it, heart and soul. How or why this should be so he could not fathom, and this mystery became part of his character, with some interesting implications for the religions with which he came into contact, and for those who revere him today. It created in him an odd division between the arrogance of one chosen to unite, lead and conquer, who was justified in using every means to achieve Heaven's purpose, and the humility of an ordinary man awed by the inexplicable nature of the assignment. It was this that lay at the heart of the paradoxical whirlwind of destructiveness and creativity, of ruthlessness and generosity, that constituted Genghis's character.

Judging by *The Secret History*'s straightforward account, his people took the story of his revelation on Burkhan Khaldun at face value. *The Secret History*'s first sentence proclaims that he was 'born with his destiny ordained by Heaven above'. It was this belief that gave him his charisma, and inspired his companions, his family, his officers and his subjects.

Temujin's next task was to rescue Börte. He turned to the

man he called 'Father', Toghrul, and was not disappointed. Had Toghrul not promised that he would help Temujin unite the Mongols? Now—

> In return for the coat of black sable
> I will crush the whole Merkit tribe,
> And bring Lady Börte back to you.

He would send his two cavalry divisions; Temujin had a small army of his own, and for additional help called on his childhood friend and sworn brother, Jamukha. He, too, had been through adversity, having been captured by Merkits and forced into servitude until he found a chance to secure his freedom and build a following. Now he was head of his own clan, as much of a man to be reckoned with as Temujin. Eager for revenge on the Merkits and eager to help his blood brother, he undertook to provide another two divisions, and sent back messengers with detailed instructions about where and when the forces were to meet.

The author of *The Secret History* was careful to record exactly what happened next, because these events teach yet another valuable lesson in the fundamentals of campaigning. The three armies were to rendezvous in the Khenti, the tangle of mountains and valleys that formed the Mongol heartland. Toghrul, having camped on the westward-flowing Tula near the site of present-day Ulaanbaatar, took his two divisions 160 kilometres north-east up the river valley, over the 2,500-metre ridge of the Little Khenti mountains. Meanwhile, Temujin and his division worked their way up the Kherlen and into the same knot of ridges and gulleys. The two armies linked up and descended together into a broad valley made by the headwaters of the Minj, one of the rivers that flowed northwards into the Selenga. There they were to meet Jamukha.

By the time they got there, Jamukha had already been in place for three days, and he was fuming – with good reason.

This was not the wide-open steppe. Here in the heart of the Khenti, pastures were hemmed in by mountains. On a rough estimate, it takes 10 acres to feed a horse for a month. Jamukha had two divisions. Though a division was called a 'ten thousand', in practice it might number no more than 3,000 horsemen. Here, then, were 6,000 men at a conservative estimate, each with two or three spare mounts – say, 15,000 horses. Each day, on average, the horses would graze 5,000 acres of grass – and that excludes the horses belonging to the families already living in the valley. Imagine Jamukha's growing consternation – thousands of men all geared up for battle, sleeping rough, eating into their food supplies, increasingly restless to get back to their herds, the pasture vanishing, the locals facing ruin. Not to mention the fact that such a force would have been no great secret; any wandering Merkit could easily have seen what was up, and galloped off with a warning. Even a day's delay threatened both the economic and strategic basis of the whole operation. This was no way to ensure victory, no way for Temujin to get Börte back. These were lessons that *The Secret History* – and, we may conclude, Genghis himself – were at pains to emphasize with Jamukha's furious words.

'When we Mongols say "Yes",' he shouts, when his allies arrive, 'are we not oath-takers?' There is no possible excuse! If Mongols agree to meet, neither snow nor rain should delay them! Didn't we say – and *The Secret History* makes its point with a couplet:

> Let us expel from our ranks
> Anyone who breaks his promise!

Temujin and Toghrul take the verbal lashing contritely. What can they say? They are at fault. It is for Jamukha to reprove in any way he sees fit, and for the future leader of the nation – and the nation itself, listening to the story – to take note.

A week or so later, the combined armies – 12,000 men or more – working their way north over the mountains towards Lake Baikal, approach the tributary of the Selenga, the Khilok, beyond which the Merkits are camped. They cross by night, each man building a float of reeds and swimming across with a horse. The operation is too huge to achieve total surprise. Huntsmen ranging the Khilok's further banks see what is happening, and gallop off with a warning. The Merkits flee, scattering in panic down to the Selenga and along its banks.

Among those in pursuit of the refugees rides Temujin, calling for Börte. A prized hostage, she is in one of the fleeing carts. She hears the call, jumps down, comes running, seizes his bridle, and as he dismounts throws herself into his arms. It makes a romantic picture: two young lovers in a moonlight embrace, a brief stillness in the midst of turmoil.

That's enough for Temujin. 'I have found what I was looking for,' he says, and calls off the chase.

It was a famous victory. The Merkits were scattered, many of the women taken as concubines and servants; Börte was saved; and Temujin was established as a Mongol leader almost equal to Jamukha. The only shadow was that Börte returned pregnant. Though paternity was never properly established, Börte's first child, Jochi, was stigmatized by his possible illegitimacy, so that he would never be considered truly in line as Temujin's heir.

For eighteen months after the successful campaign against the Merkits, Temujin's family lived with Jamukha's. The two men were inseparable, as they had been as children. They exchanged sashes, they gave each other horses, they feasted together, they slept together (this does not imply homosexuality; sodomy became punishable by death under the code established after Temujin became khan).

But this powerful friendship soured suddenly one April, when family groups were moving to spring pastures along the

Onon river. The two friends are riding along in front of the carts when Jamukha suggests that they should each make their own camp. Temujin pauses, puzzled, wondering if Jamukha is suggesting a separation. He asks Hoelun's advice, but it is Börte who speaks: everyone knows Jamukha tires of things quickly, she says, so probably he's tired of them all.

From this hint, a suspicion grows into a terrible realization. If the two are not as one, what then? If they part, they cannot be companions; if they are not companions, then they are rivals; if rivals, then one or other must dominate; and Temujin is surely not prepared to be a mere follower. Temujin makes his decision, and leads his own group onwards, without camping at all, right through the night.

He might have simply marched away into isolation, and remained a footnote of history. But by the time the stories were dictated and written there was much to be explained, and *The Secret History* does so by condensing a process of small-scale conquests and capitulations into a drama, complete with blatant *post hoc* justifications.

At dawn, strange things happen. Three brothers and their families, leading members of a minor clan, catch up with Temujin. Then another five appear, then more men, more families of more clans – Tarkuts, Bayuts, Barulas, Manguts, Arulats, Urianghais, Besuds, Suldus, Jalairs – all opting for Temujin rather than for Jamukha. They are not the greatest of families, for Jamukha has the loyalty of the established leaders. But Temujin offers something Jamukha cannot: a fierce loyalty towards all who rely on him, a hope for those who otherwise had no prospect of advancement.

Among the Mongol clans, rumours have spread that young Temujin is the one, and rumour strengthens into hope, hope into prophecy. Later arrivals report signs and omens. One man says he has heard an ox bellowing, 'Heaven and Earth agree, let Temujin be the nation's master!' And still they come – Geniges, Sakayits, Jurkins; even some of Jamukha's own clan, the Jadarans – all pitching their tents nearby. Some are relatives, like Temujin's cousin Kuchar and his second cousins Altan, son of the legendary Kutula, and Sacha, great-grandson of Kabul: all senior to Temujin in the family hierarchy, yet all drawn by the feeling that here at last was the man the Mongols needed to restore their lost unity.

The decision itself is formalized by his three senior relatives, who must balance the advantages of serving with a strong leader against the humiliation of submission to a junior. They choose to serve, and swear an oath to pursue their new khan's enemies, to bring him the finest women and the best horses, and to hunt for him. If in war they disobey, 'Separate us, and throw down our vile heads upon the ground!' If in peace they disobey, 'Exile us and throw us out into the wilderness!'

This decade-long process of assimilation, its details largely unrecorded, was complete towards 1200. The main body of Mongols had their new khan. They were a nation once more, ready to turn on their neighbours.

5

THE RISE TO POWER

TEMUJIN'S BIRTHPLACE IS ONLY ONE OF THE HISTORIC SITES associated with his rise. There are many others, and identifying them has become a minor industry in Mongolia. An atlas, a coffee-table book of photographs and numerous tour-company pamphlets pinpoint exactly where Hoelun was abandoned, where Temujin escaped from the Taychiuts, the path he took to find his family again. Most of these identifications are the result of conjecture or wishful thinking, because names are shifty things, slipping out of memory as clans move, combine or scatter. Rivers and mountains may retain their identity down the centuries, but not hills, plains and forests. If Burkhan Khaldun itself is in doubt, who can tell whether the Blue This or the Black That are the same now as then?

But there is one place that does link past and present. It is the place – a lake, a mountain and nearby pastures – where Temujin and his family settled after his great escape, and where in all probability he transformed himself from tribal chief to emperor. Blue Lake, as it was then and is now, is the heartland of his heartland. It is as secure as he could have wished, nestled into Burkhan Khaldun's southerly foothills, high up between the Kherlen and the Khorkh, a safe 60 kilometres from the open plains that sweep down to Avraga. That was the direction from which we approached: up the open valley of the Khorkh river, past forested hills, then beyond the river's source, through an open woodland of slight firs, where daffodil-like flowers dotted the shadows with yellow, and out onto the lakeside arena where Temujin became Genghis.

We left Temujin, approaching 30, in control of half the Mongol clans. To see how he came to rule the whole tribe and then neighbouring tribes as well is to enter into a complex game, played out on shifting ground. In Europe, princes seeking power were rooted in cities, territory, families, the laws of succession. On the steppe, all was fluid. Tradition dictated that leaders did not fool around with the bonds of family, clan and sworn brotherhood; but traditional dictates blew in the wind if there arose a powerful reason for breaking them (and for enduring the heartache that such acts involved). Other lesser rules surrounded feasts, marriages, alliances, campaigns and the sharing out of spoils. But there were no bottom lines, except power and survival. The world itself changed as good year succeeded bad, and the social fabric changed with it. Medieval steppe-land history is a cloud chamber in which the tribal particles collide, split, bounce away, decay, re-form and annihilate each other in an utterly random way. Family ties linked enemies; men could gallop 150 kilometres in a day to spy, or help, or betray, and no-one could tell in advance which it would be. It would take fifteen years for Temujin the clan leader to emerge as Genghis the founder of the nation, the leader with the surest instincts, steadiest ambitions and most firmly grounded character. Hindsight and the sources – which had the advantage of their own hindsight – allow us to suggest which events and character traits explain Temujin's rise. One trait has emerged already: his faith in Heaven's guidance. In what follows, watch for another emerging ever more strongly: his sense of loyalty.

In the early 1190s, he was still at best the second most powerful clan leader, and very nearly something much less. Foreseeing violence, knowing his own strength, Jamukha moved first. There was nothing sudden about this: it took a year, allowing time to look after the herds, to ensure loyalties, to mobilize armies. Then, using the killing of a relative in a dispute over horses as a pretext, Jamukha sent a force of some 20,000–25,000 men to attack Temujin. Warned of their approach by two members of an outlying clan, Temujin hardly had time to rally his own force, with catastrophic results: he fled the field to hide in the twisting gorges on the upper reaches of the Onon, protected again by the foothills of Burkhan Khaldun. *The Secret History* does not provide a coherent narrative of this process, but from the confusion a few major developments emerge. Temujin's patron, Toghrul, the leader of the Keraits, falls on hard times. Toghrul's younger brother, with help from the Naimans, deposes the older man, casting him out. The Naimans now rule the Keraits. Toghrul appeals to Temujin, his ally. The two rejoin forces. Fearful of Temujin's growing power, those tribes close to Jamukha form an alliance and make him their leader, with the title Gur-Khan ('universal ruler'). These tribes include the Taychiuts, the tribe from which Temujin had escaped so dramatically.

At this point, probably in 1202, the story again comes sharply into focus, as forces muster for a great battle on the plains of eastern Mongolia. If *The Secret History* skimps on politics, strategy and military details, its author was at pains to record examples of the one trait that Temujin valued above all: loyalty, the most fundamental of virtues to life on the steppe. Always remembering that these stories were probably sanctioned by Genghis himself, with additional spin from *The Secret History*'s editor to emphasize their messages, we are told that during the battle with Jamukha's coalition Temujin had two narrow escapes, which opened the way for shows of loyalty that bound the participants as if with a sacred vow.

At one point in the battle an arrow just misses Temujin, but pierces his horse's neck, killing it. After he changes mounts another arrow, a poisoned one, actually hits him, in the neck. In camp that night, with no food or drink to sustain him, he lapses into unconsciousness. His deputy, Jelme, sucks the wound clean, then sneaks into Jamukha's camp and steals some curds. When Temujin revives, Jelme feeds him with curds and water. At dawn, as Temujin's strength returns, he sees that he owes Jelme his life.

Later, with the battle won and Jamukha a fugitive, Temujin is out mopping up stragglers from the enemy's camp when he is approached by Sorkan-shira, the man who sheltered him when he was trying to escape from the Taychiuts in a cangue. Now free to join Temujin, he has with him a companion. Temujin asks if Sorkan by any chance knows who fired the arrow that killed his horse.

It is Sorkan's companion, Jirko, who speaks up: it was he who fired the arrow. This is quick thinking. As an enemy warrior who has almost killed Temujin, he could expect summary execution. But he is with Sorkan, the young khan's one-time saviour. Both know the truth. If Jirko keeps quiet, and his act is revealed, he will seem cowardly and deceptive. Better to come out with it, even at risk of death – a risk he minimizes by dedicating himself to Temujin, promising to obey any order, however difficult. If you kill me, he says, I'll only rot away in a plot of earth the size of your hand; but if you show mercy, I'll cut through oceans and mountains for you. On other occasions, later in life, Temujin had no time for turncoats. But there is no betrayal involved here. Both had been enslaved by the enemy. Swayed by Sorkan's presence, Temujin praises Jirko's honesty and courage. 'This is a man to have as a companion,' he says, and renames him on the spot in memory of his deed. 'He shall be named Jebe ['Arrowpoint'] and I will use him as my arrow.'

Jebe and Jelme would become two of the khan's greatest generals.

After the battle, the Taychiut chief who had held Temujin captive – 'Fatty' Kiriltuk – is himself captured by a man of a subordinate clan and his two sons. The three shove Kiriltuk on his back in a cart, and then, with the father of the two young men sitting on the captive's paunch, they set off to give themselves up with their prize. On the way, however, they recall Temujin's uncompromising views on loyalty, and begin to wonder if they are doing the right thing. They have, after all, sworn to serve the man who is now their prisoner. Rather than resort to treachery, they let their captive go, and present themselves to Temujin without him. It is a good move. Even though Temujin would have done Kiriltuk to a terrible death, he places loyalty to a leader above his own desire for revenge. 'You were unable to forsake your rightful khan. Your heart was right,' he tells the three men, and takes them into his service. (Kiriltuk gets his come-uppance anyway, being killed later by one of Sorkan-shira's sons.)

There remained two major obstacles to Temujin's total command of the region. The first was that Jamukha remained at large, at the head of an alliance of tribes. The second was his unstable senior ally, Toghrul.

Toghrul is now ageing and insecure. In a battle against the Naimans, he flees the field before battle is joined, only to be pursued by the enemy and see his wife and son, Nilka, kidnapped. Yet he still has the nerve to ask for Temujin's help. Temujin responds, yet again, sending his four best warriors to rescue Toghrul's family. Toghrul is naturally overwhelmed with gratitude, swearing again that Temujin is like a son to him. 'When we are riding against our enemies, let us ride out together with one goal; when we are hunting wild beasts, let us hunt together with one aim.'

To secure the alliance, Temujin suggests that his son Jochi should marry Toghrul's daughter, while his own daughter should marry Toghrul's son, Nilka. But Nilka, though he owes his life to Temujin, is jealous of Temujin's authority and wary of losing his inheritance as clan leader to the man his father has so recently called 'son'. He scathingly rejects the marriage proposals. Toghrul is caught between two conflicting loyalties: to his son and heir Nilka, and to the son of his blood brother, his saviour Temujin. In his dilemma he emerges as something of a tragic figure.

If Temujin, the junior partner, is rejected, Toghrul seems to the other commanders the man most likely to rule the steppe. Alliances re-form. Jamukha contacts Toghrul with a message: Temujin is not to be trusted; move against him, and I will join you. Toghrul, bound by the bonds of blood brotherhood and the knowledge of Temujin's loyalty, freezes, totally unable to resolve the conflict. Nilka twice sends messages to his father, begging him to act against Temujin. Couldn't the old khan see the truth – that Temujin intended to seize power over all of them? Still Toghrul does nothing, and *The Secret History* is at pains to reveal the agony of his indecision. 'How can I forsake my child, my son?' he says, hopelessly. 'By Heaven we shall definitely not be loved! How can all of you tell me to forsake my son?'

Nilka then resorts to treachery, sending an invitation to Temujin, offering his sister's hand after all, intending to capture and kill him. Warned of the trap by two spies, Temujin flees with a small band of men along the Khalkha river, and then to the shores of a lake (or possibly a river) called Baljuna. What followed assumed huge significance, because it marked Temujin's nadir in military terms, but a turning-point in terms of leadership. Oddly, no-one has much of a clue where Baljuna was. Scholars have argued for several different possibilities, lying hundreds of kilometres apart. Perhaps it was a pond near present-day Balzino, 150 kilo-metres over the Siberian border; or in Mongolia's far east, near the Khalkha; or 500 kilometres further west, on the Balj river, close to the spot selected as Genghis's birthplace in 1962. Wherever it was, the future emperor was again close to extinction, as recorded in a number of Chinese sources which were rediscovered and translated in the late nineteenth century. According to these, Temujin endured extreme deprivation with nineteen loyal companions, all of whom were reduced to drinking the muddy waters of the Baljuna. In the words of one of two almost identical accounts:

> Upon arrival at the Baljuna, the provisions were used up. It happened that from the north a wild horse ran up.[1] Kasar brought it down. From its skin they made a kettle; with a stone they got fire, and from the river, water. They boiled the flesh of the horse and ate it. Genghis Khan, raising his hand toward the sky, swore thus: 'If I finish "the great work", then I shall share with you men the sweet and the bitter; if I break my word, then let me be as this water.' Among the officers and men, there was none who was not moved to tears.

This was Temujin's Henry V moment, at which a leader willing to share suffering, defeat and death with his companions forged a bond like no other:

---

[1] Wild horses, a subspecies of domestic horses, were commonly hunted, because they were intractable and interbred with domestic horses. They became rare, and were only formally classified in the nineteenth century by the Russian explorer Nikolai Przhevalski. Many were captured and taken to western zoos. The *takhi*, as the Mongolians call *Equus przewalski*, went extinct in the wild in the 1960s, but has now been successfully reintroduced.

For he today that sheds his blood with me
Shall be my brother.

The future Genghis would have approved King Harry's words. The experience of 'drinking the muddy waters' was Genghis's St Crispian's Day. It united a band of brothers who would glory in their hardships and the loyalty that locked together lord and warriors. In later life, those who were part of the Baljuna Covenant, as scholars call it, stood a-tiptoe at its mention. This was a story that good men would tell their sons.

Yet despite its significance, the incident does not appear in *The Secret History*. Since the events before and after are there, the exclusion would surely have been deliberate. We can only guess at the reason. Perhaps the event was omitted *because* of its significance, as a way for an inner circle of initiates to guard their secret bond. Perhaps the Baljunians became a sort of freemasonry, fiercely protective of their special status, unwilling to have it sung by bards and written down for all the world to see. I can also imagine a more altruistic reason. By the time the *History* was written, 25 years later, many other brave and loyal men had joined the imperial ranks, and it would, perhaps, have seemed impolitic to glory publicly in an experience from which so many worthies would be excluded.

From Baljuna, where he and his happy few regain their strength over the summer of 1203, Temujin sends a long and moving message to Toghrul, in effect suggesting national unity – but on whose terms? What the message said originally is anyone's guess. All we have is the spin provided by the future Genghis and *The Secret History*. Naturally, it seizes the moral high ground. Khan, my father, Temujin asks in sorrow, why turn against me? Don't you recall how we swore allegiance? Were we not like oxen pulling together, or like the wheels on a two-wheeled cart? Did not Yesugei, my father, come to your help? Were you two not sworn brothers? Did you not say 'I will repay your favour to your children's children'? When you were cast out, surviving with five goats, drinking the blood of your camels, did I not restore you? When you were plundered by the Naimans, did I not send my four greatest men, my four 'war horses', to help you, and save your son? So why, khan my father, do you now turn against me?

Morally, Temujin's position is strong, and Toghrul knows it. 'Oh, my poor son,' he groans. 'Am I to separate from him?' Militarily, though, Temujin is weak, and can only wait for the revival that will come with the high summer's grass, drawing strength from the arrival of reinforcements from his wife's people, the Ongirads, and other local clans.

He is right to wait. In his absence, Toghrul's alliance falls apart. Jamukha, always impatient with Toghrul, plans to assassinate the old man. Toghrul discovers the plot. The plotters flee to join the Naimans. Temujin falls upon the hapless Toghrul, and after a three-day battle – there are no other details of this great clash – is victorious. Jamukha, Toghrul and his son flee westward, into Naiman lands.

There Toghrul is killed by a guard who refuses to believe the refugee is the great khan of the Keraits. Later, when his identity is established, his head is brought to the Naiman headquarters, where the queen mother orders a tribute to the Naimans' former ally. The head is placed on a white felt carpet, and becomes the centrepiece in a ceremony of wine libations and fiddle-playing. The Naiman crown prince, Bai Bukha – usually known by his Chinese title Tayang – is hypnotized by this bizarre ritual. He can't take his eyes off the severed head. Suddenly he yells: 'It smiled!' and stamps the head to a bloody pulp. His parents are appalled, especially Tayang's father. When a shaman interprets the barking of dogs as an omen of disaster, the elderly khan sinks into depression. 'I am growing old,' he mutters. 'My son was born stupid,' with no thought for anything but falconry and hunting. He fears for the future of his people under this paranoid dimwit.

Nilka, meanwhile, has fled south and west, leaving Jamukha with the Naimans. Nilka is eventually killed in Kashgar, in Uighur lands, on the far western borderlands of China.

The Naimans remained unconquered and, though living in the remote far west, they were now a threat because they were sheltering their new ally, Jamukha. Temujin knew there would have to be a showdown. In preparation he withdrew eastwards again, back to the Khalkha river, to regroup and plan the coming campaign. When all this was complete, in mid-May 1204, he began his march up the Kherlen towards the Khenti range where the Naimans, under the doubtful leadership of Tayang, were camped. By the time they encountered the enemy, an overwhelmingly superior force, the Mongol horses were exhausted. After spying out the opposition, one of the new commanders suggested making camp to regain strength, and at the same time deterring the opposition from attack by having each man light five fires. It worked. That night, Naiman guards, posted on the heights ahead, reported to their prince that the Mongols 'had more fires than the stars'.

Tayang, the weakling, becomes twitchy, and suggests withdrawal to fight another day. Now for the first time we hear of Tayang's fiery son, Kuchlug, who I imagine to be about 20. Kuchlug will have none of it, saying that his father is as useless as a tethered calf or 'a pregnant woman who doesn't go beyond her pissing place'. One of Tayang's commanders is equally outspoken: If we knew you were going to be so cowardly, he says, we would have sent for your *mother*, you little *shit*. In a paroxysm of rage, Tayang issues the order to fight.

In a preliminary skirmish on plains some 200 kilometres west of present-day Ulaanbaatar, Temujin's vanguard saw off the outlying Naiman troops. And now *The Secret History* starts to revel in the coming victory. When Tayang asks why his men are fleeing, Jamukha reminds the prince that Temujin has four great companions, his 'four hounds', the generals Jebe, Jelme, Subedei and Khubilai (not to be confused with Genghis's grandson, the future khan). They were raised on human flesh, they have

> Foreheads of cast copper,
> Chisels for snouts and
> Awls for tongues
> With hearts of iron and
> Whips for swords they go,
> Eating the dew and
> Riding the wind.

Ah, mutters the nervous Tayang, 'let us stand at a distance from these barbarians,' and backs away into foothills.

And who is that over there, Tayang asks from the new place of safety, the one that looks like a starved falcon?

The one whose body is stitched with cast copper and wrought iron? replies Jamukha. That is Temujin, my sworn brother.

There is a brief silence.

'This is awkward,' says Tayang. 'Let us climb further up the mountain and stay there.'

Now Jamukha has got into his stride. See Kasar, Temujin's brother? Their mother used to nourish him on human flesh. He eats three-year-old bulls. He can swallow a man whole, quiver and all, without it even touching the sides of his throat. He can shoot straight through ten or twenty people, even if they are on the other side of a mountain.

So it goes, until Tayang has retreated right up the

mountain. Jamukha then sends a message to Temujin, telling him how he, the faithful Jamukha, planted such fear in the prince that he has retreated. 'As for myself,' he lies, 'I have separated from the Naimans.'

Whatever the true nature of the epic battle, it ends in Temujin's victory. Tayang dies of his wounds, while Kuchlug flees to the west (to Khara Khitai, where he will build a new life for himself, and live to fight Temujin another day).

Jamukha had also fled into the mountains of the far north-west, with five other survivors, seeking the help of the Merkits, the people who had captured Börte 20 years before. A final campaign ends with the Merkits' defeat. Jamukha is betrayed by his companions and captured. According to *The Secret History*, Genghis executes Jamukha's companions for the crime of turning against their khan, then gives Jamukha a chance to recant, calling to mind their old oaths. 'We should', he says,

> Remind each other of what we have forgotten,
> Wake each other from our sleep.
> When you went away and were apart from me,
> You were still my lucky, blessed sworn brother,
> Surely in the days of killing and being killed,
> The pit of your stomach and your heart yearned for me?

In effect, he is looking for a chance to show mercy. Jamukha may have spoken against me, he says, but 'I have not heard that it was his thinking to harm my life.' But Jamukha knows he is finished; he has, after all, proved himself a dissembler, an intriguer and a traitor. 'Now that the world is ready for you, what use is there in becoming your companion? On the contrary, sworn brother, I would haunt your dreams; in the bright day I would trouble your thoughts.'

> I would be the louse in your collar,
> I would become the splinter in your coat-lining.

There is nothing left for him but to seek an honourable death. 'Let me die without shedding my blood. Kill me and lay my bones in a high place. Then I will protect and bless the seed of your seed for ever.'

This, at least, is *The Secret History*'s story. From it Jamukha emerges as a man who went astray, but in the end regains the nobility that justifies Temujin's earlier trust. And Temujin is the wise and generous leader, who would never willingly abandon the bonds of blood brotherhood. Jamukha condemns himself, and is granted a princely death by strangulation, his body not exposed like that of a criminal, but buried as befits a noble.

Temujin was now absolute master of most of present-day Mongolia, the man who had 'unified the people of the felt-walled tents'. In 1206 a national assembly – the word used then, *kuril*, is used today for the Mongolian parliament – at Blue Lake proclaimed him leader of the newly united nation, and invested with the title Genghis Khan.

This title is a matter of controversy. There were a number of traditional titles, some generously conferred by the Liao or Jürchen rulers of northern China: the leader of Khara Khitai was a Gur or 'Universal' Khan, which was also the title chosen by Jamukha; Toghrul had been the Wang (Chinese: princely) Khan. But neither traditional titles, whether Turkish or Mongol, nor any Chinese title would have seemed appropriate, for no Mongol had ever before risen to such a height. Others, yes; but never a Mongol. Something new was called for.

'Genghis' was an invented title, never conferred before or since, and its origins are much disputed. One tradition was that it was given by the leading Mongol shaman, or the oldest and most revered male, but that says nothing about its meaning. It may, perhaps, have been related to the word for 'sea', *tengis*. Oceans and lakes were objects of particular veneration; when in the sixteenth century a later khan, Altan, wished to confer grandeur on the highest Buddhist dignitary, he made up a Mongolian version of the lama's Tibetan title and called him the *dalai* lama, which also means ocean or great lake. Or perhaps the word *Genghis* was intended to recall the word for Heaven or Sky, 'Tenger', which would make the new emperor a Heavenly Ruler, matching the Chinese emperors who ruled with 'Mandate of Heaven'; perhaps, if only there were an *r* in Genghis, and some suitable grammatical *-is* ending for Tenger, which there isn't. Or perhaps it harks back several centuries to a Uighur ruler called Dengis, or even to Attila's son, Dengizikh, which might or might not equate to the modern Mongol *tengis-ikh* ('sea-great'). But, even assuming a folk memory of such obscure predecessors, why not simply go for the founders, Oghuz and Attila themselves? Nothing really works. At the time, if there were those who knew the title's origin, they kept silent. No-one saw any need to explain it.

This was the moment Temujin's loyal companions had been working, fighting and waiting for. Rewards came in plenty, as *The Secret History* records at length, reviewing the adventures and campaigns that had brought them all to this point. Those who had stood by him – 88 of them are named in a litany of praise – became commanders of one or more 'thousands'. In all, this amounted to an army of '95,000 households', though given the approximate nature of a 'thousand' this may have amounted to no more than 50,000. Those especially favoured would be forgiven for up to nine crimes. Boorchu, Mukhali, Borokul and Chilagun became Genghis's 'four war-horses', Khubilai, Jelme, Jebe and Subedei 'my four hounds'. Sorkan-shira, who had saved the new emperor's life when he escaped from the Taychiuts, became a royal aide, a quiver-bearer, as did each of his sons.

The appointments marked something new in nomadic

imperial administrations. In the past, Mongol unity had always been undermined by tribal rivalries. Genghis's own childhood had been blighted by them, and his slow rise to power constantly threatened by them. Now came a revolution, with appointments made not on the basis of inherited position within a tribal hierarchy, but on services rendered. Loyalty was the key. Sorkan-shira and his sons were not the only ones raised to power from obscurity. Shepherds, herders and carpenters were included. Jelme and Subedei were blacksmiths' sons.

A new society, especially one of this size, needed new rules, and new ways of administration. In particular, it needed *written* administration. Genghis had foreseen the need for this as his conquests grew, for one of those captured from the Naimans was a Uighur named Tatatunga, who had been the chief administrator. Using the Uighur script, he had kept the Naiman records. Now Genghis ordered him to do the same job for his new master, and also teach the scripts to the younger princes.

This embryonic chancellery would have to be overseen by one of the family – someone closer to Genghis than a captured functionary. The choice fell upon Genghis's adopted brother, Shigi, who had been seized from the Tatars ten years previously. 'While I am setting in order the entire nation under the protection of Eternal Heaven, you have become my seeing eyes, my hearing ears,' Genghis told Shigi. 'Divide up the people of the felt-walled tents ... punish those who deserve to be punished,' and record the division of possessions, the laws and the judgments 'on white paper in a blue book'. This would be a permanent record for future generations, and anyone who tried to change it would be punished. Shigi's Blue Book became famous as the 'Great Yassa', or *jasagh* (transliterations vary of the Mongol word for government or legal code, which sounds like *dzassag*). The book itself vanished – possibly because it was never accorded legal authority in China, even after the Mongol conquest – but elements of it can be derived from other sources, from China to Persia.

Hidden in the previous paragraph is another novelty, hinting at Genghis's growing confidence in his destiny. Traditionally, the Mongols honoured the Blue Heaven. Now, for the first time, comes a mention that Genghis is under the protection of *Eternal* Heaven. It is hard to know when exactly this shift occurred, but here is evidence that Genghis and his followers had begun to see faith as justified, dreams becoming reality. A clan's brief success, achieved with the fickle backing of the Blue Heaven, might last for a season; the founding of a nation suggested the support of something rather more enduring – and what could be more help in achieving empire than an everlasting deity?

Genghis's revolution penetrated right the way through society. Out went tribal regiments; in came regiments that owed loyalty to their commanders. True, some regiments remained tribal; but only if loyalty to Genghis were assured. Switching regiments became a capital offence, and commanders who failed to measure up could be fired. The whole military and social structure was underpinned by Genghis's decision to form his own elite bodyguard of 10,000 men, who were granted special privileges. This was a masterstroke, for the corps included the sons of the regimental commanders, who had a rank equal to that of their fathers – except that, in the event of a dispute, the son would be preferred above the father. Very clever, and highly original, if not unique. Before a commander entertained thoughts of disloyalty, he would recall that his son was a hostage to the khan, and that treachery would have to involve the two of them. Personal loyalty superseded tribal bonds, weaving a new and enduring social texture, devoted to one purpose: conquest.

And conquest was vital, for this was not a money economy. Troops could not be paid, except in kind. Power itself bought nothing. Once the conquered tribes had been absorbed – the men allocated to their regiments, the young women distributed, the children taken as slaves, the silks, goblets, saddles, bows, horses and herds all shared out – the warriors would look at their leader with new expectations. Old ways had been broken, new ones forged – to be served how, exactly? Only by looking to the ultimate source of wealth, which would also be the source of future challenges: the settled lands to the south beyond the Gobi.

Blue Lake is not the only possible site for the ceremony by which Temujin became Genghis Khan, but its beauty, geographical location and layout carry overwhelming conviction. I very much want this to be the place Temujin chose for his coronation. There is an open platform of grass some 6 metres above the lake, while its eastern shore rises gently to offer good grazing and a natural site for troops to gather and camp. If a commander needed an overview of his forces, he could have climbed 100 metres up the grassy peak opposite, Black Heart Mountain.

I am not alone in my opinion. Mongols have long accepted this as the most likely site of the ceremony, and have honoured the place accordingly. A rough circle of flat, lichen-covered stones marks out the base of something very large – a mobile palace, perhaps, raised who knows when and for what. It's tempting to think of it as a coronation palace, but on what evidence? It is probably the remains of some later structure honouring the memory of the coronation, as is a more recent addition – a little marble pillar, surrounded by a scattering of stones and offering-cups, and into which is set a stern portrait. Around it (the one on the cover) is a faint path worn by visitors making the ritual threefold circumambulation. Blue silk flaps in the breeze across a caption in the old vertical script: 'Here at Black

Heart Blue Lake, Temujin was crowned as Genghis Khan.'

And across the lake, Black Heart Mountain itself proclaimed the reason for its fame with enormous white letters in the old vertical script: 'GENGHIS', and then alongside a smaller: 'Khan'. I wondered how the sign was made; perhaps by scratching the grass away to reveal chalk beneath, like the white horses on English downs. The morning would offer a chance to find out.

Nights are cold up there, even in high summer, and mine was miserable, with no pillow, no groundsheet and only a lightweight sleeping-bag. At dawn, shivering banished sleep. I crawled out of my dew-soaked tent into perfection. The rising sun contoured the hills, its slanting heat on the lake raising a mist that drifted, as stagy as dry ice, at the foot of Black Heart Mountain. The GENGHIS sign, which faces due south, of course, was tinged with orange from the east. Walking fast to warm my sopping feet, I struck off over a foreshore roughened by the holes of marmots and field-mice. There was no breeze to stir the firs or the water's slowly rising veil. A distant cuckoo and a skylark invisible in the eggshell blue were the only sounds. The marmots slept and so, thank goodness, did the flies. The only moving things were me and the dissipating mist.

Squelching mud warned me that the lake's eastern end was a bog. I traced the old shoreline round to high ground, gaining a view over my vastly extended shadow straight westward, up the stream that feeds the lake. The mist was gone now, and the Blue Lake mirrored the blue sky, a perfect symbol of divine beneficence.

The GENGHIS sign turned out to be made of quite large rocks, perhaps 150 of them, all painted white. As the flies began to pester, I paced the sign out: 37 metres from top to bottom, as near as I could make out on that slope. The rocks were of all sizes, from a boulder weighing a tonne to stones that I could have lifted. I wondered who had made the sign, and when. It was well maintained, and the paint quite fresh. A recent creation, then, for Genghis had only been resurrected since the fall of communism. Frost, rain, melt-water and grazing sheep had already begun to take a toll, rolling a few stones away down the mountainside. One stone – the top left-hand corner of the first letter – was a new replacement. I could see the bare imprint of the original in the grass nearby. If this was official, which seemed doubtful, it was also a labour of love.

And what a view. I panted up to the summit, and found an *ovoo*, a pile of boulders draped with a single length of blue silk and the usual clutter of empty bottles, scattered out of either reverence or laziness. Looking back, due south, I saw forest, marching over ridge after ridge, in huge clumps separated by grassy slopes, all as if created by a landscape gardener with infinite resources to represent armies on the march. The lake's western shores were soft and green, as boggy as the eastern end, with an oozy sliver of grass and willow clumps dividing the main lake from a pond.

Later, when I made some trite remark about the timelessness of the view, Baatar made sense of the bogs and willows. 'You look at this now, and think nothing could change it? When I was young, all these lakes were bigger.' It was all to do with global warming. The lakes lie in permafrost, he explained, and in this Siberian borderland the permafrost is melting, the lakes all draining away. 'Soon, they will all disappear.'

Black Heart, Blue Lake: the colours were mysterious. From up there beside the *ovoo*, I could look down at a steeper angle, and the water didn't look blue after all. It was brown. Yet now, as I write, when I look at the picture I took, the lake is as true blue as the sky. It seems there's more than a question of angles here. The camera and the eye see different wavebands. Later, when I waded in to wash away the sweat, the water was transparent, right down to its peaty, dark brown bottom. I cupped some in my hands and drank; it was clear and pure enough to bottle. This oddity seemed to explain the name of this place. A blue lake with a dark heart, for the word *khar* – 'black' – also means 'dark'. The name recalls ancient opposites – above and below, light and dark, heaven and earth, divine and mundane, a reminder that the newly created Genghis was to be lord of an earthly empire in which, if seen aright, the divine would be reflected.

II

EMPIRE

6

THE GREAT STATE OF WHITE
AND HIGH

OUR IMAGINED GAZE NOW FOLLOWS GENGHIS'S ALMOST EXACTLY
due south, across 600 kilometres of grassland and Gobi, over
foothills where gravel gives way to pastures, between two
mountain ranges to the Yellow River, and then on up the
broad and silt-laden river for another 250 kilometres, to
the city of Yinchuan.

You can get a view of Yinchuan, capital of today's Ningxia
province, from the top of an eleventh-century pagoda rising
above the trees that shade the grassy courtyard of the city's
museum. I climbed its steep and shadowy interior because an
overview usually provides some sort of insight. Not in this
case. Yinchuan, a city of almost a million people, looked at
this first glance like a huge, drab, low-rise postwar suburb,
vanishing into a haze. To the west, mountains loomed dimly.
I thought I could see a trace of yellow in the distance: desert
sands. The haze came from the dusty desert, and the traffic
weaving around the bicycles and tricycle rickshaws, and the
factories that squat along the plains to the north.

But there is another Yinchuan, to which the pagoda itself,

and the trees and grass eleven storeys below me, were clues. The streets are tree-lined, the verges grassed and sprayed from water trucks. The hazy plains, when you drive through them, are all covered by crops – wheat, vegetables, orchards – watered by an ancient and intricate network of canals leading from the Yellow River, which runs past 12 kilometres to the east. The museum's pagoda is a reminder that this city has ancient roots, that it was once a centre of Buddhism. Indeed, the only other high-rise building is a 54-metre pagoda of angular brickwork that dates back 1,500 years. It was closed – but not out of neglect, indeed quite the opposite. The whole site was undergoing renovation. Yinchuan is rediscovering its rich past, to ensure a richer future.

That past lay in a very different and very un-Chinese world. A thousand years ago Yinchuan, which lies just one-third of the way across present-day China from the coast, was beyond the reach of any Chinese ruler. It was the centre of a culture apart, whose odd and enigmatic relics stagger first-time visitors. I had come by rail from the capital of Inner Mongolia, Hohhot, with my friend and guide Jorigt, a lecturer at the Inner Mongolian University. If you drive half an hour westwards from Yinchuan along a new highway, the hazy mountains harden into a rugged wall of rock: the Helan Shan. Against them, above the roadside trees, loom odd bullet-shaped structures, 30 metres high, that look like giant, grey termites' nests of rain-worn earth. There are nine of them, but at first glance you can see only three or four. The others are swallowed by the space around them, an apron of gravel and soil that runs for 10 kilometres along the lower slopes of the mountains from which it was washed. The domes are the tombs of emperors.

For almost eight centuries, the tombs were Ozymandian ruins, enigmatic and awe-inspiring as the vast and trunkless legs of stone memorialized by Shelley. The site is still one colossal wreck, thanks to the attention of Genghis's troops, who left no bodies and few artefacts. But they have now become a focus for archaeologists and a prime tourist attraction, touted as China's equivalent of the pyramids. They are not, of course, on an equivalent scale; but they and their site, extending over 50 square kilometres, assert the power and prestige of a culture that for 200 years dominated an area the size of France and Germany put together. It was only natural that Genghis should cast predatory eyes on it.

But why on these people, rather than their wealthier neighbours, the Jin, the Mongols' traditional enemy? To understand Genghis's strategy demands an overview of available choices.

China in the early thirteenth century was a land divided (it may help to turn to the map on pp. 56–7). The central and southern regions had long been under the control of the Song dynasty, which had presided over an artistic and intellectual renaissance. Its southern portion was still in Song hands, but the north had fallen to two 'barbarian' peoples. In the northeast lay the kingdom founded a century before by the Jürchen from Manchuria, who gave it the same name as their adopted dynastic title: Jin. Genghis's great-grandfather Kabul and his great-uncle Kutula had fought Jin, and it would eventually be Genghis's main target. But Jin was a tough nut. Now allied with its former enemy, Song, Jin had forgotten its barbarian origins and ruled its millions of Chinese peasants and its dozens of well-defended cities from behind the formidable walls of Beijing.

Next door, however, lay the second 'barbarian' kingdom, the one with the nine bullet-shaped mausoleums. Best known by its Chinese name, Xi Xia,[1] it was far more promising. Consider for a moment the implications of what Genghis

[1] Names beginning with X used to look wildly exotic; less so now, since pinyin transliteration replaced the old Wade–Giles *Hs* with *X,* both being roughly equivalent to the English *sh*. Xi means 'western', to distinguish it from another Xia kingdom that had existed further east in the fifth century.

was about to unleash. Here were three competing powers – Jin, Song and Xi Xia – in a precarious balance. In the wings were two other powers: Tibet and (from the early twelfth century) Khara Khitai. Now add in the semi-independent tribes and clans pursuing their own agendas within and between the major powers, all bound by trade routes, in particular the network we call the Silk Road – though silk was by now only a minor commodity – that linked China to Central Asia and ultimately Europe. Imagine the differences of religion – Islam in the west, overlapping with Buddhism, Confucianism, Nestorian Christianity and shamanism – and of major languages – Chinese, Tibetan, Turkic, Arabic, Tangut (about which more in a moment). This was the cauldron into which Genghis was about to cast himself and his people, injecting into an inherently unstable brew an army alien in its language, culture and religion. The long-term consequences were utterly unknowable.

Not that a would-be conqueror could afford to worry about the long-term consequences. His immediate task was to find the weakest point for an assault that would bring the quickest and most lucrative returns, and establish an unassailable position in the hierarchy of kingdoms. Of the two possible choices, Jin was too strong, with too many walled cities and too many mountains to cross on the way. Xi Xia was by comparison an open house, guarded only by the Gobi and sandy deserts that Mongols could cross in days; its cities were few; its armies smaller. Strategically, it would be better first to secure victory over the weaker, then turn on the stronger. There was a risk that Jin would enter the fray anyway, but it was currently lamed by the recent death of its ruler. The risk was acceptable, if victory could be swiftly achieved.

I said that Genghis's intended victim is best known by its Chinese name. In fact, Xi Xia is hardly known to anyone

A Persian miniature in a manuscript of the world history of Rashid ad-Din, *Jami al-Tawarikh* ('Collection of Histories'). Done about a century after the event, it does not aim at authenticity. The white yak-tail standards on the right are Genghisid authority symbols, but other elements – clothing, tent, trees – are Chinese and Persian.

RURAL MONGOLIA

The Mongolian countryside (*main picture*) is a world of *gers* and horses, as it was in Genghis's day. Horses are trained (*top left*) and camels loaded (*centre*) as they have been for 1,000 years. Summers are a time of plenty, while winters (*bottom left*) combine stark beauty with austerity.

TEMUJIN'S WORLD

Main picture: An *ovoo* overlooks the most likely birthplace of Temujin, the future Genghis, near the junction of the Onon (winding in from the right) and the little Khorkh.

Top right: Genghis's future father Yesugei snatches his first sight of the boy's mother, Hoelun, hidden in Chiledu the Merkit's cart. The old vertical script, introduced by Genghis in 1220, is a quotation from *The Secret History* describing the incident. The painting (by B. Mönkhjin, and bought by the author in 1996) is a reminder that Genghis and all related themes inspire as much as ever.

Bottom right: This makeshift cangue, or portable pillory, is like the one that held Temujin/Genghis when he was a captive of the Taychiuts.

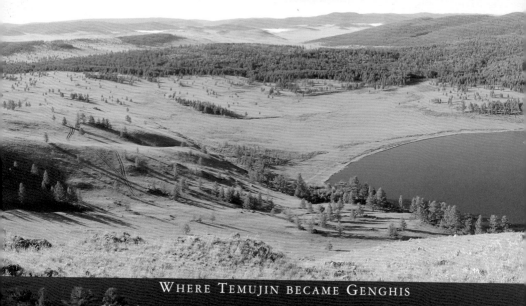

WHERE TEMUJIN BECAME GENGHIS

Blue Lake (*above*), from the top of Black Heart Mountain (*bottom right*), where Temujin was perhaps crowned as Genghis Khan. That is the claim made below the portrait and supported by the GENGHIS KHAN of whitened stones on the mountain behind (*below*).

ACROSS THE GOBI

Genghis's route southwards into Xi Xia probably took him via the Three Beauties range (*main picture*). His devastating campaigns are recalled in a Persian miniature (*left*), which shows a well-equipped army, with bows, swords, and armour for men and horses. His forces tore the roofs from the tombs of Xi Xia's rulers, leaving them bare (*top right*). The figure of Jorigt shows the scale of the site. The mountains in the background are the Helan Shan. In his final campaign, Genghis destroyed Xia Xia's northern outpost, Khara-Khoto (*right*), where, in the early twentieth century, the discovery of thousands of documents and paintings revealed the wealth of Xi Xia's culture.

قد لجمع نحت ظل رايتد الامير ضرس ناصرالدين والتونياش الحاجب وابوعبدالله
عولك قاتالهم يوم الجمعة منتصف ذي الحجة سنة ثلث وتسعون وتمانة وقعد ساعةمن المحاربة

فنثروا وهربوا الى خلف جدار القلعة فلما اجتمع سلطان الدكار كا طلب اب

ASSAULTING ISLAM

By the time Genghis assaulted the Islamic world
of Khwarezm, the Mongols were experienced in
siege warfare. In attacks on cities like this one
(*above*), both sides used the powerful little recurved
bows. But the Mongols now used trebuchets to
throw rocks, with the help of turncoats and
prisoners like the man in a turban. They also
brought siege engines, including mobile scaling
ladders (*above right*) and huge triple bows (*bottom
left*). The reconstructed siege bow (*bottom right*) is
on view near Ulaanbaatar. It was built for the
Mongol feature film *Genghis Khan*.

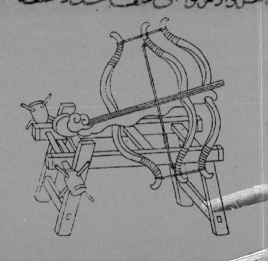

IN BUKHARA

The Kalyan Minaret (*main picture*) in the centre of Bukhara, built in 1127, survived Genghis's assault and numerous earthquakes to become the city's most famous landmark. After taking the city, Genghis addressed notable Bukharans (*right, in a Persian miniature*), telling them he was a 'punishment from God' for their sins.

ز بیم شهنشاه پیروزبخت
پلنگ اندرو شیر تند و کوه و آب
کشیدند انبار ما را بسر
شنیده جهان خورش سهمگین
بدان جایگه رفت گیتی پناه
بر منبر آمد و گفتا که من
زناگه آگاه گشتم دراز
جهانی آفرین گفت فرمان برید
زانداره بردند پیمودن گاه
ازین گونه فرمود و پرداخت تا
نهادند شمشیر در مرد و زن
بخون غوطه میخورد هر کس که بود
چو گل جامه بشسته زجان پاک

ز دل رفته آرام از کوه بخت
جهان را گرفتند چون آفتاب
نهادند چون کوه بر یکدگر
نه گاو سپهر و نه گاو زمین
بزیر آمد از باره یکسر سپاه
زناگه رسیدیم درین انجمن
برای شما میدهم پی نیاز
هر دو جهان تا زمین جان برید
ستمکاره را روز باشد سیاه
ببریدند خون پاک یک رویه را
زره در بر سیم بر سر بهن
چو خورشید رخ گشته خاک بری
چه سرو سهی پست گشته ز خاک

چنین گفت سالار لشکر نواز
ببودند یک روز بی یار خویش
تهی شد ز جو پاک انبار جاه
جهان سوزند چند اینک کردی نگاه

رسیدیم از راه دور و دراز
جهان را بخواهند پرداختن
فکندند در شهر و در خانه گاه
زن و مرد دیدی شنیده سیاه

وعظ گفتن چنگز خان بر مسجد بخارا را

مرا هرکه این شهر در دل بکشت
کشیدند شمشیر بران سیاه
بسر گشته در جوی خون گون آب

چو آتش رسیدم ز دشت
همه روی گیتی ز آتش سیاه
تن سایه پرورد شد آفتاب

ستوران ما سر برافراختند
ندانند سیری چو پیلان مست
ز جو بوم و بر بسته و کوه شد
خدیوی که چون او نیاید پدید
فرستاده بیا شهریان پی شما
در اندیشه رفتم ز بهر شما
نه در بند این دام و دانه منم
ببردند فرمان من آمدم
برانداختم از گرد ره بوم و بر
در آن روز بر دشت و بر آسمان
یکباره آتش برافروختند

نه چون مردم شهر تن پرورند
بپا ریند هرگاه و هر جو که هست
رسیدند چند اینک شنوه شد
یکی تخت در مسجد اندر دیدند
بسر بر میان و رخان برکنار
دلم خسته شد بهر شهر شما
شما راست تاوان بهانه منم
چو باد خزان در چمن آمدم
بسوزیم یکباره گی خشک و تر
نپرید پرنده از تاب آن
اگر مسجد از خانقه سوختند

THE RUINS OF MERV

Ancient Merv, though now deserted, is a treasure trove for archaeologists, boasting several astonishing ruins. Sultan Sanjar's mausoleum (*right*) was one of the greatest buildings of its age, rivalling Brunelleschi's dome for Florence Cathedral, which it predated by almost 300 years. Built in about 1150, the mausoleum once had a dome of turquoise tiles that shone out like a beacon over the desert, but only the inner shell survived the Mongol assault (*bottom left*). The weird stockade-like walls of the Great Kyz Kala (*main picture, back left*) and its smaller counterpart date from the seventh century. As well as being famous for ceramics (the shard *below* is typical of thousands), Merv had the first Islamic metal-working foundry, and was even making steel in the ninth century, several centuries before it became widespread elsewhere.

WARRIORS IN TRAINING

A Persian view of Mongol soldiers in action. This seems to be a training session, with warriors
practising their shooting techniques, including the famous over-the-shoulder 'Parthian' shot. No one
has any arrows, and one man (*second from bottom on right*) does not even have a bow.

beyond a few specialists, because Genghis did his best to wipe state, culture and people from the face of the earth. There is a case to be made that this was the first ever recorded example of attempted genocide. It was certainly very success-ful *ethnocide*. Xi Xia's successor cultures, Mongol and Chinese, had no interest in saving its records, reading its script or preserving its relics. It took the scholars of other nations, mainly Russia, to start the work of decipherment and understanding. Only recently have the Chinese sought to gain leadership in this field, establishing a research institute, retrieving artefacts, restoring monuments. Only now is this ancient culture re-emerging into public gaze on the stage from which it was so violently ejected.

The people of Xi Xia referred to themselves as the Mi. But, as usual, the terminology of the dominant culture comes out top. The Chinese called them the Dangxian, while in Mongol they became Tangut (Dang plus a Mongolian *-ut* plural). The Tanguts of Xi Xia: that's how they are known today. Under pressure from Tibetans, the ancestral Tanguts had migrated eastward from the mountains of eastern Tibet in the seventh century. Three hundred years later their base was in the Ordos, the sweep of territory within the bend of the Yellow River, where their leaders ruled the old Xia border region for the Tang dynasty; hence their later name.

When the Song came to power in 960, the Tanguts seized their chance. In 1020 they built a new capital west of the Yellow River – near or on the site of present-day Yinchuan – and then thrust further westward, over the Helan mountains, building an empire 1,500 kilometres across and 600 kilo-metres deep. The spine of their domain was the narrow pasture-rich route running between the northern foothills of the Tibetan massif and the hideous wastes of the Alashan desert, which is geographically a southern extension of the Gobi. These pastures run all the way to Dunhuang and its fourth-century complex of Buddhist caves and temples on the eastern edge of the Takla Makan desert. This part of the Silk Road, 1,000 kilometres long and in parts a mere 15 kilometres wide, was known as the Hexi Corridor (He-xi meaning 'River-West', i.e. west of the Yellow River); today it is more commonly called the Gansu Corridor, after the present-day province of which it is part. Just over halfway between Yinchuan and Dunhuang a side-road led across the desert northward along the river known today as the Shui, but to Mongols as the Etsin, which flowed through desert to a border fortress variously known as Etsina (to Marco Polo) or Khara-Khoto ('Black City', its Mongol name, though the final *o* is now redundant).

The true founder of Xi Xia as an independent empire, Li Yuan-hao, was an ambitious and talented ruler who asserted his people's status with a number of measures.[2] He renamed the royal family Wei-ming (or something like it: this is the Chinese version of the Tangut). His domain became the Great State of White and High. And he set the Tanguts apart from their neighbours by instructing the men to shave the top of their heads, leaving fringes covering the forehead and ears. His subjects had three days to comply, or be killed. In 1038 he declared himself emperor. Such moves had the Song up in arms, literally, opening six years of war that ended only when Yuan-hao lured them into a trap. Having chosen a valley in which to ambush the approaching Song, so the story goes, the Tanguts withdrew, but were faced with a problem: how to know when the Song army was in the right place for the assault. Yuan-hao's answer was to net a mass of birds, and put them in boxes along the roadside. When the Song army arrived, the soldiers, curious at the strange sounds coming from the boxes, opened them. Out flew the birds.

---

[2] Names are as complicated in Tangut as in Chinese. Li was his imperial surname; Yuan-hao was his personal name; the emperors also had posthumous names and temple names, in the Chinese fashion. And all of course transliterated differently in pinyin and Wade–Giles.

Seeing the flock from their hiding place, the Tanguts attacked, and slew 20,000 Song. In 1044 the Song signed a treaty with the Tanguts, agreeing to pay an annual 'subsidy' of 135,000 rolls of silk, 2 tonnes of silver and 13 tonnes of tea.

Resettling in the Yinchuan area beside the Yellow River was a smart move, for it brought the Tanguts into possession of a fertile valley roughly the size of Massachusetts or Wales: 20,000 square kilometres, the core of which – approaching 1 million hectares – was irrigated by ancient waterworks, and could have fed 4–5 million people, according to an estimate by one Chinese historian.[3]

Yuan-hao also enforced an order made by a predecessor that Tangut be written down, for he knew – as Genghis realized two centuries later – that writing would be the formal basis of administration and religion, and thus of a national identity. To match his ambitions, the script would have to be a supreme expression of civilization, yet also unique. The task was to select a model script to adapt. He might have gone for Tibetan, which would have been relatively simple, since Tangut was a related language and Tibetan an alphabetical script. He might then have ended up with a few dozen letters, as Mongol did. Instead, he looked to the script of the region's dominant culture, Chinese, in which each of the thousands of characters corresponds to a syllable and fits into a square. Other sinified cultures – Korean, Japanese – made use of Chinese signs to record their languages. But Yuan-hao instructed his scholar, Yeli Renrong, to assert the Tangut language's non-Chinese credentials by devising signs that were totally original. So the 6,000 Tangut characters *look* Chinese; but they are not. Even those derived from Chinese are so altered that no Chinese can read them. Anyway, phonetics alone would not have helped, since Tangut was as remote from Chinese as English from Hungarian.

[3] Wu Tianchi, in *Xi Xia Shigao*, 1980.

It was this script that was used to record laws and to translate the texts of Buddhism, which the Tangut forefathers had brought with them from Tibet and which from the start had been the state religion. Indeed, for the Tanguts Buddhism was more than a religion: it was an ideology used by the royal family to oppose Chinese Confucianism and to assert Xia nationalism. The emperor, seeking to acquire merit by performing good deeds, obtained from the Song a complete copy of the 6,000-chapter *Tripitaka*, the corpus of Buddhist canonical writing, and had it translated into Tangut. In this, Xi Xia was emulating the achievements of not only the Song, but also the Liao and the Koreans, all of whom had produced versions of the *Tripitaka* a century before. This was more than a project of translation and writing. The Tanguts, like the Song, Liao and Koreans, printed their material, carving whole pages out of wood in reverse. The *Tripitaka* required 130,000 printing blocks, each containing hundreds of characters, and each producing two pages of text. And this was just one of thousands of the Buddhist works that were either produced by or had long been available to the Tanguts. When the Mogao caves near Dunhuang, sealed up around 1000, were opened to the British archaeologist Sir Aurel Stein in 1907, he bought (for just £130, as he recalled later) a 'solid mass of manuscripts rising to a height of nearly 10 feet and filling, as subsequent measurement showed, close on 500 cubic feet' – some 40,000 manuscripts and several hundred paintings, which now form the core of massive collections in the British Museum, the British Library and elsewhere. Chinese, Tibetan, Uighur and Sanskrit documents, hidden away before Tangut culture reached its peak, indicate the weight of Buddhist tradition available as the Tanguts began to make records of their own. The effects became clear when the Russian explorer Petr Kozlov explored the abandoned ruins of Xi Xia's northern outpost, Khara-Khoto, in 1908–9: 10,000 documents, many of them in Tangut, were carted off to St Petersburg, where they still reside as a vast and still largely unread trove of Tangut Buddhist literature.

If the Tanguts' output was staggering, so too were their skill, organization and techniques. To print the *Tripitaka*, for instance, imagine producing the *Encylopaedia Britannica* by making up your own script, and then, for printing blocks, carving every page of all 31 volumes in wood – in reverse.[4]

It has long been an embarrassment to Chinese scholarship that so much Tangut raw material vanished into 'imperialist' museums. Now, as part of the Chinese attempt to reclaim the initiative, Yinchuan's Ningxia University has a fine Xi Xia Institute. It is run by Du Jian Lu, who displayed Xi Xia's legal code – 'the first complete body of law of an ethnic minority in China' – as proudly as if this copy of the St Petersburg original had been his own. Much work has been done over the past century, but those few scholars who can read the script are still finding new material to resurrect the Tanguts: 'We find here rules about clothing, even the colours ordained for ordinary people, edicts on dwelling-places, how farms were to be irrigated, how canals were to be built, how the water should flow.'

Chinese efforts to dominate this arcane field rely heavily on the lifelong labour of one man, Li Fanwen, who was by now too frail to see me. His passion for the little-known language was ignited in 1955, and he has been working on its intricacies ever since. Many of the 6,000 symbols were interpreted by Russian scholars; but symbols were only part of the problem. Li also had to wrestle with the grammar, and then

[4] The Tanguts even experimented, as the Song did, with movable type; indeed, a few Buddhist tracts in Tangut are the oldest surviving examples of such printing, predating Gutenberg's great invention by 400 years. Movable type proved unworkable, for both Chinese and Tangut lacked the alphabetical base, the presses and the paper required for such a system. But given the market for Buddhist literature, what if the Tanguts had devised an alphabetical script based on Tibetan rather than a logographic one inspired by Chinese? We might then have been honouring the Tanguts as the true originators of printing.

apply his understanding to crack multiple signs – new concepts devised by combining and inverting characters. 'Wood' added to 'carve' to make 'chisel' is a simple one. But who could have guessed that 'heart' plus 'evil' would mean 'harm', that 'knee' plus 'hand' plus 'walk' means 'climb'? Or that 'finger' written backwards means 'toe'? After almost 50 years in the field, compiling 30,000 note cards and transcribing over 3,000 tombstones, Li saw his massive Xi Xia–Mandarin Dictionary published in 2001.

The Great State of White and High developed an impressive culture, with half a dozen major cities, all equipped with skilful weavers, leatherworkers, builders and metallurgists. Its merchants traded across Central Asia, providing its elite with luxuries. In 1980 archaeologists found a hoard of 10,000 iron coins, all made in twelfth-century Xi Xia. Despite its vast deserts, it had the wonderful pastures of the Gansu Corridor along the well-watered northern foothills of the Qilian mountains. And its wealth funded a powerful army, dispersed across a dozen military districts, each commanded by a member of the royal family. In time of war the emperor would despatch messengers with silver tablets which ordered the local generals to conscript all males between the ages of fifteen and sixty; by this means he could raise an army of up to 300,000.

For the next 150 years Wei-ming emperors succeeded one another in the family business of ruling, their reigns punctuated by factional squabbles, the occasional revolt and turf wars along Xi Xia's unstable borders. Khitan exiles brought trouble when they fled the invading Jürchens in 1125; famine and earthquake sparked uprisings in the 1140s. But it was, on the whole, given the instability of the times, a stable, sophisticated, prosperous realm. No-one could have guessed that its strength was also its weakness. For it was a nation ruled by scholars and bureaucrats, and its armies were supported not by the countryside, as the Mongol troops were, but by its farmers and city-based traders.

At the time of Genghis's birth Xi Xia had a nationwide system of state schools and a college with 300 places to train bureaucrats and scholars. An academy of scholars wrote and stored historical records. The emperor, Renxiao, was like his predecessors a semi-divine Buddhist figure, preserving authority by acting the role of the virtuous ruler seeking enlightenment. In 1189 Renxiao honoured the 50th anniversary of his accession by distributing 100,000 copies of a sutra on the ascent and rebirth of Maitreya, the fifth bodhisattva (enlightened being) and 50,000 each of several other sutras, all printed in both Tangut and Chinese. But Renxiao was the last of the great rulers. He died in 1193, leaving an empire in the hands of less competent successors.

The grand, stone-paved approach to the tombs leads straight to Tomb No. 3, built by Xi Xia's founder, now situated in an immense enclosure pitted by archaeological excavations. This is where visitors are supposed to come. But it is a tiny part of the whole. Away over the plain, like distant sandcastles, are eight other imperial tombs and 200 smaller structures built for lesser generals and family members, all of them accessible to those with stamina, the right footwear and enough time. Our driver came to our aid. Beside the ticket office was a dirt road that led over a gravelly wasteland of tussocks and dried-up beds of springtime floods to Tombs 1 and 2, which were built by Yuan-hao to confer glory retrospectively on his father and grandfather. Workers were busy with wood and concrete, preparing to corral future visitors. Jorigt and I were on our own with the gravel, the scrub, the distant mountains and these very odd structures.

The weather-worn cones look like no other buildings I have ever seen. Imagine the noses of rockets pock-marked by nasty encounters with clouds of asteroids. Eroded detritus makes dusty skirts around their bases. But the cones are not worn evenly. There is a pattern to the damage done by eight centuries of rain, striations that run both horizontally and vertically. And then there are the holes, masses of them.

'Jorigt, what are those holes, do you think? They look like birds' nests.'

'Not birds.'

'Maybe they're air holes,' I said. He looked at me quizzically. 'No, really. This is a tomb. It must be hollow. It's got to have air inside.'

I was completely wrong on both counts. Actually, the evidence was right there, at our feet. Bulldozers had flattened the ground – ready, I supposed, for the hordes of tourists who would one day walk here – but in among the gravel were bits of tile, little shards of pastel green and brown. And beside Tomb No. 3 is stacked the evidence intact: a 50-metre-long collection of semicircular tiles, about 20,000 of them by my reckoning. Tiles meant roofs. The holes and the striations marked where rafters had once slotted into structures that were not hollow at all, but solids of packed earth towering over the graves themselves and their approach ramps. The rafters had supported tiled roofs, probably overlapping each other and curving upwards slightly in the style of Chinese pagodas.

At the peak of Xi Xia's power, in the early thirteenth century, this place would have looked spectacular, its nine pagodas glowing with colour in their own courtyards, with their attendant 'companion tombs', and all nine of these palatial compounds guarded and tended by contingents of troops.

All of this is made clear in a smart new museum at the entrance to Tomb No. 3, which announces itself to be 'one of the splendid pearls in the great treasure-house of Chinese history and culture'. It seemed a fair claim, backed by a model of the site, and the hundreds of statues, tiles, scrolls, coins, printed books and pots, all telling the Xi Xia story to date. It was only as our guide warmed to his task that it struck me that there was something odd about what he was saying. It wasn't that his commentary was learned by heart and delivered in a robotic monotone, for it was remarkable that there was an English-speaking guide at all. Nor was it his habit of clearing his throat after every sentence, with a sound like that made by the 'over' button on a walkie-talkie, as if he were adding a phonetic exclamation mark to every sentence. It was the assumptions behind his words that gave us pause.

Xi Xia, he said, had lasted 190 years, 'until conquered by Inner Mongolian troops [*kchk!*]'.

'*Inner* Mongolian troops!' muttered Jorigt. 'Where does he think Genghis Khan was born?'

It was no mistake. 'We see nine emperor tombs [*kchk!*].' Our guide pursued his dogged course, with its noisy punctuation. 'But we see that there were twelve emperors [*kchk!*]. The specialists think that the last three died in the war with Inner Mongolian troops.'

Hm. If our guide was also a guide to official thinking, someone in authority wished visitors to be told that the invading Mongols from beyond the Gobi actually came from a Chinese province. Were we meant to believe that the Tanguts were defeated by Chinese subjects?

The quick answer to this question is yes, for reasons I will get to in a moment. But a quick answer hardly does the question justice. It opens up other questions about the nature of identity, to which I found myself returning again and again on this trip. The matter lies at the core of so much to do with how Genghis Khan is judged, both throughout history and now.

So to the reasons behind the quick answer. Let them emerge from an imagined interrogation:

Who attacked the Tanguts in the early thirteenth century?
The Mongols under Genghis Khan.
Very good. What happened?
Genghis Khan won.

Excellent. And?

And eventually the Mongols defeated the rest of China.

They did indeed. And?

And they set up the Yuan dynasty.

And the Yuan dynasty was an essential part of the history of which nation?

China.

Terrific. So who founded this Chinese dynasty?

Genghis Khan, of course.

So – and here's the tricky bit – what does that make Genghis: Chinese or Mongol?

You see where we are heading. Looking at things from south of the Gobi, *Genghis Khan was actually Chinese.* With the further implication that all Mongols are actually Chinese. Must be. It's entirely logical.

Put like this, the past suddenly becomes part of the present, with political implications that will engage us more closely later. At that moment, listening to our insistent guide, something cast my mind back to a conversation with Jorigt on the train as we clacked slowly southwards along the Yellow River.

I should say something about Jorigt. He was born the son of a herdsman on the grasslands of Inner Mongolia. Until he was seven, he walked to school from his tent, attending a Mongolian school, speaking only Mongolian. His parents spoke no Chinese. Later, his father became a minor functionary in the town of Shilinghot. Both he and his mother, who never learned to read, were insistent that education was the way to advancement. When he graduated, doing his exams in Mongolian, he applied to do Mongolian studies in the Inner Mongolian University at Hohhot. But by now he knew that the world he inhabited was not Mongolian at all. It was Chinese. To get on, he had to learn the language. Starting when he was seventeen, he was fluent in Mandarin by the age of twenty-one. He then went on to specialize in the relationship between the Turkish and Mongolian languages, studied in Ankara, and finally, in his late twenties, started to learn English, thanks to the presence of an American professor in Hohhot. So Mongolian is his first language, Chinese his second, Turkish his third and English his fourth. He was my interpreter in his fourth language, and my debt to him is quite incalculable. He was also a pretty good runner, having won university titles in the 800 metres, 1,500 metres and 10 kilometres, and that was going to prove a useful asset as well.

'So,' I asked him, 'are you Chinese or Mongolian?'

'I am a Mongolian. But,' he paused, 'of Chinese nationality.'

To illustrate his point, he told me the story of his name. Jorigt is a straightforward enough name in Mongolian, which transliterates easily into English. But Chinese signs are mono-syllabic, each ending in a vowel sound or an *n*, and therefore do not put two consonants together. To represent his name, he had to choose signs that most closely represent the sounds of his name in Mongolian. It comes out as something like Je-Zhi-Ge-Tu. Now, this is obviously not a Chinese name, but it gives him a Chinese identity, because it can be written and spoken. The point of all this is that, whatever complex mixture he feels himself to be, to Chinese he is Chinese.

So here, in essence, was the Chinese position on identity. Once you fall into the Chinese sphere, in Chinese eyes you become Chinese. Jorigt is Chinese; and so was Genghis Khan; and that's that.

Where do those 'Inner Mongolian troops' come in? The answer makes perfect sense, but you will have to follow me closely. Once upon a time, Mongolia and China were one, under the Mongols, who thereby became in effect Chinese. Since then, the Mongol empire has vanished, and China was also diminished in other ways. Outer Mongolia – the Mongolian People's Republic, as it became – unfortunately slipped away from the family at a time of Chinese weakness in the early twentieth century. But there are more Mongolians in Inner Mongolia, which is still part of China, than in Mongolia itself, which isn't. So history's underlying reality is best served by calling all Mongolians 'Inner Mongolians', because to Chinese that's where Mongolians come from. So therefore the troops that invaded Xi Xia in the thirteenth century were 'Inner Mongolians'.

There is one further dimension to this. The territory of Xi Xia overlaps present-day Xinjiang, Gansu, Ningxia and Inner Mongolia, all very much part of China. If the Tanguts were with us today, they, like Genghis and Jorigt, would be Chinese – never mind that their language was related to Tibetan, that they established their own state by beating off the Chinese and that they were virtually extinguished or absorbed before the emergence of a unified China. They were, after all, blotted out by a Chinese people, i.e. the Mongols. So their position is unequivocally part of the great family of China as it emerged after 1949. Thus, by the ruthless application of hindsight, it is possible to see an extended struggle for control of Inner Asia involving three separate nationalities as a minor spat among members of the same family.

A wall-sized photograph of all China's 56 nationalities, which acted as a full-stop to the exhibition, summarized the story. The guide answered my obvious question. 'This photo, it telling us that in the 56 nationalities we have no Tangut nationality. But Tangut nationality has mingled into these nationalisms. Today, all nationalities get together and make our country beautiful.'

There is a good deal to admire in the official line on minorities. All but one of the 56 cultures together account for only some 5 per cent of the population, the vast majority of which is Han; but each is in theory guaranteed its own voice, language and culture. It also presents minority nationalities with the challenge of adopting the wider culture, a challenge that has always been a constant feature of borderland and migrant existence and is today replicated in ever more situations in a world of displaced minorities. But Han inclusiveness raises problems, in particular to do with history. Reclamation of historic borders or the seizure of new areas mops up borderland cultures that may not slot easily into the Chinese folder. Tibet is a prominent case in point. As for the Tanguts, it is a strange distortion of history to impose Chinese-ness retrospectively on a unique non-Chinese people who were ruled by Tibetans, if anyone, before they carved out their own kingdom.

And there are political implications in lumping former Chinese subjects with those inside contemporary borders. The part of Manchuria that is now Russian was at one time or another largely Chinese (or at least Liao or Jin, which in Chinese eyes comes to the same thing). This could make for interesting developments should Russian control slip. And take Mongolia: if, by being a successful Mongolian conqueror, Genghis becomes Chinese; and if, as a result, all Mongols are seen as Chinese; then China has a claim on Mongolia, independent though it is at present. There is a potential here for conflicting views of who might rightfully exercise authority over much of Inner Asia's borderlands – a matter that, as we shall see, is intimately connected to the legacy of Genghis Khan.

Genghis already knew a good deal about Xi Xia, because Mongols and Tanguts were as interlocked as suspicious relatives. The Tanguts had close links with his old ally and enemy Toghrul, the khan of the Keraits. Toghrul's brother, Jakha, had been captured and raised by the Tanguts as a boy; later, they even made him a *gambu* (great general or counsellor). Jakha's daughter became one of Genghis's stepdaughters, and in due course the mother of two Mongol Chinese emperors and the first Mongol Persian ruler. And when Toghrul's son Nilka fled, he did so through Tangut territory, providing an excuse for the first Mongol raids in 1205. So the Mongols knew all about the Tanguts: their sophistication, their scholarship, their deep Buddhist faith (they referred to all Tangut emperors as 'Burkhan', which meant both Living Buddha and Holy One; the same word as in the name of their sacred mountain Burkhan Khaldun). None of this mattered. What mattered was that the Tanguts were rich, and vulnerable.

There was as yet no imperial aim. Genghis, who had been absorbed in a campaign to subdue his old enemies the Merkits, needed booty for his troops, with extended payments if possible; Xi Xia was the obvious source, which meant turning Xi Xia into a tribute-paying vassal state, as fast as possible, before Jin stepped in. There would have been no thought of occupation; only a vague plan, probably, to use Xi Xia's wealth as a stepping-stone to seizing or extorting yet more wealth from Jin.

In spring 1209 came the invasion proper. For this first large-scale campaign Genghis could have chosen many different routes across the Gobi. Probably he would have marched 500 kilometres south-west from Avraga, then on down a river, the Ongi, newly unfrozen and full of meltwater, aiming for the sanctuary of the Three Beauties ranges. Here the Altai mountains finally peter out in a 20,000-square-kilometre oval of peaks, canyons, high pastures, sand and gravel. To the west lie towering lines of dunes, known now as the Singing Sands because of the odd ethereal drone produced by wind-borne sand particles; to the east are gravelly lowlands, where water is scarce and the wildlife scattered. But between sands and plains the Three Beauties, with streams, pastures and wildlife, would have made a good staging post for an army on the move. Over the centuries, the wildlife retreated as the herders advanced; but now it is a national park, and the wildlife is returning, giving a hint of its former appeal. On a recent visit I saw mountain sheep bouncing up spines of rock, listened to herdsmen complaining about wolves, saw a foal that had been mauled by a snow leopard. There was even a reported sighting of one of the rarest of mammals, the Gobi bear, a relict variety cut off from its Himalayan cousins by the spread of the desert millennia ago. In the thirteenth century the Three Beauties was also a haven for wild asses, which not only made good eating but also provided excellent training for troops, because they move in herds and rival horses in speed and manoeuvrability (once, in a 4×4, I clocked a herd galloping at 70 k.p.h. in the remote western Gobi, where wild asses, now protected, have made a comeback).

From the Three Beauties, the route led on south another 300 kilometres to the Helan mountains, which form the eastern edge of the Alashan desert. On the map this is not the obvious approach, which would seem to be down the Yellow River, where the railway now runs. But this would mean crossing well-populated farming land interlaced with canals. Fast-moving cavalrymen preferred the hard, open Alashan, with its widely spaced defences. When the Mongols seized a little fortress town, the Tanguts sent an urgent request for help to the Jin, whom they expected to set past differences aside and come to the Tanguts' aid against a common enemy. But Genghis's timing was perfect. Jin was in the hands of a new leader, Prince Wei, who complacently told the Tangut ruler: 'It is to our advantage when our enemies attack one another. Wherein lies the danger to us?'

Driving on southward, desert to their right, mountains to the left, the Mongols came to a fortress defending the only pass leading through the mountains to the Tangut capital, present-day Yinchuan. Today, you can drive through this pass in half an hour, an easy ride. In Genghis's day, the track would have followed a dry riverbed in summer, or the mountain flanks at times of flood, the ground itself rising gently only 100 or 200 metres. Horsemen could cross the steep hills, but not easily and not fast. So the pass was the only way through, as it is today. Hence the fortress: the base for a Tangut army of 70,000, hastily reinforced with another 50,000 (always remembering that these are estimates, and almost certainly generous).

Even with a siege army, forcing this point would have been impossible. Genghis's only hope was to lure the Tanguts out on to the plain. After a two-month stand-off, the Mongols used their usual tactics in such circumstances, pretending to retreat, but in fact holing up in the foothills, leaving a small contingent to act as a lure. When the Tanguts duly attacked, the Mongols leaped on them and won a stunning victory. The way to Yinchuan was open.

Now they faced a problem. Yinchuan was a well-defended city, and the Mongols were fast-moving nomadic cavalrymen. They had never tried to take a city before. They had no triple-bow siege bows, such as the Song and Jin used, capable of firing arrows the size of telegraph poles; no large-scale catapults, no incendiary bombs filled with low-grade gun-powder or molten metal; and, as yet, no captured experts to teach them the techniques of long-term siege warfare. Their experience was all in mobility and speed. They could perhaps live off the land for a while, but the troops wanted quick rewards; and besides, they could not afford to wait around until Tangut reinforcements arrived in sufficient numbers from distant parts of the Xi Xia empire.

A remedy lay to hand: Yinchuan's ancient canal system, which brought water from the Yellow River to irrigate Xi Xia's bread-basket. The Mongols had no interest in preserv-ing such an investment, tended as it was by despised tillers of the soil. So they broke the dykes and tried to flood the city into surrender. This was not a good idea. The agricultural land surrounding Yinchuan is as flat as Holland. Floodwaters spread far, but remain shallow. In cities, buildings stand clear of shallow floods; but tents and horses and carts do not. The Mongols flooded themselves out, and were forced back to higher ground.

The Tangut leaders were also in a quandary. Their enemies were still close by, their crops were ruined, and they were not going to get help from Jin.

Stalemate.

To break the impasse, both gave ground. The Tangut emperor submitted, giving a daughter (Chaka by name) in marriage to Genghis, and handing over camels, falcons and textiles as tribute. Genghis, convinced that he now had a compliant vassal who would supply tribute and troops as required, ordered a withdrawal.

But this was his first international agreement, and it lacked bite. As events would show, he was a victim of his own wishful thinking. The Tanguts had submitted with their fingers crossed, and breathed a sigh of relief. It must have seemed the storm had passed. Upstart barbarians might extort carts of booty and herds of camels, but would surely never take on a powerful kingdom of 200 years' standing, with well-defended cities and an army of a few hundred thousand – would they?

7

INTO CHINA

WHEN A JIN DELEGATION ARRIVED AT GENGHIS'S COURT TO announce a new Jin emperor and demand a ritual obeisance, Genghis is said to have spat in disdain. 'I thought that the ruler of the Middle Kingdom had to come from Heaven. Can he be a person of such weakness as Prince Wei? Why should I kowtow to him?'

He had good reasons for disdain. The new Jin emperor ruled an insecure state in which his 3 million Jürchen dominated 40 million Chinese peasants, a population now weakened by famine and economic collapse. Several senior Jin officials and a vassal Khitan leader, sensing which way the wind was blowing, had already defected to the Mongols, bringing valuable information. A border tribe, the Ongut, who straddled the transition zone between the grassland of the herdsmen and the farmland, had offered unimpeded passage to the Mongols. Information on Jin defences also flowed from Muslim merchants, grateful for the security provided by Genghis's expanding empire. As always, the system of decaying 'great walls' offered no real barrier to nomadic warriors. And his army was flush with its victory over Xi Xia.

Still, the attack would not be easy. From a population ten times that of the Mongols, the Jin emperor could draw cavalry and infantry numbering several hundred thousand, and his cities were well fortified. Two immense fortresses guarded the approaches to Beijing, which was virtually impregnable to a direct assault.

Genghis's invasion was meticulous in planning, audacious in execution. In spring 1211 the Mongols gathered in the valleys south of the Khenti and advanced across the Gobi, well spread out and in several waves in order not to drain the scattered wells and pools of meltwater. This was a huge operation by any standards: imagine something like 100,000 warriors with 300,000 horses, strung out in perhaps 10–20 groups of 5,000–10,000 each, each with camel-drawn carts, and all linked by fast-moving messengers as the army crossed 800 kilometres of gravel plain. Yet *The Secret History*'s editorial team ignored it, quite rightly. Nothing went wrong. It had been done before by both nomadic armies and Chinese, and would be done again. To a Mongolian audience, eager for personality and anecdote, it would have been routine. The only sources, therefore, are Chinese, and they are rather sparse.

As the Mongol army spilled into northern China and approached the pass then named Huan-erh-tsui – the Badger's Mouth – that led down towards Beijing, the Jin commander, Zhi-zhong, seems to have made a fatal mistake. He had a chance of launching a surprise attack when the Mongols were on a rampage of looting. Instead, perhaps to win time, he sent an officer, Ming-an, to discuss peace terms with Genghis. Ming-an promptly defected, with the information that the Jin were waiting at the far end of the pass. There the Jin cavalry, packed between ridges, was overwhelmed by arrows and a Mongol charge. Horsemen turned and trampled their own infantry. Bodies, 'piled like rotten logs', as *The Secret History* says, lay scattered for 50 kilometres along the valley that drops to Kalgan (now Zhangjiakou), the frontier town between the Inner Mongolian plateau and lowland China. The Mongols would always consider the Battle of Badger's Mouth one of their greatest victories.

Ten years later, when a Taoist sage, Ch'ang-ch'un, passed through on his way to meet Genghis Khan, the bones of the slain were still visible on the escarpments. 'A fresh breeze had cleared away the clouds, and the air was very agreeable,' wrote one of Ch'ang-ch'un's students and companions on the trip.

> Northwards lay nothing but wintry sands and withered grass. Here China – its customs and climate – suddenly comes to an end. But must not the Taoist learn to accept gladly whatever surroundings he may find himself in? Sung Te-fang and the rest [of Ch'ang-ch'un's disciples] pointed to the skeletons lying on the battlefield and said: 'Let us, if we come home safely, celebrate the Service of the Golden Tablets for their souls; for who knows whether our setting out on this journey was not in part fated that we might help them to Salvation?'

On his return in early 1224, Ch'ang-ch'un stayed at a town some 100 kilometres south of the battlefield on the route of the fleeing Jin army. Here, within sight of villages still devastated from the war, he fulfilled his promise and, for two bitterly cold nights and three days, prayed 'on behalf of the lonely dead'.

Follow-on skirmishes drove the Jin generals back to Beijing and captured several major cities and fortresses. Beijing held out, isolated, leaving the Mongols free to roam and loot at will. While Genghis headed southward for another 300 kilometres to the Yellow River, one of his star generals, Jebe, travelled even further east into Manchuria, crossing the frozen Liao river to attack the old Manchurian capital of

Mukden (today's Shenyang). This, Jin's second city after Beijing, proved impregnable by direct assault, so Jebe did what Mongols often did. He pretended to flee, leaving baggage scattered as if in panic. When Jin scouts confirmed that the Mongols were 150 kilometres away, the delighted citizens started celebrations for the New Year of 1212 by gathering up their unexpected windfall, which lured them ever further from the city. The Mongols sprang: after a non-stop 24-hour ride, they found the city open and the inhabitants partying. Surprise was total. They plucked Mukden like a ripe plum.

Content with his victories, Genghis withdrew northward to the borderlands between grass and Gobi. Victory to him and his troops still meant no more than booty, destruction and an assertion of dominance. In spirit, he was still little more than a gang leader in a turf war, with no interest in occupation or administration. But he had entered, unawares, upon a new type of warfare – the taking of cities – which would turn him into another sort of leader altogether.

In the autumn of 1212, a new assault stuttered when Genghis was wounded by an arrow, and ordered a withdrawal for rest and relaxation. He returned the following summer, retaking towns along the route, renewing the attack on the Badger's Mouth, with its two massive fortresses. Records speak of the surrounding area, as far as 50 kilometres away, being strewn with caltrops – iron balls with four spikes intended to pierce horses' feet – but two of Genghis's greatest generals, Jebe and Subedei, rode along the mountain crests to seize the southern fort at the far end of the pass, forcing the northern fort to surrender. At last the road to Beijing was open.

Jin was an empire under apocalyptic strains. Thousands of soldiers died in battle and, with the Mongols seizing food wherever they went, civilians starved. In besieged forts, occupants resorted to cannibalism. Beijing sank into political turmoil. The ambitious and erratic general Zhi-zhong, a favourite of the emperor, had been pardoned for losing so disastrously at Huan-erh-tsui, and had shown his disdain for the Mongol threat by organizing hunts outside the capital with his own private army. As the Mongols approached, he realized that such panache was likely to prove suicidal, but he had no intention of placing himself in the unreliable hands of his emperor. He staged a coup, slew the 500 soldiers guarding the Forbidden City, murdered the emperor, placed his own puppet on the throne and proclaimed himself regent, celebrating these astonishing acts with a banquet attended by the capital's most famous and beautiful courtesans.

When, two months later, the Mongols surrounded the city, Zhi-zhong despatched some 6,000 men to oppose them, threatening death for the commander, Kao-ch'i, should he fail; which he did. To avoid the fate he knew awaited him, Kao-ch'i turned assassin. He rode back at full tilt ahead of the bad news, presumably with a small band of men, cornered Zhi-zhong and beheaded him. Still carrying the head, Kao-ch'i ran to the emperor and confessed all. The emperor was, it seems, so relieved to escape the grasp of the self-proclaimed regent, or perhaps so terrified by the gruesome sight, that he instantly made Kao-ch'i vice-commander of the empire.

Not that there was much of an empire left. With the emperor pinned in his capital, and most towns frozen by fear, Genghis sent off all but a small force to ravage the country and seize cities. This was still a nomad army, without heavy-duty siege gear, but Genghis was learning. The Mongols used ruthlessness as others used catapults. Corralling prisoners by the thousand, they forced them to head assaults. The besieged, often recognizing relatives in the seething masses below their walls, could not bear to attack their own, and capitulated. Thus an army of 100,000, divided into three columns, rode south and west to the Yellow River, and eastwards to the Pacific, mopping up towns by the dozen across a rectangle measuring 750 kilometres across and 450 kilometres deep – an area the size of Germany. 'Everywhere north of the Yellow River', wrote the Chinese biographer of the great Mongol general Mukhali, 'there could be seen dust and smoke, and the sound of drums rose to Heaven.' In two months, present-day Shanxi, Hebei and Shandong were ruined.

But Beijing still held out, for a century earlier it had been turned into a very tough nut. Outside the walls were four fortress-villages, each with its own granary and arsenal, each linked to the capital by a tunnel. Into these the military and political leaders retreated, with 4,000 soldiers apiece. Three moats fed from Kunming lake protected the walls themselves, which formed a rectangle almost 4 kilometres long – 15 kilo-metres around – and some 15 metres thick at the base. A crenellated parapet rose 12 metres above the ground, with 13 gates and a guard tower every 15 metres – over 900 of them in all.

Inside these formidable defences, the inhabitants deployed equally formidable weapons. Double- and triple-bow cross-bows could fire 3-metre arrows a kilometre (this astonishing range was recorded by Persian sources during a Mongol attack on an Assassin castle in 1256). Another siege bow from Tang times could fire one of its seven types of arrow 500 metres, at which distance 'whatever it hits will collapse, even solid things like ramparts and city walls'. Artillery would have been in the form of catapults known as 'traction trebuchets': wagon-mounted levers some 10 metres long, with rocks loaded onto one end and ropes attached to the other. Hauling on the ropes, a team of six men, directed by an artillery master on the walls, could lob 25-kilo boulders 200–300 metres. And all of these weapons could be adapted to fire a weird variety of incendiary devices, for these were the early days of gunpowder. Fire-arrows from siege bows and fireballs from trebuchets – some made of wax to burn slowly, some with barbs that stuck into wood, some made of ceramic filled with molten iron – were all used to set fire to scaling ladders and assault towers. The Chinese also knew how to filter crude oil to make naphtha, which could be tossed in pots or thrown in bottles, like Molotov cocktails. Another means of defence was to use distilled petroleum, known as 'Greek fire' in the west. An instruction manual of 1044 described a crude but effective flame-thrower: a tube filled with Greek fire could be ignited from a gunpowder-filled ignition chamber, squirting flaming oil on those below. Perhaps the Chinese also deployed 'poisonous smoke bombs' filled with chemicals and excrement. Such devices held the Mongols at bay, but also acted as a salutary lesson. To take and hold cities, these weapons would have to be mastered, with the help of captives and turncoats.

The siege of Beijing lasted nearly a year, into the spring of 1214. It was a hard winter for the Mongols, who are said to have suffered an epidemic of some kind and to have resorted to cannibalism (though the evidence for this is all from non-Mongol sources, many of whom had an interest in presenting them in the worst possible light). But by the spring those within the walls were far worse off. Genghis offered to withdraw: 'Heaven has so weakened you,' he told the emperor, 'that, if I were also now to attack you in your distress, what would Heaven think of me?' He would, of course, need persuading: 'What provision will you make to still the demands of my officers?' It was an offer the emperor could not refuse. He agreed to hand over a princess, 500 boys and girls, 3,000 horses, and an astonishing 10,000 'bolts' of silk (which, if rolled out, would extend for about 90 kilometres). Promising to retreat in peace, Genghis ordered his booty-laden troops back northward to the welcoming grasslands.

The Jin emperor had learned a bitter lesson. Beijing, surrounded by devastation, threatened by nomads now familiar with siege warfare, could never again be considered invulnerable. The gap-toothed and eroded Great Wall, now a symbol more of collapse than of anti-barbarian power, would never offer protection against the likes of Genghis. There could be safety only beyond the true geographical frontier between the Middle Kingdom and the nomads. He decided to move his capital, not back to the Jin homeland in Manchuria, but way south, to the ancient Chinese capital of Kaifeng. The Jin would finally cut themselves from their Jürchen roots, and declare themselves irrevocably Chinese.

This was an immense undertaking. Sources mention 3,000 camels laden with treasure and 30,000 cartloads of documents and royal possessions, trailing 600 kilometres southward for two months, all in pursuit of security beyond the Yellow River. It achieved the exact opposite. Some 2,000 of the imperial army were Khitans from Manchuria, who saw the move as a confession of weakness, and certainly did not like the idea of moving even further from their ancestral home into the Chinese heartland. Fifty kilometres out of Beijing they mutinied, galloped back, set up their tents and sent a message of submission to Genghis.

The Mongol army was camped some 400 kilometres to the north of the ravaged Jin capital, at a lake in the grasslands of Inner Mongolia. Genghis was aghast at the news of the government's departure. A Chinese source records his words: 'The Jin emperor mistrusts my word! He has used the peace to deceive me!' It would also have struck him that he had been granted a terrific opportunity: Beijing abandoned by its emperor, and mutinous troops ready to fight for the Mongols. But he had to act instantly. A new capital in Kaifeng could be a base for a future Jin offensive, and would be much, much harder to subdue. By September the Mongols were back at the walls of Beijing.

There was no attempt at assault. As autumn turned to winter, the Mongol army just sat tight. In the spring, the emperor in Kaifeng sent two relief columns. The Mongols smashed both, seizing 1,000 cartloads of food. More of Beijing's outlying towns fell into Mongol hands. Beijing began to starve. As often in besieged cities, the living took to eating the dead. Leaders argued violently over whether to die fighting or flee. Kao-ch'i's deputy, the city's civilian commander, committed suicide. The military commander sneaked away, taking only his relatives with him (he reached Kaifeng, where he was executed for treachery). In June, the remaining inhabitants, leaderless and hopeless, opened the gates in surrender.

Genghis himself, meanwhile, had decamped to the edge of the grasslands, 150 kilometres north, and was by now on his way back to the Kherlen. Without his restraining influence, the Mongols ran wild. They ransacked the city, killing thousands. A palace went up in flames, and part of the city burned for a month.

A year later, an ambassador from Genghis's next opponent, the shah of Khwarezm, came to find out if it was really true that such a great and well-defended city had fallen to a mere nomad. The evidence was all too apparent. He reported that the bones of the slaughtered formed mountains, that the soil was greasy with human fat, that some of his entourage died from the diseases spread by rotting bodies. He even reported as true a wild story that 60,000 girls had thrown themselves from the walls to avoid falling into Mongol hands.

Now the Mongols were masters of all north-eastern China; they had sliced the Jin empire in half, leaving two rumps, south of the Yellow River and Manchuria. In the newly conquered territories, the few towns still holding out surrendered. Surviving garrisons revolted against their former masters and declared for the new ones. A million fled south through devastation and famine to the new Jin heartland around Kaifeng. But Genghis was not yet content, for the Jin emperor newly settled in Kaifeng refused a final submission. A knock-out blow was needed – actually, a double blow: the total reduction of Jin power in Manchuria, and a final assault on Kaifeng.

Manchuria was a rural backwater of farmers, herders and hunters, in which the strongest Khitan leader, Liu-ke, had declared allegiance to Genghis in 1212 and made himself warlord of most of Manchuria, master of 600,000 families. The rest of the region had long sent young men off to the Jin army. Manchuria would be a walkover.

So it proved, when Mukhali and Genghis's brother Kasar swept across all Manchuria in 1214–16. Mukhali – reputed for his powerful build, curly whiskers, superb archery and meticulous planning ability – was, at 45, already one of Genghis's greatest generals, having been with him for fifteen years, and he would become the anchor-man in the long struggle to subdue north China. One major task was to capture the old Liao provincial capital of Pei Ching, which fell into his lap in an extraordinary fashion. A Mongol officer named Yesen, who spoke both the local Turkish language and Chinese, ambushed a new Jin commander arriving to assume control of the city, took over his documents, persuaded the guards that he was actually the incoming general, and then, as the city's new boss, ordered all the guards off the walls. Mukhali walked in virtually unopposed, taking possession of the city's 100,000 households, together with their food and weapons. After that, resistance elsewhere crumbled. To punish two towns that had the temerity to hold out, Mukhali ordered every inhabitant killed, except carpenters, masons and, of all things, *actors*. The Mongols must have been hungry for light relief.

A small force raced onwards for a final 300 kilometres to the end of the Liaodong peninsula; it reached the Pacific by the autumn of 1216, leaving another column to pursue several thousand Khitan insurgents across the Yalu river into Korea. After killing many and capturing others, a brash Mongol emissary journeyed on to the Korean court in Kaesong, the rich and cosmopolitan river-port that today lies

The campaigns, 1206–1227.

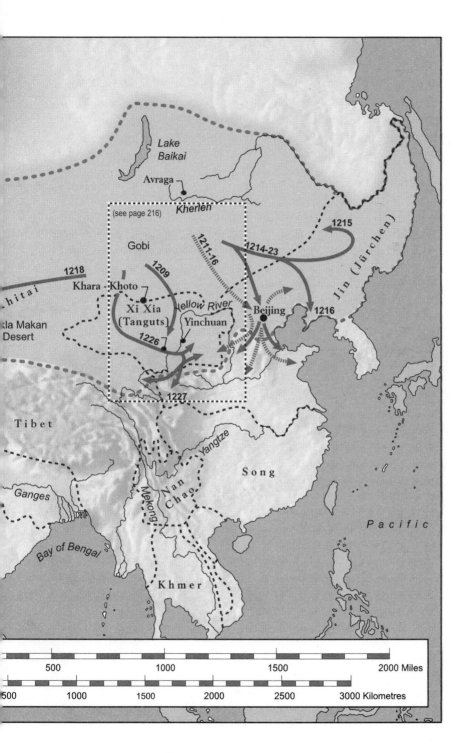

Lake
Baikai

Avraga

Kherlen

(see page 216)

Gobi

1218

1209

1211-16

1214-23

1215

Jin (Jürchen)

hitai

Khara - Khoto

Xi Xia
(Tanguts)

Yellow River

Yinchuan

Beijing

1216

kla Makan
Desert

1226

1227

Tibet

Yangtze

Song

Ganges

Mekong

Nan
Chao

Pacific

Bay of Bengal

Khmer

| 500 | 1000 | 1500 | 2000 Miles |

| 500 | 1000 | 1500 | 2000 | 2500 | 3000 Kilometres |

on the border between North and South Korea. With no respect for court etiquette, he carried sword and bow into the royal chamber to greet the king with the news that Korea had just been saved from marauding Khitans. What could the king offer by way of recompense? In the circumstances, quite a lot, including 100,000 of Korea's largest sheets of paper; it seems that Genghis wished to keep his newly literate officials well supplied with stationery.

So much for what is now southern Manchuria. An area half the size of France (or equal to the state of Wyoming) had been added to the Mongol domains, with a compliant if resentful monarch to the east.

When news of these conquests reached Genghis, he demanded and received 30,000 troops from his new vassal, Xi Xia, and despatched a force into the Ordos, south along the Yellow River, in a drive to take Kaifeng from the rear. This was another immense, year-long campaign, in which the Mongol and Tangut armies, numbering some 60,000 men, advanced 1,000 kilometres against vastly superior forces, through territory bristling with strongholds to the very outskirts of Kaifeng. They engaged in half a dozen major battles, most of them in winter, before finally retreating when Jin defences proved too much for them. During the most bitterly fought section of this campaign, along the Yellow River, the army covered some 800 kilometres in 60 days. Compare this with a mechanized army on the move at speed. In early August 1944, after the D-Day landings of June, the Americans under General Patton rolled along at 30 kilometres a day for just three days, with virtually no opposition, over the long, straight, paved roads of southern Brittany; in the autumn of 1216 the horseborne Mongols covered 13 kilometres a day, cross-country, fighting four major battles and in constant danger of further attack, for two full months.

Not surprisingly, the Jin sued for peace. One Chinese source quotes Genghis's response, posing a question to his generals: 'We have taken all the deer and other beasts; only a rabbit is left; why not let it go?' This was a challenge to the spirit of his generals, one of whom spoke up: surely there could be peace only when the emperor was emperor no more, but merely a royal vassal of the khan? This was the answer Genghis wanted. The war would go on, and it did, ending in complete victory over the Jin almost 20 years later.

Victory would have come a lot more quickly if events far to the west had not claimed Genghis's attention, opening another chapter in the history of the Mongol conquests.

8

THE MUSLIM HOLOCAUST

THE STORY OF THE MONGOL CONQUESTS HAS ALREADY JOINED
two distinct cultures, taking us from the Mongolian grasslands to the urbanized wealth and assurance of Xi Xia and
northern China. So far, the effects have been bloody, but not
entirely unprecedented. Now the story is about to involve a
third culture, Islam, with a human and cultural impact utterly
new in world history. No culture before had wielded such
destructive power as the Mongols; no culture had suffered as
the Muslim world was about to suffer. Deaths in China must
have measured in the tens of thousands. Events now about to
unfold multiply that figure at least tenfold.

The numbers – almost certainly exaggerated by Islamic
writers, but appallingly high nevertheless – suggest the release
of some terrible racial or religious hatred, or the grim
application of ideology. But it was not like that; there was no
crusading ambition to assert the grand truths of shamanism
over other beliefs, no master-race determination to exter-
minate despised opponents or win *Lebensraum* in Central
Asia. The only overriding consideration was conquest,

because, for whatever obscure reason, that was the destiny imposed on Genghis by Heaven. Destruction was a matter of strategy. Sometimes this became personal, when a leader or city caused particular offence, but mostly it remained coldly impersonal, born of a rock-solid sense of superiority, not over any one group, but over all. Racism is selective, and this the Mongols were not. Absolutely everyone else owed them deference (an attitude shared by a few other peoples at the height of empire, like the British around 1900, eighteenth-century Chinese, neo-conservative Americans in 2003). Cities, regions, kingdoms and empires tumbled with no other purpose than to assure the next victory, to which death and destruction were incidental. Whatever achieved victory was good; whatever delayed it was bad. Simple as that.

The first link in this chain of events had been forged years before when the scion of the Naiman ruling house, Kuchlug, had escaped westward at the head of his few surviving troops. He had ended up in another vast realm, which, like Xi Xia, has been obscured from modern eyes by its remoteness in time and space. Yet however obscure and remote, Kuchlug and his new base play a vital role in this story, because they drew Genghis westward into the world of Islam, which in turn became a base for yet more western conquests.

To understand what happened, we have to wind the clock back a century. When the Khitan, ruling as the Liao, were driven from the Dragon Throne by the Jürchen in 1124, a member of the Khitan ruling house, Yeh-lü Ta-Shih, had gathered 200 followers and fled westward for 2,500 kilometres, beyond the deserts of Xinjiang and over the Tien mountains, far beyond the reach of new rulers of northern China. Here, a decade later, in an anarchic section of Inner Asia peopled by a mixture of Turkish tribes and Islamic peoples, Ta-Shih carved out a realm of grass, mountain and desert the size of western Europe. It was centred on present-day Kyrgyzstan, but also included what are now western China, southern Kazakhstan and Tajikistan. It was Ta-Shih who took the title Gur (Universal) Khan and named his kingdom Khara Khitai, 'Black Cathay', after his own Khitan tribe. Once established, he began to extort tribute from his Muslim neighbour (of whom more shortly).

When, 70 years later, Kuchlug arrived, he was welcomed by the current Gur Khan, securing his position by marrying the khan's daughter. Then, in the words of the late thirteenth-century Persian historian Juvaini, he 'leaped forth like an arrow from a strong bow' to seize power. His treachery won him few friends. And he made things worse: at the behest of his new wife, he turned Buddhist and became violently hostile to Islam, demanding that Islamic leaders renounce their faith, thus alienating his own new subjects. When the imam of Khotan in southern Xinjiang reviled him – 'Dust be in thy mouth, thou enemy of the faith!' – Kuchlug had him crucified on the door of his own *madrasa*. Clearly, in Genghis's eyes, this unstable fanatic would one day wish to use his new base to avenge his father and grandfather. For the sake of the future security of the Mongol nation, he had to be eliminated.

After years of hard campaigning in China, this did not look too hard a task, and in 1218 Genghis entrusted it to Jebe. There would be no great sieges for his 20,000 men. Geography was perhaps the greatest challenge: a march of 2,600 kilometres, first across Mongolia's grasslands, then over the 3,000-metre Altai mountains, and after that through the rugged heights of the Tien Shan, where peaks reach up over 5,000 metres. The army, following one of the Silk Road trails, would have skirted Issyk Kul, the world's second largest alpine lake, with its own ecology. Depth, thermal activity and salinity combine to make the lake a heat-store, granting the valley a climate mild enough to plant vineyards and raise mulberry trees for the breeding of silkworms. Some

80 kilometres from Issyk Kul's western end lay Kuchlug's capital, Balasagun, now vanished except for its only surviving relic: the 25-metre stump of an eleventh-century minaret known as the Burana Tower.

Militarily, success came easily, as Genghis had foreseen. At the Mongols' approach, Kuchlug fled south for 400 kilometres over the high Tien Shan, probably via the 3,750-metre Torugart Pass, and down to the Silk Road emporium of Kashgar, on the western edge of the Takla Makan desert. When Jebe went in pursuit, he banned pillaging, which meant that Kashgar's Uighur inhabitants were happy to see him. Kuchlug fled again, over the desert towards the Pamirs, which rear up 100 kilometres to the south-west of Kashgar, perhaps aiming to follow the precipitous ravine of the Ghez river, which leads up into what is now Pakistan. 'Chased like a mad dog' by the Mongols, as Juvaini relates, Kuchlug and his followers entered a dead-end valley. Coming upon some local hunters, the Mongols told them whom they were after, at which the hunters, seeing a chance for glory and cash, caught Kuchlug and handed him over. Having paid the hunters, the Mongols cut off Kuchlug's head and, to confirm their conquest, paraded it through the cities of their new domains. Thus ended Genghis's struggle with three generations of Naiman rulers.

The Mongol victory over Kuchlug brought them into contact with his Islamic neighbour, a kingdom straddling much of present-day Uzbekistan and Turkmenistan, over-lapping into Iran and Afghanistan. It was known as Khwarezm (in one common transliteration; there are half a dozen), after its core province. This unruly region on Islam's eastern borderlands, for two centuries part of the Seljuk empire, had become the core of a new kingdom half a century before, leading to a continuous state of war among several participants, including the khans of Khara Khitai, who at one point controlled most of Khwarezm and continued to extort tribute from it. By the end of the twelfth century, Khwarezm had also expanded into the neighbouring provinces of Khurasan and Transoxania. It thus controlled the great Silk Road emporia – Samarkand, Bukhara, Urgench, Khojend, Merv, Nishapur – as well as the traditional frontier river, the Amudar'ya, known in classical times as the Oxus. The region known as Transoxania or Transoxiana – the land 'across the Oxus' – reached for almost 500 kilometres over the Kyzylkum desert to the barren banks of the Syrdar'ya (the ancient Jaxartes). The struggle for this region, well supplied with meltwater from the Pamirs, rich in farmland, pastures, minerals and trade goods, left few records; historians deduce what they can from coins. It was a confused and brutal time: Samarkand alone endured 70 attacks by Khara Khitai forces, almost one a year. Under this pressure, in about 1210 Khwarezm's shah, Mohammed, concluded a brief alliance with Kuchlug, then on his way up. The result was that when Kuchlug seized power in Khara Khitai, Mohammed was free to begin building an empire, thus starting a train of events that led to the next stage in Genghis's journey towards transcontinental dominion.[1]

The key to what follows was the character of Khwarezm's shah, Mohammed. No-one has a good word to say for this appalling creature, who brought to his people and his religion their greatest disaster. His mother, Terken, who ran her own court, also bears a good deal of the blame. It was perhaps on her initiative that he, a volatile and insecure Turk, had tried to impose his will on his mainly Iranian people by force. One sultan, a certain Othman, led an uprising in Samarkand, starting his brief revolt by killing all the Khwarezmians in town, and literally butchering them, hanging up their bodies

---

[1] Sources differ on the order of almost all these events. Perhaps, as Juvaini suggests, Mongol contacts with Khwarezm preceded the defeat of Kuchlug. But even with a different narrative, the cause of the war and the chain of causes and effects that led Genghis westward would remain the same.

in bits in the bazaars. When Mohammed seized the city again 10,000 died, including Othman; so when the shah made it his capital, it had to say the least a disaffected populace. In addition, he had fought with Islam's supreme head, the caliph in Baghdad, so there was no chance of his presenting himself as the defender of Islam. Finally, he was a notorious libertine. Juvaini portrays him 'constantly satisfying his desires in the company of fair songstresses and in continual drinking of purple wine'. If you felt generous, you might say that in trying to bring peace to this strife-torn region he was attempting the impossible. On the other hand, you could call him an unpopular, unscrupulous, isolated, mother-dominated, sex-obsessed drunkard; a disaster in waiting.

Genghis had no interest in embroiling himself in this mess, saying that all he wanted was a trade link. Shah Mohammed, though, had heard reports of the rape of Beijing, from the ambassador who had reported those mountains of bones and lakes of human fat. Was it really likely that a bloody warlord like Genghis would be suddenly converted to the cause of peace? As it happens, the answer was quite possibly yes, for northern China had not yet been conquered, and would not be for another 20 years. But Mohammed's reaction was a quintessence of foolishness, the five essences being weakness, naïveté, ignorance, xenophobia and arrogance. They were all the same, these idolaters: 'There is for me no difference between yourself, the Gur Khan and Kuchlug . . . Let there then be war in which swords are broken and spears are shattered!'

Genghis still insisted he was intent on trade, for war here would mean yet another extension to the Mongol realm, another campaign, yet wider borders to defend, and perhaps, who knows, defeat. Besides, there was a good opportunity for trade. Three merchants from Bukhara had arrived in Mongolia eager to exploit the route that had suddenly opened up with the Mongol advances into northern China. When they returned, Genghis had them accompanied by a huge trade delegation of 100 (as *The Secret History* records), or perhaps as many as 450 (as others say), all Muslims except for a Mongol leader, to set up business in Islamic lands. Journeying across the grasslands for 2,700 kilometres and several weeks, this delegation carried another message to the shah from Genghis, stating that they came 'in order that they may acquire the wondrous wares of those regions; and that henceforth the abscess of evil thoughts may be lanced by the improvement of relations'.

Or something like that. There are various versions of what Genghis actually said, all from the Islamic side, none suggesting overt hostility. According to one source Genghis claimed equality, or called Mohammed 'the best-loved of my sons', which, while it would have struck any leader as patronizing, was hardly a declaration of war. Yet Mohammed took it as such.

In 1217 the delegation arrived in Otrar, on the Syrdar'ya river. Today it is Otyrar, in the far west of modern Kazakhstan, and little remains of it but a few grassy hillocks and scattered ruins. In the early thirteenth century, it was a thriving border town covering 20 hectares, governed by the other villain in this story, named in the sources by his rank or title, Inalchuk ('Little Lord') or Qadir-Khan ('Mighty Khan'). Governor X, Inalchuk as he is usually known, was a relative of Mohammed's dominating mother, and would not have risked acting on his own initiative. It was he who, with a nod and a wink from his overlord, opened the gates of hell, in a double outrage. First, he accused the merchants of spying, and arrested them all. Genghis was appalled at this insult, but refused to be provoked. He offered one last olive branch, sending three envoys, who gave Mohammed a chance to disclaim all knowledge of his governor's act and hand him over for punishment. Mohammed, the idiot, at once chose to inflict instant and unforgivable injury. He had at least one of the envoys, and possibly all three, killed.

And then, 'Without thinking or reflecting,' writes Juvaini, 'the shah at once gave orders for that party of Muslims [Genghis's merchants in Otrar] . . . to be put to death,' and their rich goods to be seized. 'Little Lord' Inalchuk killed the whole delegation. And these, remember, were all co-religionists, except for the leader. This was hardly an act designed to win the admiration of his own people. Mohammed had, in effect, lost the war for hearts and minds before the first battle was joined. Juvaini rises, as often, to near-poetry to lament the rashness of an act that, as events showed, 'desolated and laid waste a whole world . . . for every drop of their blood there flowed a whole Oxus.'

To kill a single envoy would have been enough to provoke war, let alone 100, let alone 450, or however many there were. When the news reached Genghis, Juvaini describes him flying into a whirlwind of rage, the fire of wrath driving the water from his eyes so that it was only to be quenched by blood. He 'went alone to the summit of a hill' – I think we can assume that if he did it would have been Burkhan Khaldun – 'bared his head, turned his face towards the earth and for three days and nights offered up prayer, saying: "I am not the author of this trouble; grant me strength to exact vengeance."'

Thus began a new phase in Genghis's career. Up to this point, tradition had ruled. It was part of a Mongol ruler's heritage to invade China; for this, tribal unity was a pre-requisite; this in turn justified the pursuit of a rival chieftain, even if he had fled to a far state, in this case Khara Khitai; and this, as any good strategist would have understood, also meant dealing with Xi Xia. But no nomad chief, while still wedded to his home base, would ever willingly have under-taken the task of subduing an empire so far from home, let alone one that was the dominant power of Inner Asia. But in Genghis's eyes, he had no choice. Not only had he been humiliated and directly challenged; if the threat were not met, he would almost certainly become a victim of an ambitious shah eager to expand his authority to China's rich lands. As *The Secret History* says, he had no doubts about what had to be done: 'Let us ride out against the Islamic people, to gain vengeance!'

Genghis's decision seems to have inspired a discussion among his family on the subject of succession. The problem was posed by Yisui, one of his wives, of whom there were now several. In words placed in Yisui's mouth by *The Secret History*,

> When your body, like an old and withered tree,
> Comes crashing down,
> To whom will you bequeath your people?

Genghis saw the point, for by tradition his heir would be the clan's senior member, as long as he could assert the claim, though he would not necessarily be the best qualified to rule, and probably not any one of the chief's children. Now, however, the heir had something rather more than a clan to administer, and the sons were all experienced commanders in their own right. The rules would be changed. A son should rule. But which? Genghis opened the problem to all four, in public. The mantle might have fallen naturally to Jochi, the eldest; but Jochi could have been fathered by a Merkit when his mother was a captive. The suggestion started a heated argument, recorded at length in *The Secret History*.

Chagadai, the second son, burst out: 'Are you saying we have to be governed by this Merkit bastard?'

Jochi seized his brother by the collar. 'Our father the khan never said I was different. How come you do? You think you're so much cleverer than me? Only more violent!'

Two generals, Boorchu and Mukhali, held them apart while a shaman, Khökhö-chos, calmed things by recalling the dangers surmounted by Genghis to quell anarchy and found the nation: when the khan had only his spit to drink, he struggled on until the sweat of his brow soaked his feet. And what about your mother? She went hungry for you, and hauled you up by the necks to make you the equal of others.

Chagadai accepted the rebuke. OK, he would work with Jochi, he said, and suggested the third son, Ogedei, as a compromise: 'Ogedei is merciful; let him receive the dignity.' Genghis further defused the tension. No need for his two eldest to be partners; Mother Earth was wide and her rivers many; each would get his own portion of the estate. Tolui, the youngest, might have made a good khan – he had shown his military skill in China; but his wife was a Kerait princess who was a Nestorian Christian, and a woman of formidable ambition and intelligence. Perhaps under her influence Genghis's heirs would no longer respect their own traditions. (He was right to worry about her. The princess, Sorghaghtani, would emerge as one of the most powerful women of her age; and it was her sons who would finally divide the imperial mantle.)

What had Ogedei to say? Ogedei knew he was not the obvious choice. Gifted and generous, yes; but for 'merciful' read 'not sufficiently ruthless'. Besides, he was a heavy drinker. His humble, stuttering response reflected both his strengths and weaknesses. Well, um, he would do his best, though he could not vouch for his descendants. It was not much of a speech, but it was enough. The heir was chosen, the clan and the nation were still united.

And the political foundations were laid for expansion westward.

Genghis, taking personal charge of a campaign that needed meticulous planning, sought all the help he could get.

Help, in particular, with something no Mongol leader had ever tackled before: the administration of conquered territory.

It must already have struck Genghis as foolish to undertake the same conquest time after time, as he had in China, where some cities had been besieged and taken three times. A few of the Mongol princes had a rudimentary idea of administration, having learned the Uighur script adopted a few years previously. But there was as yet no bureaucracy. He would need one, if he did not wish to repeat the pattern of the Chinese campaigns.

It was perhaps at this moment that he, or someone, recalled one of the prisoners taken in Beijing three years before, when his adopted brother Shigi had made an inventory of the imperial treasure and any notable captives. Among the Jin officials one had stood out – literally: a very tall young man (8 *chu*, supposedly, which is about 6 feet 8 inches), aged 25, with a beard reaching to his waist and a magnificent, sonorous voice. He was a Khitan, one of the people who, as the Liao, had once ruled in north-eastern China and been displaced by the Jin. His name was Chu-tsai, and his family, Yeh-lü, was one of the most eminent in the Liao empire, tracing its lineage back 200 years to the founder of the Liao dynasty. Actually, his father was adopted, but Chu-tsai considered himself a Yeh-lü through and through. His father had worked for the Jin, first as a translator – he spoke Chinese, Khitan and Jürchen – and then as a senior imperial official, becoming rich and influential. Chu-tsai, born with every advantage, was a brilliant student, poet and administrator with a predilection for Buddhist literature. When Genghis invaded he was a provincial vice-prefect. Recalled to the capital, he served throughout the siege. The sack of Beijing was a horrific experience, and he determined to make sense of it in his own way, by studying Buddhism. He sought the guidance of a Buddhist sage, went into retreat for three years, and emerged strengthened in his belief that truth and virtue were best served by combining the doctrines of the Three Sages – Confucius, Buddha and Lao-tzu, the founder of

Taoism. Now he found himself summoned to Genghis, who needed someone to set up and run an imperial bureaucracy. It was an honour; and Chu-tsai was expected to show due humility in return for his release from his previous masters.

In an exchange that later became famous, Genghis addressed him: 'The Liao and the Jin have been enemies for generations. I have avenged you.'

Chu-tsai replied with astonishing composure: 'My father and grandfather both served the Jin respectfully. How can I, as a subject and a son, be so insincere at heart as to regard my sovereign and my father as enemies?'

Genghis was impressed, and offered this self-possessed and clever young man the job. And 'Long Beard', as Genghis called him, saw that conquest was proof that Heaven's Mandate had settled upon Genghis. From now on, Chu-tsai would play an important role in moulding the character of the khan and his empire, working on his master's curiosity about spiritual matters. It was almost certainly Chu-tsai who in 1219 drafted a long appeal to the Chinese sage Ch'ang Ch'un, presenting Genghis as a warrior ascetic, wedded to a life of austerity, fighting only to impose virtue.

> Heaven has wearied of the sentiments of arrogance and luxury carried to their extreme in China. As for me, I live in the wild regions of the North, where covetousness cannot arise. I return to simplicity, I turn again to purity, I observe moderation. In the clothes I wear or the meats I eat, I have the same rags and the same food as the cowherd or the groom in the stables. I have for the common people the solicitude I would have for a little child, and the soldiers I treat as my brothers. Present at 100 battles, I have ever ridden personally in the forefront. In the space of seven years I have accomplished a great work, and in the six directions of space all is subject to a single law.

A return to nomadic simplicity? Not quite yet, for unity and virtue were not yet universal, Heaven's will not yet accomplished.

Genghis sent out requests for troops to his vassals in the borderlands of Mongolia, in Uighur lands, in northern China, in Manchuria and, finally, in Xi Xia. He had conquered Xi Xia; he had received tribute; its Buddhist king, the Burkhan, the Holy One, had promised aid when necessary; this was a vassal state good and proper, and would surely respond as befitted a vassal. Genghis sent off his request to the king: Remember you promised to be my right hand? Well, I need to settle scores with the Mohammedans, so 'become my right hand and ride with me!'

What Genghis received, however, was a slap in the face as sharp as the one from Khwarezm's shah, Mohammed. The slap came not directly from Xi Xia's ruler, but from his military commander or *gambu*: the power behind the throne, Asha. When Genghis's messengers explained what was required and why, it must have seemed to Asha that he had been presented with a terrific opportunity to regain Xi Xia's independence. The Mongols had yet to achieve final victory in northern China, and were now facing another war over 2,000 kilometres away to the west. Surely no power on earth could fight a war on two such widely separated fronts. Asha pre-empted his king with a contemptuous rejection: 'If Genghis is really that weak, why did he ever bother to become khan?'

When the reply came, Genghis could do nothing to express his anger as he wished. His first task was to march against Mohammed. But then, 'if I am protected by Eternal Heaven,' oh, then there would be a reckoning indeed.

In 1219 Genghis led his army westward, swatting minor tribes along the way. This was a different sort of army from the one that had swept across the Gobi into Xi Xia and northern China; different also from the one led by Jebe in pursuit of Kuchlug. With something like 100,000–150,000 soldiers, each with two or three horses, it retained the fast-moving, hard-riding flexibility of long-established nomadic armies, able to despatch contingents that could cover 100 kilometres a day, cross deserts, swim rivers and materialize and vanish as if by magic. But there was now a hard core that was something entirely new. The sieges of Beijing and other Chinese cities had provided the Mongols with the best in siege technology and expertise. Tied onto horses and camels, dragged in wagons or on their own wheels, were battering rams, scaling ladders, four-wheeled mobile shields, trebuchets with their many different types of fire- and smoke-bombs, flame-throwing tubes, and the huge double- and triple-bowed siege bows, which could fire arrows like masts to punch holes in baked-earth walls a kilometre away. It's a fair assumption they had taken these and their crews from China: 40 years later, in 1258, 1,000 Chinese siege-bow crews accompanied the Mongol armies in their assault on Baghdad. This formidable combination of nomadic cavalry and siege weaponry had never been seen before.

There was more. Armies on the move had always lived off the land, by robbery and pillage. That, after all, was the only reward on offer, for officers and men alike. But previous armies, whether nomadic or urban, were limited by their expertise. Nomads on the move were supreme specialists, and could do nothing much with their victims, except send artisans back to HQ, kill the men, rape the women, enslave the children. Prisoners and slaves had to be supervised and made productive, and would, en masse, undermine the very flexibility that made conquest possible. That was why, traditionally, nomads had come, seen, conquered and left. By contrast, armies drawn from land-workers and cities were, in essence, machines for overrunning territory, taking over other land-workers and cities, and so had an interest in avoiding the total destruction of what would soon be theirs. This Mongol army had a new agenda, granted them in China by the lethal combination of nomadism and military technology. Now prisoners had a triple use: as a slave-labour force of specialist artisans; as soldiers in the army's non-nomadic contingents; and as cannon-fodder, a particularly nasty expedient in which civilians could be driven ahead of the army to fill in moats, take the full force of the defences, and possibly blunt them as defenders held back from incinerating their own flesh and blood.

So what rolled westward in 1219 was a juggernaut, steered by its cavalry. With wagons and siege engines, it was a cumbersome beast which demanded the building of roads and bridges, especially through the Altai and Tien Shan. But it was more than cumbersome: not just self-sustaining but ever-growing. The old cavalry regiments lost none of their manoeuvrability. And with every city taken, its non-nomadic contingents strengthened in wealth, numbers, weapons and power. Given one initial success, it would roll on explosively, limited only by geography, climate and the agenda of its supreme commander.

No-one saw all this at the time, or foresaw the consequences. The supreme commander had no long-term agenda, other than to redress wrongs, pay his troops and guarantee security. He could not have realized that he was embarking on something to which there was no natural limit; for what ruler – especially one who had been an outcast – would ever say he was rich enough and secure enough?

When the army arrived at the borders of Khwarezm it confronted a potentially far greater force. But the shah was unloved, and could not risk creating a unified command structure under a general who might simply turn against him. So when the Mongols surrounded Otrar, the shah's forces were scattered among the major cities. All of this Genghis knew from disaffected Muslim officials who came over to the Mongols. He exploited these divisions to the full, encouraging his Muslim merchants to reassure the local populations, offering towns and fortresses the chance to surrender peacefully without any pillaging by the Mongol troops.

Centres of resistance were another matter. Otrar, whose governor had sparked this bloody war, received special attention, in an assault known in Central Asia as the 'Otrar Catastrophe'. Genghis wanted the governor taken alive, to ensure him a suitably public execution. The siege – recalled by a dramatic diorama in Almaty's Historical Museum – lasted for five months, until a senior commander tried to flee through a side gate. His action hastened both his end – he was caught instantly by the Mongols and executed for his treachery – and the city's. The Mongols forced entry through the same gateway used by the fleeing commander. Their quarry, 'Little Lord' Inalchuk, barricaded himself in the inner sanctum with several hundred defenders. Since the Mongols had orders to take Inalchuk alive, there followed a slow, methodical attack that lasted another month. Realizing they were doomed, the defenders staged suicide assaults on Mongol spearmen and bowmen, 50 at a time, until finally Inalchuk and his few surviving bodyguards were trapped on upper floors, where they tore bricks from the walls to throw at their attackers. The siege ended with Inalchuk being led away in chains to his execution, which one source says was effected by molten silver poured into his eyes and ears – an unlikely and unnecessarily expensive end, I think; it would probably have been something rather more efficient. The city itself was flattened into the piles of rubble that have only recently, almost 800 years later, been revealed by archaeologists.

Meanwhile, Genghis had divided his army, sending Jochi northwards to sweep round in a vast pincer movement that would eventually snip off all Khwarezm's northern regions.

During January 1220 Genghis had sent a second force to mop up Otrar, while he himself led the other pincer-arm straight across the Kyzylkum desert – a mere 450 kilometres of freezing sand-and-tussock wilderness – towards Bukhara. Crossing the frozen Syrdar'ya, he came to a small town, Zarnuk, where he made his policy clear: resist and die, or surrender and live. Zarnuk's inhabitants did not take long to choose the path of wisdom, and survival. The citadel was destroyed, a contingent of young men levied to join the ranks and everyone else allowed to go home. A second town – Nurata, then known as Nur – hesitated only briefly before making the same decision.

As the Mongol army approached Bukhara in February or March 1220, a 20,000-garrison made a pre-emptive attack, and was blotted up on the banks of the Amudar'ya. The remaining troops made a hasty retreat into the citadel, the Ark, while the townspeople, unwilling to be killed for the sake of a shah they despised, opened the gates. Genghis rode in, through alleys lined with the wooden houses of the common people, past palaces of baked-earth brick, into the inner city, the Shahristan, and to its largest building; thus for the first time in his life finding himself in a city rich in ways he could not possibly have known.

The civilization that now lay at Genghis's feet was a glory comparable to that of China, though a newcomer by comparison. It had been founded over 500 years before, when Arabs, drawing inspiration from Islam's founder, Mohammed, swept outwards over Persia, Syria, Iraq, Egypt, North Africa, Central Asia, even Spain, until Arabs briefly controlled territory from the Pyrenees to western China.

For a while, this empire was unified by its new religion and Islam's holy book, the Qur'an, which – just as the King James Bible did for English – distilled and stimulated a language at a crucial moment in its evolution. Muslims point to its beauty as a proof of Allah's existence. On this foundation arose another doctrinal source, the *sunnah*, the deeds and sayings of the Prophet and his successors. Together, these two streams of doctrine infused every aspect of Islam – government, law, knowledge, behaviour, creativity – for Islam makes no clear distinction between church and state, sacred and profane; all should be sacred. Islam, more intensely than its paler rival Christianity, was a 'brotherhood of believers'.

Ruling an empire was very different from building it. Territories and sects took wealth and power for themselves. The Shiites claimed a right to rule based on 'Shi'at Ali', the Party of Ali, Mohammed's son-in-law. Another faction, favouring the claims of Mohammed's uncle Abbas, arose on the empire's fringes, notably in Iraq. Under the Abbasids, the empire's centre of gravity jumped eastward to Baghdad. By 1000 the Islamic world, created as one imperial river by the Arabs, had divided into a delta of five major streams and dozens of minor ones. Still, unity of a sort endured. Muslim scholars from the Hindu Kush to southern Spain all worshipped the same god, honoured the same prophet, shared Arabic as a lingua franca and inherited the same astonishingly rich intellectual mantle. All Islam shared in its economic strength, with trade linking North Africa, Europe, Russia, the Middle East, India and China. Since Islam accepted the enslavement of non-Muslims, all benefited from a lucrative trade in slaves, whether African, Turkish, Indian or Slav. Arab coins found their way north as far as Finland, and Muslim merchants wrote cheques honoured by banks in major cities from Cordoba to Samarkand. One trader had a warehouse on the Volga, another near Bukhara and a third in Gujarat, India.

Fuelled by staggering wealth, medieval Islam hungered for learning and inspired brilliant scholarship. Paper displaced papyrus, bookshops thrived, libraries graced the homes of the rich. Since Arabic was the language of divine revelation, the written word was venerated and calligraphy became an art form valued above painting. This was not a world of inward-looking fundamentalism, for medieval Islam, assured of its superiority, was innovative, curious and surprisingly tolerant. The Arabs, looking back to the Greeks for the foundations of science and philosophy, translated Greek classics en masse. Many other languages and creeds – Persian, Sanskrit and Syriac; Christianity, Judaism and Zoroastrianism – also formed part of this rich amalgam.

The arts and sciences flourished. Urbanized literati patronized poets, historians honoured Islamic achievements, architects built domed mosques, predating Italian Renaissance domes by centuries. Stuccoed and frescoed palaces set an ornate style emulated throughout Islam. 'Arabic' numerals, derived from Indian ones, provided a far more powerful mathematical tool than any previous system, as Europe later discovered. Though Arab scientists remained convinced that gold could be produced by the transformation of metals, their rigorous search for the 'philosopher's stone' that would cause this to happen created the bridge between alchemy (*al-kimiya*, 'transmutation') and modern chemistry. Muslim travellers wrote reports of China, Europe and much of Africa. European languages, enriched by translations from Arabic into Latin, still contain many tributes to Arab scientific predominance: zero (from *sifr*, 'empty') and algebra (*al-jebr*, 'integration'); star-names such as Betelgeuse (from *bayt al-jawza*, 'the house of the twins') and Altair ('the Flier'); zenith, nadir, azimuth.

Among the great centres of Islamic culture, Baghdad was the greatest. Straddling the Tigris river, it was planned as a perfect circle: a triple rampart guarded by 360 towers. The Round City, as it was known, soon became a magnet for traders, scholars and artists from as far afield as Spain and northern India, growing to become one of the largest metropolises in the world, equalling Constantinople – about the same size as Paris at the end of the nineteenth century – with wealth to match. The city's wharves harboured vessels bringing porcelain from China, musk and ivory from east Africa, spices and pearls from Malaya, Russian slaves, wax and furs.

For four centuries the ancient Persian oasis cities of Samarkand, Bukhara, Merv and Gurganj, the eastern outposts of Islam, were worthy counterparts to Baghdad. Looking back to their eighth-century Persian ancestor, Saman Khudat, the Samanids had built their own Persian brand of Islam, spreading east into Afghanistan, holding off the Arabs to the west and a new challenge from the north: Turkish nomads, eager for the wealth of Islamic society.

These four cities, all located on rivers running from the Pamirs into the wastes of the Kyzylkum, all sustained by intricate canal systems and underground channels (*qanat*), all walled against enemies and the encroaching sand, had long been the rich bulwarks of the provinces of Khurasan and Transoxania. All were trade emporia linking east and west. Watermelons packed in snow were couriered to Baghdad. Paper from Samarkand, made with techniques imported from China, was in demand all over the Muslim world, and would soon catch on north of the Pyrenees. Caravans the size of small armies – one consisted of 5,000 men and 3,000 horses and camels – ranged back and forth to eastern Europe, trading silks, copper bowls and jewellery for furs, amber and sheepskins. From China came pottery and spices, to be exchanged for horses and glass.

Bukhara, with a population of 300,000, almost rivalled Baghdad itself. Its scholars and poets, writing in both Arabic and Persian, made it the 'dome of Islam in the east', in a common epithet. Its royal library, with 45,000 volumes, had a suite of rooms, each devoted to a different discipline. In the words of an eleventh-century anthologist, al-Tha'alabi, it was the 'focus of splendour, the shrine of empire, the meeting-place of the most unique intellects of the age'. Perhaps the greatest of these great intellects was the philosopher and physician Ibn Sina (980–1037), known in Europe by the Spanish version of his name, Avicenna, who was born not far from the spot where Genghis now stood. He poured out over 200 books, most famously his medical encyclopedia, *Canons of Medicine*, which when translated into Latin became Europe's pre-eminent medical textbook and remained so for five centuries.

All of this came briefly under threat when the Turks arrived, part of a westward drift of Turkish tribes that had been going on for centuries. But Islamic civilization endured because, as they settled, the Turks converted to Sunni Islam, and acquired Muslim names and titles. So when in 999 the Turks entered Bukhara, they did so peacefully, and the Samanids were bundled off into ignominious exile. Ismail Samani's mausoleum, a gem of early tenth-century architecture, almost vanished beneath drifting sand (which was why, perhaps, Genghis never noticed it, and why its patterned brickwork, intricate as knitting, can be admired by visitors today). In the early thirteenth century, Khwarezm, under its uninspiring leadership, had inherited these religious, artistic and intellectual traditions, of which Genghis knew little; and its wealth, of which he had heard much.

Juvaini records what happened next in vivid detail. Genghis was right by one of the glories of medieval Islamic architecture, the Kalyan Minaret, built 80 years earlier by an ambitious Turk, Arslan Khan. It was, and is, a wonder, not only because of its height – almost 50 metres – but because it is one of the few buildings to survive the region's many earthquakes. As guides tell tourists today, Arslan's architect, Master Bako, knew from experience what to do. His foundation was in the form of an inverted pyramid 10 metres deep, made of mortar, lime, plaster, camel's milk and egg-white. He let his odd but well-tried cement harden for three years, then added a layer of reeds; and on this tooth-root, with its shock-proof matting, he created a building that remained Central Asia's tallest for over 700 years. Its twelve bands of baked brick still proclaim Bako's name in swirling calligraphy. Locals call it the Tower of Death, because – my guide Sergei said as we clambered up the 105 dim and dusty steps – criminals were thrown from the top.

Beside the tower was a grand entrance, leading to a courtyard 120 metres long, surrounded by a multi-domed colonnade. Was this the palace? Genghis asked through his interpreter in one version of events. No, he was told, it is the house of God, the Friday mosque. He dismounted, entered the courtyard, climbed a few steps of the pulpit and . . .

Or perhaps it was more complicated than that. According to the attendant sitting by the seedy little carpet-stall inside the entrance, what actually happened was that Genghis looked at the Kalyan Minaret—

'The Tower of Death?' I prompted, with a knowing glance at Sergei.

'Tower of Death!' The attendant threw up an arm in a dismissive gesture. 'It was never a Tower of Death! It is a holy place. The executions all took place in the Registan. But there is a story of a widow who was offered marriage by a neighbour. When she refused, saying she would be true to the memory of her dead husband, he accused her of whoring, and had her condemned to be thrown from the tower, but her clothes acted like a parachute, and she survived, so that proved she was innocent. No, no, not a Tower of Death.'

Anyway, the attendant continued, Genghis stared at the minaret, and as he was raising his eyes to the top, his hat fell off. He stooped to pick it up, and then declared: 'This minaret is the first thing I have ever bowed to.'

The attendant's story gathered pace, and detail. Genghis points to the pulpit and asks: Is this the throne? No, he's told, this is for preaching; the throne is in the fortress. So Genghis goes to the fortress, tells the guards to surrender, kills a few when they don't, returns to the mosque, kills 200 sheikhs, throws their heads down the mosque's well – it's there to this day, beneath that octagonal platform – and only now, according to this version of events, does he climb the pulpit . . .

To utter infamous words, on which Juvaini, Sergei and the attendant all agree:

'The countryside is empty of fodder; fill our horses' bellies.'

While the horrified imams and other notables held the Mongols' horses, troops emptied grain stores, brought fodder to the mosque, and tossed Qur'ans from their wooden cases to make feeding troughs. After a couple of hours, the contingents began to return to their camps outside the walls to prepare for the assault on the citadel, leaving the holy texts torn and trampled beneath the horses' casual hooves.

Some historians have seen this as deliberate desecration, inspired by Genghis himself. But that doesn't fit. Genghis, favoured by Heaven, regarded others as inferior, but did not despise them on religious grounds. Juvaini himself makes no judgement on the trampled Qur'ans. It was just that Genghis and his unheeding troops focused on the practical concerns of conquest.

Yet there was a lesson in this careless dominance, and Genghis saw it instantly. Here, in the ease of conquest, was yet more evidence that he was right to believe in Heaven's backing, and he was keen that his enemies should understand, and comply. On his departure from the city he went into the *musalla*, a court-yard for prayers during festivals held outside the city walls. Here he decided to give a speech to a carefully selected audience.[2]

---

[2] That is if you believe the source of the story, Juvaini. Many don't, including the expert W. Barthold (see bibliography), who calls it 'quite beyond belief', though he doesn't explain his reasons. Yet Juvaini has corroborative detail, stating clearly where the lecture was given. Many writers have transposed the event to the mosque itself, presumably because it adds to the drama.

First, he told the assembled citizens to select the wealthiest and most eminent among them. Two hundred and eighty men – fearful but curious men, I imagine – gathered inside the *musalla*'s simple walls. Juvaini is quite explicit about the number: 190 were residents, 90 merchants from other cities. Genghis mounted the pulpit, and gave them his explanation for his rise and their fall:

'O people, know that you have committed great sins, and that the great ones among you have committed these sins. If you ask me what proof I have for these words, I say it is because I am the punishment of God. If you had not committed great sins, God would not have sent a punishment like me upon you.'

As a Muslim, Juvaini has a point to make, though always with an eye to the Mongol rulers under whose auspices he wrote. There was nothing personal or vindictive in Genghis's words. Actually, they fitted the circumstances well, given Khwarezm's appalling leadership and the way Muslims had torn apart their own society over recent decades. It was not up to him to impose gratuitous punishment, provided that he received enough booty to keep his army happy.

Which is what happened. His cowed audience were Bukhara's leading merchants and civilians, and each was given a guard to ensure they were robbed only by Genghis or his generals, not by ordinary troopers. For the next few days, with the shah's soldiers and their families penned in the citadel and the townspeople in their houses, the rich and their escorts filed out of the city to Genghis's tent, where they handed over their wealth – cash, jewellery, clothing, fabrics.

To complete 'God's punishment', two matters remained: the capture of the central citadel, which was a base for night-time raids by a hard core of Mohammed's troops; and the disposal of the population. To clear the ground for the assault, the surrounding wooden houses were set on fire. Most of the city, except for the main mosque and those palaces made of baked-earth bricks, went up in flames. Now the mangonels and catapults and great double- and triple-bowed siege bows could be wheeled into position. Below the walls, locals were driven forward beneath bombardments of flaming naphtha to fill in the moat with corpses and rubble. For days the battle raged, until the Ark was battered and burned into submission, and its defenders lay dead, killed in action or executed, including all males 'who stood higher than the butt of a whip'. The surviving citizens were herded together by the *musalla* to be distributed, the young men into military service, women and their children into slavery, the blacksmiths, carpenters and goldworkers to join teams of Mongol artisans.

Then the Mongol juggernaut rolled on eastward towards Samarkand, with enough troops for a sideshow to seize Khojend, the border town that guarded the fine, productive soils of the Fergana valley. Samarkand, Shah Mohammed's new capital, 'the most delectable of the paradises of this world', was defended by between 40,000 and 110,000 troops (or perhaps that was the number of people; the sources vary hugely), sheltering inside a moat, and city walls, and a citadel, all hastily strengthened in the weeks since the siege of Otrar began. The defenders included a brigade of 20 elephants, presumably brought by some enterprising merchant from India. Driving crowds of prisoners, every tenth one waving a standard to give the impression of a vast Mongol army, the Mongols set up camp right around the town, where the last contingents from Otrar joined them. In a vain attempt to break the siege, the defenders sent out their elephants, which panicked, turned and trampled their own men before escaping onto the open plain. Again, it was Mohammed's hopeless leadership that did for the city, as it did for his empire. He himself fled, urging everyone along his route to gather their goods and get out, because resistance was useless. The merchant princes and clerics of Samarkand, unprepared to risk death for such a man, sued for peace, and received similar treatment to the inhabitants of Bukhara, with Mongol commanders and their families taking their pick of possessions, women and artisans.

The conquest of Khwarezm would, of course, necessarily include the capture or death of the fleeing Mohammed, a task given to Jebe and Subedei, who hounded him across present-day Uzbekistan, Turkmenistan and Iran. Desperately searching for a place of safety, with the Mongols one day's gallop behind him, he arrived at the shores of the Caspian, where local emirs advised him to hole up on a small island. Leaving his treasures to be seized, he and a small retinue (including his son, Jalal ad-Din) rowed to the island, where he died of shock and despair. His dreadful mother had followed in his footsteps, ending up in a fortress just south of the Caspian, to be starved out by Mongols and carted off to many years of abysmal captivity in Mongolia.

Meanwhile, the Mongol pincers closed on the great city of Gurganj, or Urgench as it later became (and still is). From the north, in late 1220, came Jochi, now conqueror of half a dozen lesser towns. From the south-east came Chagadai and Ogedei, reinforced by Boorchu with Genghis's personal corps. Together, there could have been 100,000 of them; not enough, however, to cow the inhabitants, who settled in for a battle that would last at least five months. This was the Mongols' hardest fight. Here, in the flood plain of the Amudar'ya, there were no stones for the catapults, so the Mongols logged mulberry trees to make ammunition. Prisoners, as usual, were forced to fill in the moats and then undermine the walls. With the walls down, the Mongols had to fight for the city street by street, razing houses as they went by lobbing flaming naphtha into them. When this proved too slow, the Mongols determined to flood out the city by diverting the river, an attempt that ended in disaster when the locals surprised and killed 3,000 Mongols working on the dam. By the time victory came in early 1221, the Mongols were in no mood for mercy. Those with any skill – 100,000 of them – were led away as captives; the rest were slaughtered. Juvaini speaks of 50,000 soldiers despatching 24 men each. That makes *1.2 million* killed.

Finally, with the whole empire almost his, Genghis designated Tolui to mop up in the western regions, beyond the Amudar'ya. It took him just three months to deal with the three main cities of Merv, Nishapur and Herat. Nishapur fell in April, its people killed, the town razed and ploughed over. Herat wisely surrendered, and its people were spared, except for its garrison of 12,000. It is Merv that deserves particular attention.

Of those cities that have suffered catastrophe, there are few that retain their scars. Hiroshima has built a new urban skin over its dreadful atomic burn. The ruins of St Pierre on Martinique, flattened by a volcanic blast in 1902, once recalled Hiroshima's; today, vendors' stalls and playing children hide the scorched stones. Hamburg, Berlin, even Dresden: there are few reminders now that they were bombed and burned to rubble half a century ago.

Not so Old Merv. In the early thirteenth century, this oasis city was the pearl of Central Asia, a city of mosques and mansions, of walls within walls, of mud-brick suburbs covering 100 square kilometres, all sustained by cool water flowing through tunnels from a dam across the River Murgab. Its ten libraries contained 150,000 volumes, the greatest collection in Central Asia. A century before Genghis arrived, Omar Khayyam worked in its long-lost observatory. Today, Old Merv is a shadow. If you stand on one of the little mounds near its centre, you are surrounded by dusty ridges and mounds of rubble by the acre. The only resurrection here occurred 30-odd kilometres away to the west, where new

Merv – Mary – casts its industrial pall into the sky. Out on the plain, the uneven heaps form the very image of desolation, accentuated by stark and isolated ruins: the dome of Sultan Sanjar's twelfth-century mausoleum, once covered in turquoise tiles that could be seen glittering from a day's march away across the desert, and still one of Central Asia's greatest architectural wonders; the Great Kyz Kala – the 'Maidens' Castle' – a roofless rectangle of organ-pipe columns as weird as an artefact dumped by aliens, and as baffling.

Something happened here to turn town to desert. There is no indication of what it was. It is like observing the ruins of Hiroshima, or St Pierre, or Dresden without a knowledge of atomic bombs, or volcanoes, or fire-storms. All around there is evidence of an explosion, but no immediate clue to its cause. To understand what happened, you have to dig into the past, into the earth,[3] and into written records.

It did not happen all at once – much of the desolation is down to wind and rain – but the process started in January 1221, when the Mongols arrived outside the walls of Merv. The city's spirit had revived under one of the former shah's commanders, a puffed-up aristocrat named Mujir al-Mulk, whose dreams of sultanship Juvaini reviles: 'In the core of his heart the delusion became implanted that the heavens could not revolve without his leave.' When a contingent of 800 Mongols probed Merv's defences, they were chased off; but 60 of them were captured, paraded through the town and then executed. This was a humiliation which, when Genghis and Tolui heard of it, ensured a terrible fate.

Their army was not large, some 7,000 men, each with his bow, arrows and knife, each in his toughened leather armour,

---

[3] For details, see the International Merv Project, directed by Georgina Herrmann, the driving force behind one of Central Asia's most ambitious archaeological sites (http://whc.unesco.org/whreview/article24.htm).

each with several remounts. As often, they were vastly out-numbered. They faced an army of 12,000 and a city whose normal population of about 70,000 was swollen to over ten times that figure by refugees from the surrounding villages. Merv's leaders had made the mistake of resisting, and its citizens knew what that meant for them. The city was hypnotized by fear. Soldiers and civilians alike bolted the doors and waited, immobile. 'The world donned garments of mourning,' wrote Juvaini, 'and the Mongols took up positions in several rings around the fortifications.'

For six days the Mongol commander patrolled the walls. At one point, 200 men tried a break-out, only to be driven back inside. Seeing no alternative, Mujir al-Mulk sued for peace. The Mongols demanded 200 of the richest and most in-fluential citizens, who were duly delivered and interrogated about their wealth. Then the Mongols entered the city, un-opposed, set upon vengeance. For four days, they drove the docile crowds out on to the plain.

Then the killing started. The place was ransacked, the buildings mined, the books burned or buried. Hiroshima was destroyed in seconds, St Pierre in four minutes, Dresden in a night, and the deaths were in the tens of thousands. Merv took days to die, and lost almost everything and almost everyone.

> The Mongols ordered that, apart from 400 artisans whom they specified and selected from amongst the men and some children, girls and boys, whom they bore off into captivity, the whole population, including the women and children should be killed, and no one, whether man or woman be spared. The people of Merv were then distributed among the soldiers and levies and, in short, to each man was allotted the execution of three or four hundred persons.

Then, when the Mongols departed, came the reckoning,

conducted by an eminent cleric. 'He now together with some other persons passed 13 days and nights in counting the people slain within the town. Taking into account only those that were plain to see and leaving aside those that had been killed in holes and cavities and in the villages and deserts, they arrive at a figure of more than one million three hundred thousand.'

One million three hundred thousand? And this in addition to the 1.2 million supposedly killed in Urgench? Many historians doubt the figure, because it sounds simply incredible. But we know from the last century's horrors that mass slaughter comes easily to those with the will, the leadership and the technology. In the Armenian massacres of 1915, Turks killed 1.4 million out of an Armenian population of 2.1 million; the Nazis slew 6 million in the Holocaust; in the Khmer Rouge atrocities in Cambodia in the mid-1970s, 1.7 million (out of about 8 million) died; 800,000 were killed in the Rwanda genocide of 1994 (out of a total population of 5.8 million).

So 1.3 million is a more than possible death toll for Merv – and attained in far less time than any of the examples in the previous paragraph. The Holocaust was spread over five years; the Khmer Rouge murders over three; and the Rwandan genocide – which Samantha Power has called 'the most rapid genocide the world has ever known'[4] – over just three months. But, unless we dispute the definition of the word 'genocide', none of those mass killings can match what the Mongols achieved in Merv. For a Mongol, an unresisting prisoner would have been easier to despatch than a sheep. A sheep is killed with care, in order not to spoil the meat. You cut a small hole in the chest, reach inside, grab the heart and stop it. The sheep seems to feel nothing, and the whole operation is over in half a minute. There was no need to take such trouble with the inhabitants of Merv, who were of less

[4] *New York Review of Books*, 6 Jan. 2003.

value than sheep. It takes only seconds to slit a throat, and move on to the next. We are not talking years or months here, but hours. For 7,000 men, the slaughter of a million would have been a hard morning's work.

Over a million dead in Urgench, over a million in Merv, tens of thousands in several other cities – this was undoubtedly a holocaust on an unprecedented scale. Given the Mongols' attitudes to non-Mongols, their obedience and their slaughtering skills, it is technically possible for them to have killed perhaps 3 million or more people in the two-year course of their invasion of the Muslim empire.

But were these figures true?

It's instructive to look at the fate of Merv as recorded by Juvaini after the reported massacre of 1.3 million – that is, supposedly, of everyone within and around it. That was in February 1221. Yet in November of the same year, rumours of Jalal ad-Din's resistance sparked a rebellion. The Mongol *Gauleiter*, Barmas, ordered 'the artisans, etc.' into a camp outside the walls, tried to summon 'the notables', failed, 'slew numbers of people whom he found at the gate' and took many more off to Bukhara. Within Merv, rebels and pro-Mongol forces struggled for dominance. One rebel 'repaired the walls and the citadel . . . improve[d] agriculture and mend[ed] the dam.' When another rebel, one of Jalal's men, came, 'the common people revolted and went over to him,' and he in his turn undertook agricultural schemes and dam-building. Shigi himself arrived to quell the revolt, for 'strangers from all parts, attracted by its abundance of wealth, had risen from their corners and turned their faces towards Merv,' joined by the townspeople. The new siege ended in the by now familiar fashion: 'Putting camel-halters on believers, [the Mongols] led them off in strings of ten and twenty and cast them into a trough of blood [i.e. executed them]; in this way they martyred 100,000 persons.' A local governor, left by the Mongols, then had the sneaky idea of calling survivors to prayer, 'and all that came out of the holes' were seized and imprisoned, 'being finally cast down from the roof. In this manner many more people perished,' until 'in the whole town there remained not four persons alive.' Yet a new emir, Arslan, assumed leadership – of what or whom, may we ask? – gathering an army of 10,000 and ruling for six months. A Mongol general returned, 'slaying all that he found'. Then came Shigi again, and 'began to torture and torment the inhabitants'. And again, 'except for 10 or a dozen Indians . . . there was no one left in the town.' Yet in the 1240s the governor, Arghun, came to a village near Merv, where 'for several days they feasted in the royal palace, and each of the ministers . . . began to lay out a park and erect a mansion.' In 1256 Merv was among those provinces from which 'wine was drawn like water and unlimited provisions' taken for the benefit of the Mongol ruler Helugu. In this tale of repeated catastrophe, there were always more people to kill, always an economy still worth robbing; which, if true, indicates that each catastrophe was not quite so apocalyptic as Juvaini suggests.

How many did die, really? It is impossible to say. There was no census, and all numbers are little more than guesses. But there are a few guidelines for speculation. In the whole of Khwarezm there were about 20 substantial cities, with an average population of 100,000 each, giving a rough total of 2 million city-dwellers. Geographers quoted by Barthold list 223 villages in the rich valley of the Zarafshan river, on which Bukhara and Samarkand lay. Let's give each village 1,000 people – say 250,000 all together – then assume another 750 villages for the less well-endowed regions, making 1 million villagers. This gives us 3 million in all. Now look at more recent figures for the region once covered by Khwarezm: in the early twentieth century Uzbekistan and Turkmenistan, then part of 'Russian Turkestan', had about 2 million people, while the Iranian region of Khorasan had about a million: again, some 3 million in all (against a current population of the whole region of about 30 million). So if Juvaini is correct, assuming numbers were then much the same as they were before the imposition of communist rule, the Mongols killed not only every inhabitant in some major cities, but *the whole population of their new domain.*

But they didn't. Even in the most extreme cases, cities went on operating, with rebellions crushed, armies raised, taxes paid and reconstruction undertaken. A simple assessment of destruction based on surviving sources hardly does justice to the complexity of events. So the assumptions and/or the sources must be wrong, leaving the truth buried, unrecoverable. Perhaps all we can do is assume a higher level of population and a lower level of death, something like 25 per cent of 5 million: a level that would allow a crushed and brutalized society to continue life, of a sort, until the passing years freed them from oppression.

That still leaves us with 1.25 million deaths in two years, as a conservative estimate.

It was still one of the biggest mass killings in absolute terms in history; and in proportional terms, perhaps the biggest, an equivalent of the 25–30 per cent population cut meted out by Europe's greatest catastrophe, the Black Death.

The Khwarezmian massacres have modern equivalents. What happened in Merv, in Urgench and across the region suggests a comparison with the Nazi Holocaust itself, for there are some terrible similarities in the attitude of Tolui's Mongols and that of those who perpetrated the Final Solution. What strikes me most strongly is the banality of this evil, in Hannah Arendt's famous phrase. The Mongols were, one and all, master slaughterers of animals; the killing of sheep was utterly routine to them, and the killing of these humans was merely a job to be done – just as the managing of gas chambers and ovens was no more than a technical and bureaucratic challenge to Rudolf Hoess, the commandant of

Auschwitz. But the comparison does not follow through. The Holocaust was the consequence of state policy, carried through over years, with no military or economic aim; no purpose other than to fulfil Hitler's antisemitic obsession. The Khwarezmian massacres were the sum of one-off applications of a decision to use terror to back strategy – not genocide exactly, but the killing of towns, a strategy that deserves its own term: urbicide. For the Mongols, vengeance was not racial or religious in motivation; it was local and strategic.

The slaughter of Merv was not quite the end. Mohammed's son, Jalal ad-Din, was very different from his father. He rallied the surviving forces and retreated southward, into present-day Afghanistan, pursued by Genghis. In spring 1221, at Parvan, just north of Kabul, he inflicted the first defeat the Mongols had suffered in this campaign. (The Mongol general, by the way, was Genghis's adopted brother and possible editor of *The Secret History*, Shigi. Genghis was understanding. Shigi had never experienced fate's cruel knocks, he said. This was a salutary lesson for him.) Jalal, trying to preserve a core of resistance, fought on even as he retreated for another 400 kilometres, through the Hindu Kush and down via the Khyber Pass onto northern India's stifling plains, until he was trapped between the Indus and the advancing Mongols. It was the end for his army – but not for Jalal himself, who, in Juvaini's dramatic account, forced his horse into the water and reached safety on the far bank. Watching with his hand to his mouth in astonishment and admiration at his courage, Genghis let him go, saying: 'Every father should have such a son!' Jalal lived to fight again, though to no great effect, writing himself into legend as a hero. No-one knows for sure how he died. Possibly he was murdered in 1231 by Kurdish robbers who had no idea who he was. Rumours of him continued to circulate for years.

Juvaini records two pseudo-Jalals, both of whom were put to death for their claims.

Genghis did not follow up his victory by advancing into India. One story tells that he was put off by meeting a 'unicorn' that spoke to him. It was probably a rhinoceros, a sight so awe-inspiring that when Genghis heard Chu-tsai's wise interpretation – turn back at once! – he did, and switched his attention elsewhere, to his destiny: to the rebellious vassals who had dared defy him before the campaign began, and to the unknown lands that lay further to the west.

9

THE GREAT RAID

THE ONLY LAW OF HISTORY IS THAT THERE AREN'T ANY OTHERS. But there are a handful of near-certainties. Here is one:

Empires expand for as long as they have the power to do so.

New conquests create new frontiers and reveal new threats, which when confronted lead to new conquests. What was true for the Romans, British, Russians, French, Chinese and now for the Americans was also true for the Mongols.

With Mohammed dead and the Khwarezmian empire about to be bundled off into history, Subedei, Jebe and their victorious troops on the shores of the Caspian stared round for some new challenge. Territorial conquest beyond Islam was not uppermost in Subedei's mind when he galloped back to discuss matters with Genghis in Samarkand in early 1221. The Islamic world was quite enough of a challenge. Its centre – Baghdad – would not fall easily. But to the north-west there lived a Muslim people who called themselves Bulgars, fur traders who did good business with Khwarezm. Ethnologists now assume a distant relationship with the other, southern Bulgars, later of Bulgaria, but at this point all contact between the two groups had long since been lost. These Bulgars, Islamic since the tenth century, were a proto-nation of hunters and fishers who had made themselves rich by trading furs with the Russians and the Islamic world. As Muslims and allies of Khwarezm, the Bulgars were fair game. But how far away did they live? And who and what lay en route, in the rugged Caucasus mountains the other side of the Caspian? Genghis agreed it would be good to find out. He himself was just off to chase Jalal ad-Din southward, and Tolui was about to give Merv his close attention. Genghis could spare Subedei for a year or two. No-one was better qualified than the 45-year-old one-eyed veteran of China, Manchuria, Khara Khitai and Khwarezm. He and Jebe could meet up with Jochi, now freed from further commitments in Khwarezm, and the three of them could ride around the Caspian and see what treasures they could prise from the Bulgars. The expedition was bound to repay itself many times over in terms of loot and information.

Thus was born one of the most astonishing adventures in military history: a 7,500-kilometre gallop which for the first time brought the Mongols into contact with the Christian world.

The first kingdom in the line of march was Georgia, which had been Christian for almost 1,000 years, independent for 100. It was at this moment at the height of its power and prestige, thanks to its heroine–queen Tamara, whose empire stretched from the Black Sea along the Caucasus into present-day Azerbaijan. Georgians look back to Tamara's reign (1184–1213) as a golden age, a Renaissance of literature, architecture, scholarship and art, funded by fertile soils and merchants who turned Tbilisi into an entrepôt linking

Europe, Russia and Khwarezm. Rustaveli, whose national epic *The Knight in the Panther's Skin* was written a few years before the Mongols arrived, was familiar with Chinese and Greek philosophy. With its palaces and monasteries, its icons and gold-worked gospels, Georgia was just what Jebe and Subedei needed to fund their great adventure.

In fact, it was in that very year, 1221, that Christian Europe had its first rumour of what was happening in Central Asia. At that moment, Christianity needed help. For the past three years, the French and German armies of the Fifth Crusade had been trying to conquer Egypt, and had been cut to pieces by the Saracens. The pope had turned for assistance to the Georgians, rich and powerful fellow Christians. But Tamara's heir, Giorgi the Resplendent, was not the only possible source of aid. News came from the French bishop of the crusader town of Acre, Jacques of Vitry, writing to the leaders of Christian Europe in Rome, London, Vienna and Paris, that 'a new and mighty protector of Christianity has arisen.' His name was King David of India, and he was the grandson of that legendary Christian king Prester John, with whom he was soon confused. Apparently, David/Prester John had sprung from the depths of Asia at the request of the head of the Nestorian church in Baghdad, and having defeated the hordes of Islam was on his way to rescue Christian Europe and restore Jerusalem to its rightful owners. This nonsense, echoing travellers' tales from Khwarezm and Georgia, con-flated several facts, chief among them that there *had* been a Nestorian king (Toghrul) and that there *had* been victories over Islamic powers (by Ta-Shih, the founder of Khara Khitai; and now by Genghis himself).

Then came a sort of backhanded confirmation of Jacques' rumour, from Georgia itself, inspired by the arrival of the Mongols. The attack had come with whirlwind speed, and with no apparent logic. The Mongols rode almost to Tbilisi, cut the flower of Georgian knighthood to bits, vanished back into northern Iran, decided against an attack on Baghdad, swung north again, shattered the Georgian army for a second time (killing Giorgi the Resplendent) and then moved on through the Caucasus, leaving the Georgians unaware that the Mongols were merely on a reconnaissance mission, wondering why they had been spared a further onslaught.

Whatever the reason, there could be no thought of sending help to the crusaders in Egypt now. Giorgi's heir, his sister Rusudan, wrote a stunned apology to the pope. 'A savage people of Tartars, hellish of aspect, as voracious as wolves in their hunger for spoils, and as brave as lions, have invaded my country. They must be of Christian origin . . .' She apparently thought the Mongol flag, a flying falcon, was a distorted cross. Now they had left – chased out, she lied, by Georgia's brave knights. 'Alas,' she concluded, 'we are no longer in a position to take up the Cross as we had promised your Holiness.'

On the lowlands north of the Caucasus, in present-day Chechnya, the Mongols came up against another, greater enemy. These nomadic Turkish people – known to the Russians as Polovtsy, to Turks as Kipchaks and to Europeans as Kumans – dominated the grasslands that ran north of the Black Sea, across the Don to the borderlands of the Russian state and its capital, Kiev. The Polovtsy, who had contacts with Georgia, Byzantium and Russia, were more than a match for the Mongols, with a flexible mix of heavy-duty war machines and mounted archers. Besides, they were on their home ground and had more warriors, reinforced by other local bands. For a long moment, Jebe and Subedei, trapped between superior armies and the glaciated passes of the Caucasus, faced defeat. They did the only thing possible, which was to send an envoy to the Polovtsy with offerings of herds laden with treasures picked up in Georgia. Why should the Polovtsy risk this sudden windfall in fighting? They took it and galloped away overnight, leaving the smaller local groups to fall easy prey to the Mongols. But then, of course, the Mongols, unburdened by carts, treasure or war machines, caught up with the fleeing Polovtsy, defeated them, and snatched their treasures back again. The survivors fled on into Russia, leaving the Mongols in charge of the steppe north of the Crimea.

Now Jebe and Subedei divided their forces. While Jebe secured a base on the banks of the Don, Subedei headed south into the Crimea, mopping up Polovtsy. And here, for the first time, Mongols met Europeans. These were from an empire of a different sort from theirs – the merchant empire of Venice. Their enclave, which spanned the entry to the Sea of Azov, was one of two Venetian bases in the Crimea, the other being Cherson, near today's Sevastopol, with the rival Genoese outposts of Sudak (at that time known as Soldaya) and Feodosia (Kaffa) between them. The Venetian merchantmen at once saw the potential of the new arrivals. The Mongols were rich, with silvered saddles and harnesses, and silks beneath their chain-mail; they had a virtual army of interpreters; they had a corps of eager Muslim merchants; and they could grab whatever they wanted by force of arms. And for the Mongols the Venetians had their uses, with their sailing ships and trade contacts and access to a new world of goods. A deal was done. Subedei burned the Genoans out of Sudak, gave the Venetians a monopoly of the Black Sea trade, and headed back to join Jebe on the Don.

In late 1222 the two then struck west together, across undefended steppe, to the Dniester. Scouts brought in prisoners for interrogation, scholars from China hired teams of interpreters, bureaucrats gathered information on peoples, cities, armies, crops and climate. Spies were recruited, paid and sent home as sleepers, to await further developments. Then, rich with information and booty, Jebe and Subedei galloped back to the Dnieper for the long haul north to the Bulgars.

Not quite yet, however. Though the Polovtsy had a spiky

relationship with the Russians, the Polovtsian khan Khotian (or Khöten in an alternative spelling) had secured his position by becoming an ally, indeed the son-in-law, of a local Russian warlord, Mstislav Mstislavich the Daring. Khotian proposed to Mstislav a military alliance against the Mongols: 'They have taken our land today; tomorrow it will be your turn.' Princes of other Russian provinces came on side, from Volynia, Kursk, Kiev, Chernigov, Suzdal, Rostov, all massing on the Dnieper's west bank in the spring of 1223.

Confronted by this immense force, the Mongols hesitated. Messages came that Jochi, working his way westwards north of the Caspian, had been ordered to join them; but Jochi was, as usual, proving a hard man to order about. He was apparently 'ill' – probably unwilling to lose his independence of action. In his continued absence, Subedei and Jebe sent a peace delegation to the Russian princes. Our quarrel was not with you, the Mongols said, but with the Polovtsy. All we want is a promise that you will not help our enemies. But, as Shah Mohammed had done four years before, the princes rejected the proposal, accused the Mongols of being spies and killed them. Now as then, this was an affront that demanded vengeance.

The Russian force slowly gathered on the banks of the Dnieper where it spreads out below rapids, now drowned by the lake made by the huge hydroelectric dam at Zaporizhzhya ('Beyond the Rapids'). Spreading on to the island of Khortytsya, later to become a famous Cossack base, they amounted to some 80,000 men: the mounted archers of the Polovtsy, Galician foot soldiers arriving by boat, cart-loads of equipment and food, heavily armoured Russian cavalrymen with their conical helmets and iron face masks and longswords and maces and iconic banners. They looked fearsome. But they were, at heart, an army used to fighting European-style, with set-piece engagements backed by castles and ramparts. And the various units were under princely commanders who were as ready to fight each other as to tackle a common enemy. There was neither time nor will to create unity in command structure, intelligence or strategy.

Compare this to the rigid discipline of the 20,000–25,000 Mongols, their speed in the field and their unity of purpose, secured by a messenger service that was in constant touch with Genghis's headquarters: the Mongol pony express, with regular changes of horse and rider at relay stations, could cover 600 kilometres a day – a speed not equalled again until the coming of the railways, and infinitely more flexible than the iron horse. Moreoever, these were now superbly armed cavalry, equipped not only with their own bows, but with Muslim armour and lightweight swords of Damascene steel.

For the Russians lined up on the west bank of the Dnieper, their first sight of the enemy elicited nothing but disdain. Groups of Mongols, armed only with bows and sabres, loosed off a few arrows and then fled across the open steppe when a detachment of Russian cavalry crossed the river. Russian confidence mounted when they scattered a small Mongol contingent and captured and executed the commander – he had hidden by a burial mound, perhaps planning to operate behind enemy lines. The main army hastened to cross, using a bridge of boats. Still the Mongols retreated, seemingly happy to abandon their herds and local prisoners, which the advancing army swept up in its triumphant progress until, in the words of an anonymous Russian chronicler, 'the whole army was full of cattle'.

For nine days the Mongols fled on their fast little horses, and the advance continued, ever deeper into the grasslands, the Russians with cavalry guarding the carts ever more confident of victory, the Polovtsy delighted to get their lands back. On 31 May the Russians reached a little river, the Kalka, scarcely more than a fold in the low hills from which it flows over steppeland to the Sea of Azov, 40 kilometres to the south. First across, naturally, were the Polovtsy, for they were on a par with the Mongols for speed. Behind came the Russian cavalry, and then the foot soldiers, leaving the carts and heavy gear on the far bank of the little defile. Soon, the army was like a smear of water being dragged into a line of droplets.

Now the Mongols attacked – in an utterly unconventional way, heavier cavalry routing the lightly armed Polovtsian archers, the horsemen then assaulting the Russian cavalry, moving in with their lances, spears and lightweight swords, until both advance forces were in chaotic flight, sweeping into their own rearguards, pressing the lot into the shallow valley. Six princes and 70 nobles lay dead. Across the river, the stolid Kievans just had time to get their carts into a defensive formation and begin a slow retreat, as the other forces galloped and ran for their lives across the steppe. Days later, some survivors reached the Dnieper and sailed off downriver; others were harried to their death as they fled over the grasslands. Of the leaders, only Mstislav the Daring of Galicia managed to escape, back to his home on the borders of present-day Hungary and Ukraine.

Eventually the surviving leaders, including Prince Mstislav Romanovich of Kiev, surrendered, on the understanding that no blood would be shed. Subedei and Jebe had no intention of forgoing vengeance for the killing of their ambassadors, but they kept their promise, granting their opponents the respect due to princes of a bloodless death. The method of execution chosen was nasty, brutish and deliberately drawn-out, not purely to give the Mongol leaders sadistic satisfaction, but to send a grim warning to the waiting west. The captives were tied up and laid flat on the ground, where they became the foundation for a heavy wooden platform on which Subedei, Jebe and their officers feasted, while Prince Mstislav and his allies suffocated slowly beneath them.

At this moment, in early June 1223, Jochi, who had lingered north of the Caspian, was on his way with reinforcements. After one brief foray across the Dnieper, Subedei and Jebe turned back towards the Volga, where the two forces met. Working their way upriver for 700 kilometres, they came up against their most formidable opposition yet, in the form of the so-called Volga Bulgars. They had two towns, Bulgar and Suvar, dominating the Volga near present-day Kazan. This was the original target of the whole expedition. But it proved a near-disaster. The sources give no details, but the Bulgars proved too tough, and the Mongols, having suffered their first and only defeat, backed off – taking a memory of the humiliation that would endure until revenge became possible fifteen years later.

The Great Raid on Russia and its crucial encounter on the Kalka river had extraordinary consequences. As the Mongols rode back to rejoin Genghis on the Irtish river, they brought with them excellent knowledge of the land, its resources and the opposition. It would take a much larger force to vanquish the borderland tribes, after which the Russians, lacking a unified command, could be picked off province by province and the cities pillaged.

And beyond, as they now knew from Polovtsy prisoners, was another sweep of grassland rich enough to sustain any Mongol army driving westward. With proper planning, Genghis could pursue his manifest destiny by creating a third focal point for his nomad empire. In the centre, his homeland; in the far east, the rich cities of China; in the far west, a new objective – the rich plains of Hungary. It took little imagination to see Hungary as the new Mongolia, Europe as another China, ripe for the plucking.

10

SEARCHING FOR
IMMORTALITY

BUT WHAT WAS THE MEANING OF IT ALL? OBVIOUSLY, EVENTS proved to Genghis that he was ordained by Heaven for world dominion; he was well on the way to fulfilling the promise implicit in his salvation 40 years before on the slopes of Burkhan Khaldun. But why him? And what was the nature of this hidden Power that had elevated him, and, through him, his nation? It must have been doubly puzzling, first to be snatched from obscurity, and protected, and rewarded for his obedience with unprecedented conquests, and then granted no insight into the Truth with a capital *T*, the underlying nature of the universe.

This is conjecture; but such speculation was in the air he had breathed from childhood, when shamanism and Nestorian Christianity were rivals among Mongol and Turkish groups. As a young man he knew that Mongolian shamans, with their drums and masks and trances, did not offer the only route to spiritual knowledge; that other priest-hoods claimed deeper insights; and that other political leaders made similar claims of divine backing. As a leader and conqueror, his experience widened. The Chinese emperor ruled by the Mandate of Heaven, the king of Xi Xia was a Burkhan, a Holy One, a Living Buddha. Everywhere he saw monuments that stated religious belief, the pagodas and royal tombs of Yinchuan, the temples of Datong and Beijing. Now, from the letters written by Subedei's scribes and brought by pony express, he learned of other great monuments, the Christian cathedrals of Georgia. It seemed to him that all these faiths – shamanism, Confucianism, Buddhism, Christianity – might all be groping towards the same obscure Truth. This is the conclusion to be drawn from one of his edicts, in which he ordered that all religions were to be granted equal respect, a law that underlay one of the most remarkable qualities of the Mongol emperors from the time of Genghis onwards: their religious toleration.

The open-minded search and the lack of prejudice also seem to have woken in Genghis other, rather less spiritual thoughts. If such uncertain faiths could produce such empires and such monuments, what power he would wield if he could command the *true* Truth! Especially if that involved (a) knowledge of, and assured survival in, the next life; and (b) of rather more practical significance, an ability to prolong this one.

Genghis had with him two men who were better qualified than most to encourage such speculations. One was the Khitan Yeh-lü Chu-tsai, 'Long Beard', who had endured the siege of Beijing and then sought enlightenment in a Buddhist retreat before joining Genghis as his closest adviser in 1218. The other was the khan's Chinese minister, Liu Wen, also renowned for his skills as a herbalist and in whittling bone into whistling arrowheads. It was from these two, while he was gathering his forces for the invasion of Khwarezm, that Genghis first heard of a Taoist sect known as Ch'üan-chen ('Complete Perfection') and its eminent head, the sage Ch'ang-ch'un.

The Complete Perfection sect, rooted in a combination of high-mindedness and eccentricity, was founded by Wang Che, nicknamed Wang the Madman, to whom the doctrine was revealed in 1159 by two mysterious strangers when he was out walking. It was, in essence, a form of Taoism, which had evolved over 1,700 years from the teachings of the semi-legendary Lao-tzu. Taoists believe that life is best lived in finding and following the Way – the Tao or Dao. By this they mean understanding the original purity of people and things – their 'natural state' before they were corrupted by life – knowing their destiny as decreed by Heaven, and then achieving again that prelapsarian purity by fulfilling that destiny. One of Wang's two main contributions to this ancient teaching was to insist on an extreme, mystical, fakir-like asceticism, which included sleeping as little as possible, an abstention known as 'smelting away the dark demon'. Inspired by this insight, he dug himself a 3-metre pit in which he remained for two years, later changing his abode to a hut. After four more years of isolation he set fire to his hut, and was found dancing in the ashes. Only then, presumably well honed in mind and body, did he found an institution, the Golden Lotus Congregation, to promote his syncretic teachings – the Three Doctrines, which united China's three main religions, Confucianism, Buddhism and Taoism, with Taoism as the fundamental faith. To its ideals in ethics, behaviour and government, it added a commitment to social welfare; and all of its precepts applied equally to men and women, the involvement of women being one of its most distinctive features.

One of Wang the Madman's disciples was a teenager called Ch'iu, who won wide acclaim for his prodigious memory and elegant verses. When Wang died in 1170, Ch'iu, now aged 22 and styling himself Ch'ang-ch'un ('Everlasting Spring'), was one of those who spread Wang's word. He was therefore well versed in Tao's huge body of alchemical literature, and the belief that certain substances – jade, pearl, mother-of-pearl, cinnabar, gold – could, if made artificially, be used to make a life-prolonging elixir. Like many Islamic and European alchemists, Ch'ang-ch'un was more interested in the symbolism of alchemy – this was all about *spiritual* transmutation – than in its practical application. But it was the idea of a longer life that partly explained the sect's growing popularity. Complete Perfection was patronized by the Liao court in Beijing, and began to acquire its own temples. In addition, at a time of war with the Song, when towns were burned and brigands roamed the countryside, the sect's philanthropic principles also won converts among the common people.

Such a man as Ch'ang-ch'un would have been of interest to Genghis and some of his officials for several reasons. Chu-tsai's agenda included introducing Genghis to any system that might give Heaven a helping hand by transforming a murderous barbarian chief into a civilized and spiritualized imperial administrator. Politically, Genghis would have seen the sense in co-opting a man with such a benign influence over his restless Chinese subjects. But it was alchemy's practical application that clinched matters. Genghis was now over 60, and could not go on campaigning for ever – unless what he heard from Liu Wen was true, that Ch'ang-ch'un was 300 years old, and *could teach others the secret.*

In 1219 Ch'ang-ch'un, in fact aged 70 and the sect's leader, had already received and declined an invitation from the Song court. Now, to his temple 500 kilometres from Beijing in Laizhou, on the Shandong peninsula, came a delegation from the far north-west with a more pressing invitation: a long letter drafted in Chinese by Chu-tsai, the one later engraved on several stelae in which Genghis adopted the guise of an austere Taoist sage. It was brought by Liu Wen, accompanied by 20 Mongols. Liu Wen had been at a Naiman camp in central Mongolia when he received Genghis's order. It had taken seven months to cross the grasslands, the Gobi and the war-torn countryside of northern China to Ch'ang-ch'un's temple.

At the first realization of what the journey would involve the ancient adept hesitated. Genghis's invasion of Khwarezm was well advanced, and he was getting further from China every day. Liu Wen became nervous. What if the old man refused, as he had refused the Song? 'The Emperor has sent me as his special envoy across mountains and lakes, commanding me, whether it takes months or years, on no account to return without you.' I imagine that at this point there would have been an appeal to Ch'ang-ch'un's ambitions. If things worked well, wouldn't a meeting with Genghis be the best possible thing for his sect and his religion?

Clearly, 'no' was not an option. Very well: it was the will of Heaven. Ch'ang-ch'un prepared for a journey that would cover 10,000 kilometres and take almost four years. A record of his journey was made by a disciple, Li Chih-ch'ang (and beautifully translated by the orientalist Arthur Waley in *Travels of an Alchemist*, from which the quotations in this chapter are taken). It provides a unique survey of the lands and peoples of Inner Asia at a crucial moment. Never before in these much-contended lands had it been possible for any-one, let alone an ageing monk, to travel from the Pacific to the heart of Islam, even to the borderlands of India, while under the protection of a single authority, that of Genghis's coalescing empire. Ch'ang-ch'un's journey is the first example of the unprecedented freedom established by the un-precedented brutality of the previous 20 years. The Pax Mongolica would make it possible for numerous western travellers to cross Eurasia from west to east over the next century and a half, including Catholic priests, merchants and explorers – the most famous being Marco Polo.

But the first to make the crossing came in the other direction, at the behest of Genghis himself.

A few days after his meeting with Liu Wen, accompanied

by nineteen followers and with a mounted escorted of fifteen, Ch'ang-ch'un set out for Khwarezm, or wherever Genghis might be in however many months it would take to get there (Afghanistan, in two years' time, as it turned out). With Liu Wen and his troops guaranteeing safe passage, and Taoist clergy staging processional welcomes, Ch'ang-ch'un arrived in Beijing, where crowds besieged him, begging the Master to utter a verse for them or grant them a religious name. Pressures to delay grew. There were full moon ceremonies to be performed, priests to be consecrated. A message came saying that Genghis had moved even further westward. The journey would be long, the way hard, and the Master was getting older. Perhaps, Ch'ang-ch'un suggested, it would be better if the meeting took place upon the khan's return? No, not possible. And then, all of a sudden, Ch'ang-ch'un found out that Liu Wen was bringing a mass of girls to join the khan's harem.

'I am a mere mountain-savage,' said the old man, severely. 'But I do not think you ought to expect me to travel with harem girls.'

Messages were sent, arrangements revised. They would travel slowly, reverently and in safety, taking a giant dog's-leg via the headquarters of Genghis's younger brother Temuge in eastern Mongolia, circling the unreliable Tanguts and the barren heart of the Gobi. The journey continued, with stopovers at temples to recover from the heat of summer. Ch'ang-ch'un's mere presence caused miracles: a drought broken, an umbrella-shaped cloud shading a crowd from the sun, an empty well filling to the brim. Summer gave way to autumn. In the mountains south of the Gobi, a solicitous message arrived from Genghis himself (probably again written by Chu-tsai). 'The way before you, both by land and water, is indeed long; but I trust that the staff and leg-rest [i.e. the comforts] I shall provide will make it not *seem* long.' Winter was spent in another temple, and the journey continued in March 1221. Taking leave of him, Ch'ang-ch'un's disciples 'asked him, weeping, when they might expect to see him back from this immense journey'. He prevaricated, claiming that he could not tell whether his own Tao would harmonize with that of the Mongols, but at last, when pressed, said he would see them again in three years. It was soon afterwards that he and his entourage, travelling through the Badger's Mouth pass, came upon the heaps of bones left by the first great Mongol victory in China, and promised to say masses for the departed on their return.

Then they were out over the treeless expanses of eastern Mongolian grassland, the Master riding a horse or reclining in a cart, accepting the hospitality of herders or pitching their own tents, until six weeks later they came to the massed wagons and *gers* of Temuge's camp. After a three-week rest, they were off again, westward now, their little expedition turned into a large one by Temuge's gifts of ten wagons and several hundred oxen and horses.

They were following the Kherlen's southern bank when, to their growing astonishment, the air grew cold, the sun dimmed and an all-embracing shadow rushed at them. It was a total eclipse of the sun, an event that gives their experience an exact date and place. It was late morning on 23 May 1221 by today's calendar, and they were not far from Avraga, which lay 10 kilometres away to the north of the river. At this spot my own travels very nearly overlapped Ch'ang-ch'un's, and I see the scene through Li's eyes as the wagon-drivers and the horsemen pause, amazed, watching the river edged by newly green willows and the waves of grass dotted with little yellow star-like flowers and the distant snow-capped hills all vanishing into icy shadow; and above, the moon's black disc, briefly ringed by the hidden sun's corona, standing in a twilit sky suddenly studded with stars.

The party pressed on along the Kherlen; that they did not cross the river to stay in Avraga suggests that the old capital was already being displaced by the new one planned at Karakorum. Where the Kherlen's course turned northward, leading upriver towards Burkhan Khaldun, they veered away south-west, being given delighted welcomes at each *ger*-camp from the Mongols, to whom the field-mice told all grassland secrets and who had been awaiting Cha'ng-ch'un's arrival for months. Through the summer they made their way south-west, passing close to the site where Karakorum would soon stand – Li makes no mention of it – and on along a winding track into the pine- and fir-clad Khangay mountains. Here, on high pastures, they found 'hundreds and thousands' of wagons and tents; 'the palanquins, pavilions and other splendours of this camp would certainly have astonished the Khans of the ancient Huns.' This was the summer camp of two princesses, one being the Tangut given to Genghis when Xi Xia surrendered in 1210, the other the Chinese handed over when Beijing surrendered in 1214. While awaiting the khan's return they seemed to get on well, living as befitted their status, generously offering bread baked with flour brought by camel from beyond the Tien Shan, some 700 kilometres away. On then, over a ridge and down across a valley where they saw their first Muslim, who was digging a canal to irrigate a field of barley (barley grows well even in the Gobi if there's water, which can be led from the many small springs along the base of the mountains).

Somewhere to the north was the headquarters of a commander called Chinqai, a Muslim from Khwarezm who had left his home, joined the Keraits, entered service with Genghis in time to 'drink the waters of the Baljuna', and become a trusted aide. Chinqai himself arrived the next day. The Master pleaded with him: couldn't he please spend the winter here, and await Genghis's arrival? Impossible, replied Chinqai; it was more than his job was worth: 'If the Master stays here, I shall certainly be blamed.' But Chinqai himself would lead the expedition from now on. He knew the way through the precipitous Altai mountains ahead, down to desert, across the Domain of White Bones, where a whole army had simply collapsed and died, and then, with the snows of the Tien Shan glinting on the horizon, round the eastern edge of the great Dzungarian basin, where progress over sand dunes 'was like that of a ship over the crests of huge waves', and the heat, even now in September, was fatal by day; travel had to be by night. Ch'ang-ch'un's companions trembled at the thought of goblins and elves leaping at them out of the darkness, until their Master laughed their fears away: 'Do you not know that ghosts and evil spirits fly from the presence of honest men?'

Now they were in Uighur country, rejoining the Silk Road at Beshbalig, one of the oasis towns east of present-day Urumqi. Here the local ruler lodged the Master upstairs in a large house overlooking vineyards and sent him wine, fruit and perfumes – not quite the things for an ascetic who ate no fruit, but they must have gone down well with his military entourage. In the evening, a troupe of Chinese dwarves and musicians provided entertainment.

Winding on westward towards Kazakhstan, they turned left at Sairam lake, hauling carts over the ravines and torrents of the new Pine Tree Pass military road, with its 48 wooden bridges, built by Chagadai for the Mongol invasion the previous year. From there they followed the Ili river, with its meadows and mulberry trees, past Almalik, named (like Kazakhstan's present-day capital Almaty) after the region's famed apples (*alma*); and so, tracking the north-facing foothills of the Tien Shan, past Balasagun, the old capital ruled briefly by Kuchlug until his defeat, they passed through Tashkent, across the mouth of the Fergana valley, to ruined Samarkand.

Samarkand's former population of over 100,000 house-holds – let's say 350,000 people – had been reduced by 75 per cent as a result of Genghis's assault (and this was a town that had largely *escaped* Mongol wrath). It was under new international administration, with Chinese, Khitans and Tanguts managing the farmland, and Chinese artisans busy rebuilding. Liu Wen, who had ridden on ahead, returned to report that the pontoon bridge over the Syrdar'ya had been destroyed by bandits. Winter was at hand. Genghis was far away, mopping up in Afghanistan. Wouldn't it be better to arrange the meeting for the spring? The Master assented. The governor, a multilingual Khitan named A-hai, billeted Ch'ang-ch'un in Shah Mohammed's palace, which A-hai had rejected as his own HQ in case the locals rebelled. That made the new arrivals nervous, until the Master reassured them. 'The man of Tao lets fate lead him whither it will,' he said, with his innocent optimism. 'Good and Evil go their own way, without harming one another.' The governor urged the Master to accept wine, gold brocade, rice, corn-flour, fruits and vegetables, all of which he refused, except for a hundred pounds of grapes for his visitors. It is hard to be ascetic when one lives in a palace, surrounded by admirers, with access to every comfort and luxury, but Ch'ang-ch'un did not let his ideals slip: 'It was his habit to give what grain we could spare to the poor and hungry of the city . . . and in this way saved a great number of lives.'

Among the many visitors to the illustrious guest was a Chinese astronomer. Since astronomy and astrology were two sides of the same coin, the two men compared notes, and carefully worked out the path of totality of the eclipse experienced near Avraga. On the Kherlen, the moon had covered the sun completely; further south, it had covered 70 per cent; in Samarkand, 60 per cent. 'It is just as though one covered a candle with a fan,' the Master concluded. 'In the direct shadow of the fan there is no light, but the further one moves to one side, the greater the light becomes.'

Spring came. The bridge was repaired, the bandits scattered. Chu-tsai arrived to escort the Master to the khan. Had the moment arrived? Ch'ang-ch'un was uncertain. Genghis was 500 kilometres to the south, deep in the Hindu

Kush, snowbound. The Master had heard there were no vegetables south of the Amudar'ya. He would wait until his diet was sorted out, a decision with which his followers had no problem. Rather than tackle the Afghan snows, better to remain for a few weeks longer, in the company of the admiring Chu-tsai, enjoying spring in Samarkand, exchanging poems, chatting with astronomer–astrologers, admiring the freshly blooming almond trees, the terraces, lakes, pagodas, orchards, vegetable gardens and woodlands, where one could discuss the mysteries of Tao, resting on soft grasses and sipping wine.

But at last there could be no more prevarication. A message from the khan arrived. 'Adept! You have spared yourself no pain in coming to me across hill and stream, all the way from the lands of sunrise. Now I am on my way home and am impatient to hear your teaching.' The intervening two years had merely increased his eagerness to learn the secrets not only of long life but of real power, the sort of power that seemed to flow from religious convictions. He had seen the way many Khwarezmians had fought, not for their leaders, nor simply to preserve their wealth, but for their religion. He had gazed in awe at the towering Kalyan Minaret in Bukhara, at the mosques that dignified every Muslim city and (almost certainly, for he had passed right by them) at the two great sandstone Buddhas, 40 and 50 metres high, that stared out from the cliffs of Bamian, just north-west of Kabul, until they were blown to bits by the Taleban in 2001 (there are plans to put them back together again). Any leader of imagination would have yearned for the commitment and respect that lay behind such creations.

Another stiff journey lay ahead for the Master: southward through the Iron Gates – the Buzgala Defile, a needle's eye between precipices so narrow that the way had once been barred with double doors – over the Amudar'ya, where the frontier of Uzbekistan now runs, and up into the mountains of northern Afghanistan where, as the messenger said, 'the snow was so deep that when I plunged my riding-whip into it, I did not get near the bottom.' But the snow was melting and Boorchu was waiting with an escort of 1,000 men to lead the way south, through Bamian to Parvan (today's Charikar, 80 kilometres north of Kabul).

In the second week of May, with the heat of early summer beginning to warm the Afghan highlands, the Master and the khan met at last, speaking through an interpreter. The two old men were almost equals, each pre-eminent in his own domain, each recognizing the other's hard-won authority. Senior monks did not kneel to emperors. After the pleasantries – Genghis expressing delight that such a man, having refused another emperor, should come 10,000 *li* to see him; the Master, a humble hermit of the mountains, replying that the meeting was Heaven's will – Genghis came right to the point:

'Adept, what Medicine of Long Life have you brought me from afar?'

The Master did not miss a beat.

'I have means of protecting life,' he said, 'but no elixir that will prolong it.'

Genghis liked straight talking, and swallowed his disappointment. Tents were set up, questions asked about what to call his guest (Father? Master? Adept? Genghis settled on 'Holy Immortal'). Now for the main purpose of the trip, as conceived by Chu-tsai and the Master himself. The Holy Immortal, now aged 73, would give the ruler of Asia's heartland (aged about 62) a tutorial on good living and good ruling. But these regions were still not properly tamed. Genghis still had to deal with bandits in the mountains, a task that would take a month or so. The Master said that in that case it would be best to return to Samarkand. Wouldn't that be tiring? asked Genghis. Oh, no, it was only a three-week journey there and back, nothing to one who had already travelled 10,000 *li*.

Back in Samarkand, the Master lived in some comfort through the summer heat, cooled by soft winds on his verandah and bathing in a lake, sustained by aubergines and melons – sweeter than any available in China – grown in a field presented by the deputy governor. In September came the return trip into Afghanistan.

Genghis was about to set off for home, but made it plain that Ch'ang-ch'un and his entourage were to travel with him. On the way, the two old men had several chats, culminating in a discourse by Ch'ang-ch'un on the Tao, the Way that underpins all things in Heaven and Earth. Genghis had the Master's words recorded in Mongol and Chinese; it was 20 November 1222. 'Most men only know the greatness of Heaven,' explained the Master, with A-hai, Samarkand's governor, acting as interpreter. 'They do not understand the greatness of Tao.' When Man was first born, he shone with a holy radiance and his step was light. But his appetite and longing were so keen that his body grew heavy and his holy light dim. Agitated by sensuality and emotional attachment, his life essence became unbalanced. Those who study Tao seek to regain that balance by quietism, asceticism and meditation. In this lay the true elixir – that symbolic combination of minerals – of long life. The khan should curb his appetites, live without desire, reject luscious tastes, use only foods that are fresh and light, abstain from lust. Which reminded him about Liu Wen and those harem girls in Beijing: 'Once such things have been seen, it is hard indeed to exercise self-restraint. I would have you bear this in mind.' Try sleeping alone for a month. Better still, he could have added, try sleeping less, to banish the 'Yin ghosts', the base sexual impulses that cause such havoc in the unguarded sleeping mind. You will be surprised what an improvement there will be in your energy. As the ancients said: 'To take medicine for a thousand days does less good than to lie alone for a single night.'

During the return journey, with the reclusive Master

travelling a little apart to avoid the din of an army on the move, the lessons continued, with a few more raps over the knuckles. Forget Mongol taboos, like not bathing in rivers in summer and not washing clothes. There were more important things. 'It is said that of the three thousand sins the worst is ill-treatment of one's father and mother. Now in this respect I believe your subjects to be gravely at fault, and it would be well if your Majesty could use his influence to reform them.'

The khan was pleased: 'Holy Immortal, your words are exceedingly true. Such is indeed my own belief.' Then to his ministers and officers he said: 'Heaven sent this Holy Immortal to tell me these things. Do you engrave them upon your hearts.' (But they didn't: Ch'ang-ch'un is not mentioned once in *The Secret History*.)

Now the Master begged to be allowed to return to China. He had promised to be back in three years, and if he were to fulfil that promise he should leave now. Just a few more days, urged Genghis, because his sons would arrive soon. The delay was worthwhile, for it gave the monk a chance to proffer one more piece of advice. While out hunting boar the khan fell, and his prey, instead of rushing in to gore him, stood still. Ch'ang-ch'un said this was a sign from Heaven reminding him that all life was precious – in this case the boar's. (Apparently Ch'ang-ch'un did not take the opportunity to say anything about the million or more humans recently slain, the evidence for which was all around; perhaps that was the will of Heaven, of which Genghis was merely the helpless tool.) Anyway, the khan was getting old. He shouldn't hunt.

'I know quite well that your advice is extremely good,' replied the khan. 'But unfortunately we Mongols are brought up from childhood to shoot arrows and ride. Such a habit is not easy to lay aside.' Still, he tried, and gave up hunting for two months.

And in a final interview came the reward for which the Master and his followers must have been hoping. Genghis

asked Liu Wen if the Master had many disciples back in China.
Oh, yes, Liu Wen replied, when he was escorting the Master, he
himself saw many disciples – and the lists drawn up by tax-
collectors who wanted their share of the income they collected.
At this Genghis ordered that Ch'ang-ch'un's disciples – in effect,
his whole organization – should be free from tax, an edict that
was then written and given the imperial stamp. This was a smart
move: Chu-tsai had prepared the ground, but intended the law
to apply to all monks. For some reason Chu-tsai was away at
that moment, with the result that only Taoists benefited.
Chu-tsai never forgave the astute old man.

At a stroke, Genghis had set in train a minor revolution that
would serve both himself and his spiritual adviser. As soon as
Ch'ang-ch'un arrived home, Buddhism would be on the
retreat in the face of a new, centralized and highly ambitious
form of Taoism. Ch'ang-ch'un, travelling fast with the help of
the imperial post-horses, arrived back in Beijing in early
1224, to be greeted by vast crowds of admirers. Eager to put
Genghis's edict into effect, the Master urged his followers to
accept Mongol rule with equanimity. Tax relief had a
wonderful effect on recruitment. From being a small sect,
dominated by its parent and rival Buddhism, Taoism boomed,
its growing bands of disciples building new temples – Beijing's
governor gave land for one – and taking over decaying
Buddhist ones. For Taoists, it was a time of miracles and
omens. Cranes circled overhead, a brackish well became
sweet. The planet Mars entered Scorpio, threatening calamity,
which the Master was able to avert by performing the correct
observances. On several occasions he ended famines by the
power of his prayers.

In 1227 Ch'ang-ch'un was made head of the whole expanding, tax-exempt Taoist movement, in effect becoming a sort of
Taoist pope, his Vatican being a renovated and enlarged

temple renamed after him. But he knew his time was near (as one might when one is 79 and suffering from dysentery). When a great storm caused the bank of one of the palace lakes to collapse, the Master smiled and said: 'When the hills fall and the lakes dry up, is it not time for me to go the same way?'

On 22 August, six months short of his 80th birthday, he died. By a strange coincidence, it was the very month and year in which his greatest pupil also died; a story for another chapter. Li Chih-ch'ang records his death in words as simple as brushstrokes. That afternoon, the Master wrote a poem on fleeting life and its enduring essence, looking forward to the moment when he would slough off the shell of his body and ascend to holy immortality. 'He then went up to the Pao-hsuan hall and returned to Purity. A strange perfume filled the room.'

It should be said that the mood surrounding his departure was not all universal devotion and ethereal piety. Ch'ang-ch'un was very smart in the service of his sect, and infuriated mainstream Buddhists, who delighted in his end and its circumstances. He died of dysentery, they noted, while in the toilet, and jested crudely about the nature of the perfume surrounding his death.

But his followers were many, his fame growing. When his body was displayed, 10,000 a day paid their respects – princes, officials, scholars, commoners, Buddhist priests and nuns as well as Taoists, whose adherents grew in number daily. Volunteers raised a temple in his honour in just 40 days. Wang the Madman and his apostles would become the subjects of plays and stories, and the teachings of the Complete Perfection sect would become a major part of modern Taoism, a fulfilment of the poem the Master and Adept Ch'ang-ch'un wrote on the afternoon of his death:

> The transient foam comes and vanishes;
> but the stream goes on untroubled.

11

THE LAST CAMPAIGN

BY 1224 GENGHIS WAS FREE AT LAST TO TURN ON XI XIA, THE Tangut kingdom that had refused him reinforcements five years previously. He had taken the refusal as a slap in the face from an inferior, an unforgivable insult and a threat to the new empire's very existence. Xi Xia was the key to Inner Asia, and thus the key to future expansion in China. Xi Xia had to be destroyed.

But he faced a strategist's nightmare. Four powers were now battling for supremacy in Inner Asia: the Mongols, Xi Xia, the Jin in northern China (still only partially defeated by the Mongols) and the Song in the south. The next stage in this struggle came to a head in 1227, the year of two turning-points which occurred almost simultaneously – the death of Genghis and the final solution to the problem of Xi Xia.

Xi Xia had a new young ruler, Xianzong,[1] who was not the man to steer his state back to its former pre-Mongol stability. Perhaps guessing what was coming, he signed a peace treaty

---

[1] Hsien-tsung in Wade–Giles. Weiming Dewang was his given name.

with his rivals and neighbours the Jin, who needed a respite from war on three fronts. To gain time, the devious Xianzong also proposed a peace treaty with Genghis, dangling the possibility that he might, after all, acknowledge his predecessor's fault and do as he was told in future. Genghis agreed in principle, for an assured peace with the Tanguts would allow him to turn safely on the rest of China. But Xianzong had to prove himself in earnest by sending his son as a hostage. There followed a brief respite, allowing Genghis to regather his forces, ready for whatever happened next. No princely hostage arrived. When Mongol envoys demanded him, the emperor, reassured by his peace with the Jin, refused outright.

Now Genghis's war machine shifted gear. He faced two allied enemies, and had to move fast if he were to pre-empt their joining forces. In the autumn of 1225 he advanced south. As before, his route lay across the Gobi and through the mountain ranges known as the Three Beauties, where, in the rolling intermontane basins, herds of wild asses roamed. Genghis, as active as ever in his mid-sixties, was not one to miss a chance for a good hunt. At one point, his ochre-and-grey horse shied, and the khan fell. His injury – a dislocated shoulder, perhaps, or a bruised rib – demanded rest.[2]

That night Genghis developed a fever. Plans had to change. Leaders met and talked. Tolun, Genghis's *cherbi* (a sort of chamberlain), who had been with his master during the invasion of China thirteen years before, spoke up. The Tanguts were city people, he said, they weren't going anywhere; best to withdraw, allow the khan to recover, then attack. But when this suggestion was passed to Genghis, he would have none of it: 'The Tangut people will say that our hearts have failed us.'

---

[2] Actually where and when he had his accident is not clear. Some say it was a, or the, cause of his death. But he remained campaigning almost to the last, so it couldn't have been too bad.

Better to stay where they were and play for time, sending a message recalling the cause of the war, hinting that it was still not too late for the Tanguts to make peace if they wanted it.

When the emperor heard what Genghis's ambassadors had to say, he was eager for a way out. After all, he wasn't personally to blame for refusing aid to Genghis five years before—

No, broke in the acerbic commander-in-chief, Asha, 'it was *I* who uttered the insulting words!' And he went on to fling at the envoys an uncompromising challenge. 'You Mongols should know how to fight by now. So if you want to fight, I've got latticed tents and laden camels and people in Alashan, my homeland. Come to me in Alashan! We'll fight there!'

Genghis, still recovering from his fever when the reply came, was incensed. The arrogance of it! The Tanguts were meant to be vassals! Now this – treachery on treachery, insult upon insult. His anger must have been all the more intense when he recalled that he had actually let these people off the hook 20 years before. There could be no mistake this time, for he could not have such an opponent on his flank when the time came to finish off Jin and attack the rest of China. There was more than imperial strategy at stake. This was deeply personal. 'In the face of such mighty words, how can we possibly withdraw?' *The Secret History* has him saying. 'Even if it means my death, God knows, we can't just go!'

Asha's challenge was more than a provocation; it revealed his hand. It echoed a centuries-old tradition by which settled states across Eurasia had resolved their quarrels. If there were to be battles, commanders had to know where the opposition was to be found, and there had to be rules of engagement, in order to know the outcome. Not so for Genghis. He now knew the strategy that Asha expected the Mongols to follow – a fast sweep in from the north across the Gobi, and a good clean fight in Asha's backyard, where the Tanguts could draw on their two main cities, Yinchuan and Wu-wei, for reserves

– so he would therefore do the exact opposite. But there was no rush. This would, as always, have to be a campaign fought on his own terms. Anyway, winter was upon them. The troops scattered into the valleys of the Three Beauties, where they hacked frozen water from streams and hunted wild asses and mountain sheep, keeping the meat frozen until required. Many probably returned to their homes for the winter months, leaving their siege machines standing with their ropes frozen until their return.

In spring, as the slow warmth unshackled the landscape, the forces regathered. Genghis, nursed back to health, was well enough to lead his army across the 160 kilometres of sand and gravel that separates the Three Beauties from today's Chinese border, over the borders of Xi Xia, to Xi Xia's northern stronghold, the city the Mongols knew as Khara-Khoto, the Black City.

This had been a fortress outpost for over 1,000 years. It guarded a grim landscape of gravel pavements across which the wind drove snaking dunes, but it was a thriving outpost of perhaps several thousand people standing on a T-junction where a sub-branch of the Silk Road ran in from the east to join the headwaters of the Etsin river, as the Mongols called it (its Chinese name was the Juyan then, the Shui today), which flowed through a forbidding desert wilderness to the soft, green foothills of the Qilian Shan, the Snowy Mountains, 300 kilometres to the south. Now all that's left of the town is a square of 10-metre sandblasted walls surrounding the low and scattered remains of fallen buildings.

Imagine an army of nomadic warriors who were now also adept at siege warfare, with catapults able to throw gunpowder-filled bombs some 200–300 metres, flame-throwers, multiple bows, and perhaps by now the first true fragmentation bomb, the 'heaven-shaking thunder', the existence of which was recorded only a few years later, at the siege of Kaifeng in 1232. It consisted of an iron casing filled with gunpowder that exploded so violently it could be heard several kilometres away; any soldier within 10 or 12 metres of it was 'blown to bits, not even a trace being left behind'.

Khara-Khoto didn't stand a chance. Its seizure was the first step in a roundabout approach to ensure that Xi Xia would have no reserves when the showdown came; and if Asha dared send a force across 500 kilometres of desert from Yinchuan, his troops would arrive exhausted, at the limit of their supply lines and utterly unfit for battle. The Tanguts, heirs to a refined and urbanized culture, preferred to place their faith in strong walls. No army swept westward to confront the unsporting Mongols.

This was a policy that suited the Mongols perfectly. They could gather their forces wherever they might have the greatest effect, while their opponents were divided and stationary. Besides, once one city had fallen, the Mongols would as usual be able to draw on prisoners, defectors, supplies and weapons to take the next one, by negotiation if possible, by force if necessary. As in Khwarezm, this was no blitzkrieg, but a steady advance that fuelled itself, with the momentum of a slow-motion avalanche.

Two months later and 300 kilometres further south, where the Etsin is turned eastward by the Qilian mountains, Genghis could afford to divide his army, now reinforced with Tangut food, weapons, animals, prisoners and traitors. Subedei headed west to oversee the assault on the most distant cities of Xi Xia, while the main force struck east towards the heart of the rebellious domain.

A hundred and sixty kilometres to the east lay the Silk Road city of Kan Chou (Ganzhou in pinyin). Today it is the industrial city of Zhangye, but in Genghis's day it was an oasis town famed for its pastures and its horses and its Buddhist temple, with its 34-metre reclining Buddha (both temple and Buddha are still there). Genghis had been here before, briefly, in the campaign of 1205. At that time a young boy, the son of the city's commander, had been captured. The boy had adopted Mongol ways, fought, proved himself, acquired a Mongol name – Tsagaan (White) – risen through the ranks and now commanded Genghis's personal guard. Tsagaan's father, however, was still the city's commander. Now Tsagaan shot over the walls an arrow carrying a message to his father, requesting a meeting. The father agreed. Representatives were talking terms when the second-in-command discovered what was afoot, staged a coup, killed Tsagaan's father and rejected the very idea of submission. Furious, Genghis, according to one source, threatened to bury the whole population alive. But in the event, when the town fell, Tsagaan interceded to save the inhabitants of his former home – all except for the 35 who were involved in the coup that had killed his father.

In August, while Genghis escaped the heat in the Snowy Mountains, his troops were at the gates of Wu-wei, Xi Xia's second greatest city. Since the whole area of today's western China was in Mongol hands, the inhabitants of Wu-wei looked to the capital for help. None came. Seeing death as the only alternative to surrender, the citizens surrendered, and lived.

Now it was autumn. Genghis, returning from his summer break, rejoined his army at the Yellow River, crossed it, and—

I must interrupt. The sources do the Mongol advance less than justice. The Yellow River is not an obstacle to be leaped in two words. In this stretch, where it skirts the Helan mountains before heading north past Yinchuan, the river is a kilometre-wide gruel of silt, not yellow at all to my eyes, but a muddy brown. It is too broad to break into white water, but it flows at a fair clip in midstream, and although nomadic cavalry, with their leather floats, could swim their horses across, it is too deep for wagons. Besides, the water is thick enough to eat. I swam in it, opened my eyes underwater, and could see nothing at all. I came out filthy, wading through mud up to my thighs. This is a river that demands boats, a form of transport not much in demand in Mongolia. Luckily, however, the locals had river transport, in the form of sheep-skin or cowskin floats (they still have, actually: in the river-town of Shapotou, tourists can take river trips paddling platforms resting on skin floats). Fourteenth-century sources recorded how several skin floats spanned by a platform, manned by rowers, formed a good enough vessel to ship cargoes of grain and salt down the smoothly flowing river to Yinchuan, and beyond. This was clearly not a new tradition. Such floating platforms would have been known to the Mongols, and quickly adapted to ferry wagons, carts, oxen and laden horses across the river; on the other side they could march away, carrying the floats and platforms with them.

Having crossed, the Mongols circled north, approaching Yinchuan from the south-east – a direction precisely opposite to the one Asha had proposed in his challenge.

It was enough to fill any ruler with terminal terror, which is exactly what seems to have happened. The ineffective emperor, Xianzong, died, and the poisoned chalice of kingship fell to a kinsman, another of the Wei-ming clan also named Xian. His reign was so brief and what followed so destructive that he is virtually nothing but a wraith to us.

In November the Mongols encircled Ling-wu (Ling-zhou, as it was then, or Turemgi – 'The Aggressive [City]' – to the Mongols), a mere 30 kilometres south of Yinchuan. Now, at last, the Tanguts made their move. Ling-wu, like Yinchuan, was a place watered by a large system of canals. Most of the year, these would have acted as a protection. But it was winter, and the canals and the river itself were frozen solid. As the Tangut army approached along the opposite bank, the Mongols broke off their siege, galloped across the frozen river, shattered the demoralized Tanguts and returned to their siege. No details of the battle survive, but it must have been clear to both sides that the Tanguts were finished.

Ling-wu fell in December. The only detail we have of this episode is that the rampaging troops went down with some sort of disease, typhus or dysentery perhaps. We know this because the scholar, humanitarian and imperial aide Chu-tsai, returning from Central Asia, witnessed the scenes of pillage and suffering, and did his best to minimize both. While 'all the Mongol officers contended with each other to seize children, women and valuables, His Excellency [Chu-tsai] took only a few books and two camel-loads of rhubarb,' which he used to treat infected soldiers. It's a strange detail. Rhubarb might, I suppose, have helped young men short of fresh food, but we have no other explanation.

Then, while one Mongol force besieged Yinchuan, another went off not only to secure other smaller cities to the east and south, but also in pursuit of a wider scheme that foresaw the neutralization of Jin. While mopping-up operations and the siege of Yinchuan continued in Xi Xia, Genghis, now rejoined by Subedei, headed south and west, over the Jin border just 100 kilometres away. The purpose of this advance was to slice across a narrow tongue of western Jin some 150 kilometres wide – mainly covering present-day Ningxia and Gansu provinces – to prevent Jin troops coming to the rescue of their Tangut allies, and to prepare for the final conquest of the Jin heartland. To do this Subedei crossed the northern reaches of the Liupan mountains, covering some 450 kilometres as the crow flies, perhaps double that on the ground, given his zigzag progress from town to town, in February and March: an astonishing achievement for an army that had already been in the field for a year. He celebrated his success by sending his lord and master 5,000 horses as a gift.

Genghis, meanwhile, struck due south; and thus came upon, or at least came near, another extraordinary monument that spoke to him of that other-worldly universe which now seemed so close.

*

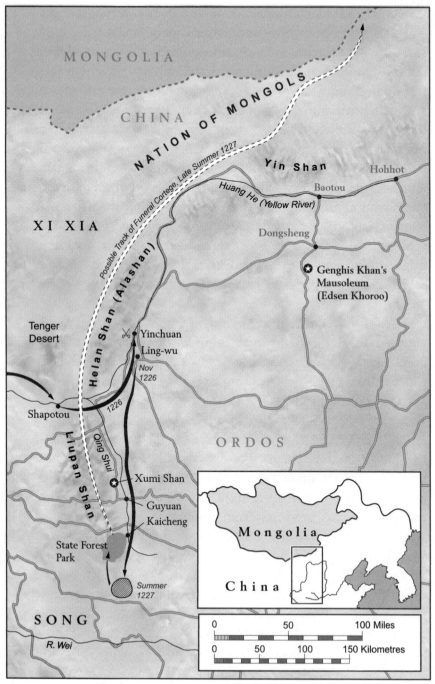

The last campaign and death, 1226–1227.

The route taken by Genghis's army followed the Qing Shui river. At first glance, the valley looks like good, flat going. In fact, the overburden of dark red earth is crossed by ravines cut by streams flowing from the Liupan Shan to the west and the Shang and Luo hills to the east. There were probably wooden bridges; and, since it was summer, the Qing Shui itself was a mere trickle, with sun-hardened shoulders beneath its steep banks. But whether on road or dry riverbed, progress would have been slow for wagons and siege engines. Contingents of cavalry would, of course, have been free to roam widely ahead and either side, scouting for the best routes, for food, for opposition. So Genghis would have been told of what lay 20 kilometres up the tortuous track that hugged the steep sides of the Si Kou ('Temple Mouth') river, which joins the Qing Shui at the dusty truck-stop town of San Ying.

As you round a bend in the road that loops along the contorted strata of red sandstone, you see a cliff face honeycombed with holes. There are over 100 of them – all the cells of Buddhist monks dating back to the sixth century, linked by vertiginous stairways cut from the rock. This is Xumi Shan, 'Treasure Mountain'. Once, it was a wonderful place to seek enlightenment: remote, austere yet beautiful, with views over the reds and greens of sandstone ravines and grass-pimpled uplands. Today, there are no monks, just a couple of aged guardians with gold teeth and glasses held together with massive hinged clasps. Gnarled pines scrabble at the rocks with twisted roots, and schoolkids scar the soft rock with knives. If the spirit of Xumi Shan has power to punish graffiti writers, Wang Yujin and Gu Yijing from Shanghai, among others, will be beetles in their next reincarnation.

And there *is* a power here. It looms around a rocky corner in the form of a Buddha, enshrined by the rock from which it was cut. The half-closed eyes and the formal folds of the robe present a traditional image of serenity and enlightenment.

The real impact comes from the sheer size of the statue. Though seated, the Buddha is 20.7 metres – 67 feet – tall; his distended ears alone are 3 metres long. George Bernard Shaw once defined a miracle as something that creates faith, and for centuries this rock-carved giant must have worked just such a miracle for awed novices. He might still do so, if any novices still come here, for he has survived rather more than the ravages of time and weather. In the 1960s, during the Cultural Revolution, Red Guards bent on destruction battered away his lower legs before giving up. Now he has been repaired, and sits, with his legs plastered in concrete, staring out eastward across the river gorge as he has for the last 1,400 years.

In the presence of this immense proclamation of faith, scepticism takes a back seat and humility seems appropriate. For two *yuan* the attendant, who was no more a Buddhist than we were, burned six sticks of incense, set a many-holed silver bowl ringing with a tap from a wooden mallet, and chanted a prayer for us. Jorigt and I bowed our heads.

I like to imagine that Genghis felt something similar when he passed this way in the spring of 1227 – but with a more personal agenda. He was on the point of destroying a line of kings whose grand tombs would soon be empty and roofless, reminding future generations of ultimate failure. Here was something created by faith and artistry that had been worshipped for centuries, and would be a focus for worship for centuries to come. By now, with two nasty falls, a fever and advancing years all reminding him of his mortality, Genghis would, I speculated, be considering his posthumous reputation, hoping to be remembered for rather more than corpses and shattered cities. How? No true nomad would be interested in mere monuments, Jorigt commented over the piped chanting that came from Xumi Shan's abandoned monastery. Temples and tombs so easily vanish into dust. But get yourself worshipped, and you live in hearts and minds for ever.

*

A few weeks later, directing the siege of Longde, Genghis guessed that Yinchuan, the capital, should be ready to capitulate. He sent his Tangut officer, Tsagaan, to negotiate. Tsagaan found that six months of starvation and sickness had indeed taken such a toll that Xian was prepared to give up. All he needed, the emperor said, was a month's grace to prepare suitable gifts. Xian, who had only been in power for a few weeks, must have hoped for easy treatment and a long reign as vassal. Genghis had no intention of granting either. But nor did he want to hint at his true purpose, which was, as always with those who resisted, and particularly with this twice-treacherous people, to be utterly ruthless. No grounds for trust or reconciliation were left. The Tanguts had insulted him, broken promises, refused him troops and failed to surrender cities, in particular their capital Yinchuan. As *The Secret History* grimly states, Genghis decreed: 'While we eat, let us talk of how we made them die and of how we destroyed them. Let us say: "That was the end, they are no more." ' As a first step in this dreadful process, the Tangut ruler had to die. So Genghis agreed to a formal capitulation, sent his chamberlain Tolun to act as regent, and kept his real plans to himself.

Now it was summer. Genghis based himself in the Liupan mountains, near present-day Guyuan, where he continued to juggle war with politics, striking where necessary, always staying open to the possibility of getting his way by negotiation.

Xi Xia was as good as finished, and the Jin rulers knew it. In the same month that Xi Xia agreed to capitulate, the Jin emperor, according to the official Yuan history, sent an embassy to sue for peace. The audience would have been a grand and formal occasion, during which Genghis offered the two envoys honeyed words. He recalled that there had been a conjunction of five planets a few months back, an omen that had inspired him to promise an end to killing and plundering. 'But in my haste I failed to authorize the order,' he told his followers. 'Now let the order be announced far and wide, at home and abroad, and make sure these ambassadors know my royal command!'

Apparently an end to killing and plundering did not mean peace, exactly, for the advance through Jin continued, commanded by Genghis himself. But 100 kilometres to the south of the Liupan mountains, just short of the Jin–Song border, Genghis fell ill – so seriously ill that he was rushed north again, setting off the strange events that put his life's work in jeopardy.

III

DEATH

12

THE VALLEY OF DEATH

GUYUAN, IN THE SOUTH OF NINGXIA, IS NOT A PLACE FOR tourists. It is a poor city in China's poorest province, with a Muslim minority, the Hui, who are the poorest of the poor. To the south of the Yellow River the fertile plains watered by the canals of Yinchuan turn into problem areas. The soil is rich enough – sometimes over 50 metres thick – a single undifferentiated layer of dark earth dumped over millennia by the winds of the Gobi. But the earth does not stay around to be cultivated. Rains wash it away, sun bakes it solid, winds whip it into dust clouds, torrents carve out unstable ravines. Here a field made fertile by one year's blessed balance of rain and sun can be whipped and washed into wilderness for the next ten. Nothing is fixed, neither crops nor the dark-red mud-brick houses, and the cycle of poverty has not yet been broken by brick and cement, by canals and lakes and lasting buildings.

Education is obligatory, but few Hui country families can afford the £15 annual contribution required. At best, family groups club together to send a single child to school, which may be a two-hour walk from home. Even then he (and it is usually he) may have little to sustain him other than a crust of bread, or less. This I learned from a foreign teacher in Guyuan, Moira Laidlaw. The town has 100,000 people, and I was there for a day. But foreigners were exotic rarities, so we met as inevitably as lodestones. A student accosted me. 'You are English. There is an English teacher. She is my friend. Come.' Over tea and noodles, ordered by sign language from a menu of pictures, Moira told me of her work in these grim circumstances. Not that they are a cause for despair. The conditions are well known both to the government and to foreign aid agencies (hence Moira's presence); but change will take years, perhaps decades. Meanwhile, students, knowing their future depends on education, droop with hunger, and out of town many children remain at home to work the land, for who can invest time and energy in education for tomorrow when food is needed today?

So it was a surprise to find that Guyuan has a fine museum, reflecting a rather wealthy past. Once upon a time Guyuan was not a backward provincial town at all, but an entrepôt on the Silk Road, with a double wall 13 kilometres around and ten gates, all on show in a scale model of the whole town as it still was in the late middle ages. It had been that rich for centuries. A sixth-century regional boss, a general named Li Shien, rated an underground tomb, approached by a sloping tunnel 40 metres long, and guarded by his own army of 237 terracotta soldiers. Perhaps it was Li himself who bought the museum's greatest treasure: an elegant sixth-century silver vase, decorated by scenes inspired by the legends of ancient Troy. It seemed to me very odd that 'A-Foo-Do-Te' – Aphrodite – should be dancing here with Menelaus, Helen and Paris, on a Persian vase made 2,000 years after the fall of Troy, in a Chinese city, 4,500 kilometres from Persia and 7,000 kilometres from Troy itself.

Guyuan fell to the Mongols in 1227 without a murmur, so

easily that no-one mentions it. Genghis would have known exactly why he wanted this place, for only eight years before he had been further west down the same route, in Bukhara and Samarkand. If things worked out, the Mongols would soon control the whole length of the trade route that linked China through Central Asia to Europe.

And right nearby there was the most perfect military base, which Jorigt and I were to see in the company of the museum's deputy director, Yan Shijong. Our destination was the Liupan Shan State Forest Park, to which, as Mr Yan and everybody else seemed to know, Genghis Khan had been taken in his last days.

For 70 kilometres, the road south of Guyuan rolled over soft hills, their summer mantle of grass and crops broken here and there where rain had carved brown ravines. To our right, green as emerald, ridged like a lizard's back, towered the Liupan mountains. Just before the southern tip of Ningxia province, you turn towards them and head up a steep-sided valley. After a few kilometres, two lines of buildings flank the park's weird gateway: a white dragon contorted into a rectangle, its spiny concrete backbone straddling the road.

Beyond lies a wilderness of astonishing beauty, and – despite being popular with day-trippers – equally astonishing isolation. It is totally unknown to foreigners, not rating a mention in any guide book, for it is a new park, hard to get to, with an access road still being finished and nowhere to stay except for ten spartan rooms at the dragon entrance. But a visit is worth all these inconveniences, for it is an enormous, untouched glory: 679,000 square kilometres, the size of two English counties, larger than the state of Delaware. That's its square measure on the map. On the ground it is all three-dimensional wrinkles, range upon range of forested ridges and peaks and stream-carved ravines, which must almost double its surface area. Inside the gateway, the new road looped upwards round hairpin bends, with ever grander views of terraced lowlands vanishing into haze behind us. We were on our way to the heart of the park, the road's end – Genghis's last campsite. I imagined *gers* and pastures, a vision I could not square with these beetling forests. The pass peaked and dropped into a ravine of firs and rocks and fast-flowing water, and then climbed again, to a sight that made the heart sink.

Genghis Khan's last camp consisted of three 'Mongolian tents' made of nice new smooth concrete, their pointed domes strung with a streamer of little coloured flags. Half a dozen cars and various motorbikes filled the car park. In an open space behind the concrete *gers* stood a couple of horses and an old wooden farm wagon, like a Chinese version of ye olde mock-Constable haywain. I had hoped for authenticity, and found kitsch.

But wait. As Jorigt and Mr Yan, the archaeologist from Guyuan, began talking to the camp's guide, some of the more agile motorcyclists took turns on the horses. I wandered up to watch; and found myself staring at something that didn't fit with concrete tents and tourists. It was a table with eight seats; a table made of one huge, circular, carved stone, and seats that were stool-sized cylinders of stone, all obviously ancient.

The others joined me, to discuss the vital question of a lunch to honour this rare visit from Mr Yan. Yes, yes, lunch, of course, but what on earth were these old stones?

'Yuan dynasty,' said the young guide, a 22-year-old Hui named Ma. 'You see the hole in the middle? It's a flag support. Genghis Khan used this.'

'What? How do you know?'

Ma, a graduate of Yinchuan's Tourism College, told the story with utter assurance, pointing to an official guide book as evidence.

'In 1227, Genghis stayed here for the summer. It is very interesting. When he attacked Xi Xia, he fell from his horse, and was injured. But he had a duty to fight, so he came here, and trained his forces here, and hunted, and looked after his body. But this had no effect. So he died here. It was hot so his body began to decay. So he was buried here. Only his saddle and his other equipment was taken away for burial elsewhere.'

This was an astonishing claim. No other source suggested that Genghis might actually be *buried* here, in the Liupan Shan. It would undermine the whole story, not to say the basis of my research. Actually, it was so preposterous that I at once began to doubt everything he said.

What, in historical terms, was so special about this secret, overgrown, hard-to-get-to valley?

'It's cool in summer, and a very good place for training. That is my opinion. It's a very important military position, central for Mongolian forces from Gansu and Shanxi provinces. If you occupy this place—' he waved a hand at the surrounding hills, 'no enemy forces can get you, and you can control all the surrounding region.'

That much was true, as a glance at the map showed. The Liupan mountains were 200 kilometres from the Xi Xia border and 150 kilometres from the Song border, right in the middle of Jin's western wing.

'You think Genghis Khan was really here?'

'Oh, yes. We know this. Just up the road there is the place where Genghis called his generals together to brief them. This is the Training Centre. And there is another place called the Command Centre.'

Hm. Was it really likely that a whole army, siege machines and all, could make its way over the precipitous pass? And once here, how would they camp? How train? The place was all forest, no pasture. Ma was still talking, rambling on about the emperor of Xi Xia coming to meet Genghis here and Khubilai Khan, Genghis's grandson, being the one who finally destroyed Xi Xia. More nonsense. I needed evidence.

'The stones are evidence.'

'But you mean these stones were found right here?'

'No, but nearby, just up the road.'

The sky was clear, the sun not too hot, and lunch hours away. We had time to stroll further on, where the road turned into a track rising through fir forest. We joined a small group of soft Chinese visitors seeking *natural things*, as Jorigt the Mongolian snidely commented, by feeling unpaved earth beneath their slip-ons and high heels. Ma stopped and pointed vaguely down the fir-clad slope.

'They found the stones here.'

'Who found them?'

'Archaeologists. But soon no-one will know where they found them, because these trees will all be fully grown.'

I should have seen that these were young trees. And I should have guessed why, because Moira Laidlaw, the English teacher in Guyuan, had mentioned one of the battier excesses of the Cultural Revolution, when China's great leaders had embarked on a campaign to eradicate sparrows. Obviously, the sparrows would die if they had no trees to nest in; so the campaign against sparrows turned into a campaign against trees. This, naturally, proved disastrous, denuding cities, stripping hillsides, encouraging erosion and having absolutely no effect on the sparrows. Eventually the pendulum swung, anti-sparrowism was forgotten and a new initiative taken. Everyone, everywhere had to plant trees. This, newly declared a national park, was to be made into instant forest. Hence, I guessed at last, the fast-growing blanket of firs.

There was one small gap in this growing forest of explanations: If this had been forest before the Cultural Revolution, how come the stones were there?

'No trees before,' said Ma.

'Why not?'

'Because they had been cut.' He was being very patient.

'So there were people here?'

'Many. Farmers and hunters.'

Suddenly I saw the park in a different light. This had been not a primeval wilderness, but a hidden valley where a whole community had once lived, cutting trees for firewood and to clear fields, planting crops, raising animals, hunting the forests for boar, rabbit and deer, keeping in contact with the outside world along the precipitous pass we had just crossed – not a new road at all, but an ancient path, open to horses and wagons. And if there had been people in this fertile and secure valley until a few years back, there would surely have always been people here, for centuries. In 1227 this valley might have been a huge glade of crops and pastures, a perfectly wonderful base to hide a nomadic army.

I needed something to make sense of all this. Maybe folklore would help. Perhaps there were some old people to talk to.

'Oh, no. There is no-one here. Because this is a State Forest Park, everyone was moved out. The last people left four years ago.'

By now we had wandered further up, beyond the firs and into the cool and gentle embrace of deciduous woodland. By pure chance I glanced through a gap in the slender birches and saw what looked like dark spots a couple of kilometres away, backed by steep flanks of green.

'But look. Aren't those houses?' Houses that were standing in remarkably open countryside, soft and pale green as if with a mantle of ripening grain. It looked as if the mountains had poured out a carpet of welcome. 'And aren't those fields? Maybe there *are* people.'

'No people!' Ma was adamant. 'All people have been moved!'

'Well, somebody is still farming those fields.'

'No, no.'

'Yes, they are. That's new grain, new crops.'

'Not new crops. It is impossible. In four years no-one comes here!'

This was agonizing. If there were crops, that meant people, and people meant informants and folklore, and maybe more evidence about what really happened here.

'Look, a path.' I pointed to a gap in the roadside bushes. 'And car tracks.' Actually, if they were car tracks, they were made by a very small car.

'The police,' said Ma. He was struggling now. 'On motorbikes.'

Going where, to see whom or what? There was a silence. Despite himself Ma was obviously intrigued, as was Jorigt, who had been acting as interpreter and peacekeeper. If the path led to the houses, it would take only an hour to make the round trip. Lunch could wait.

The three of us set off, finding ourselves in a woodland idyll: an open path leading over sweet streams pure as bottled water, beneath a canopy that filtered sunlight into a dappling of green. The tracks, only a few days old, were not made by a car or motorbike. They were made by one of the small two-wheeled tractors with long handlebars that you steer sitting on the trailer.

But when we arrived, past a pond and the field I had seen from the road – it was not wheat, but something like barley, only slighter – we entered a ghost village. The half-dozen stone houses were tumbledown and overgrown, their roofs of grey curved tiles misshapen by age. The paths between the houses were rank with grasses.

'*You ren ma?*' yelled Jorigt. 'Is there anyone there?'

No echo came from the hills beyond, and no answering voices, no sounds except for the crickets and the birds. It was eerie. The tracks and the field pointed to a human presence; but here all was silence, decay, collapse. Various dramatic scenarios flicked through my mind. Everyone had fled. Everyone was dead. We were about to meet a survivalist, a Chinese Ben Gunn crazed by years spent alone in the wilderness.

Then, across the overgrown yard, I saw something that added another dimension. It was a huge stone bowl, a metre across, well carved, with the marks of a stone chisel scoring the inside surface. No mere peasant farmer would have carved this, and it wasn't recent, either. Connections flashed like Christmas lights. That table back at the camp . . . 'Yuan dynasty' . . . now this – a cattle-trough, a Mongol horse-trough. Had to be. The conclusion clunked into place like a well-oiled lock.

I think now I was wrong. But it was further inspiration, beyond the glorious view over the field down the valley, which, once stripped of trees in my mind's eye, turned into perfect grassland, complete with river. Surely someone could tell us what had once been here? We would have to come back and find people. How and when I had no idea; nor did the others.

We set off back in thoughtful silence, past the inexplicable field, down the path, over the stream.

And there, suddenly, right in our way, was a woman, a reserved and dignified figure in a grey shirt, dark trousers and a white head-dress shaped like a chef's hat, marking her as a Muslim Hui. She carried a toddler of about three, with cheeks as red as her overalls – it was very obviously a girl, because she was wearing trousers conveniently split at the crotch – and held the hand of a boy a couple of years older, clad in a frayed grey jacket faintly printed all over with the name 'Snoopy'. Over her shoulder was a bag. She was collecting an edible, asparagus-like fern which she called *qie cie*, unknown to both Ma and Jorigt. In an instant, she solved many mysteries. Her name was Li Bocheng, and it was her husband and brothers-in-law who farmed the fields we had just left. They had once lived here, and even after the authorities had moved them away had refused to abandon their small-holdings. Every summer they returned to plant and harvest. Oh, yes, she had heard about Genghis Khan, but if we wanted to know about him we had better talk to the men. They would return with the cows later.

By mid-afternoon we were back, to find six men, along with the woman and her two children. A house stood open, revealing a brick oven and a stone sleeping platform scattered with mattresses, built on top of a fireplace to offer central heating at night. In front of the house was a plastic sheet neatly laid with medicinal roots, which they called *sho-you*. We squatted down on bits of stone and old sacking while the woman brought green tea in jam-jars. The woman's husband, a wiry man in his thirties wearing a shirt of black-and-white stripes, took on the role of spokesman, telling us of Genghis as if he had been the previous owner of the house.

All this – with a sweep of his arm towards the valley – belonged to Genghis. This was the Training Place, where his bodyguard lived, and up there, where the cattle are, that's where he lived, the Meeting Place. Down there, below the flax field (oh, it was *flax*, not wheat or barley) was the Command Centre. 'That's what my father told me, because that's what the old people told him, when he came here, fifty years ago. I remember my father and grandfather talking about it. And right up there, that was what they called the Sitting Place of Genghis Khan.'

'You mean the terrace?'

'No, no, that's the Meeting Place! I mean high up.' He pointed at the mountain that overlooked the whole valley. 'Up there, there's a platform, you can see over everything.'

I imagined some sort of structure, like a reviewing stand.

'If you go up there, do you see stones from Genghis Khan's time?'

'Many stones! Feeding troughs, and other things. When I was a child, you could see them everywhere, but now they're mostly buried and overgrown.'

I had a vision of making a great archaeological discovery. Could he show us? Yes, he could. But it was a hard climb through undergrowth. We would have to wear long trousers and watch out for poisonous grass. I raised my eyebrows at Jorigt's leather slip-ons, but he was game. 'I am Jorigt. I am a Mongolian,' he said, disdaining any physical challenge.

We were off at eight the next morning, over the terrace above the house, with two brothers, Yu Wuhe and Yu Wuse, as guides. While we walked through firs, the Yu brothers told their story.

When the family came, this had been a community of 30 families. Once, 100 years ago, there had been a Buddhist temple here, though with the influx of the Muslim Hui it had been cannibalized for building materials (hence, I guessed, the solid stones for the village houses). Then the valley had been deliberately overgrown in a policy called Stop Farming – Grow Trees. Now everyone else had gone. They were the last, coming only in the summer, walking over the mountains with a few dozen sheep and some cattle to tend the fields and collect medicinal roots in the forests. 'We won't go until they give us our compensation. Or maybe they will offer crops instead of cash. So we'll just go on farming as long as we can.'

We were into thick woods by now. One of the brothers pointed to a dark pile on the ground. Bear droppings. There were *bears* here, as well as poisonous grass? Oh, lots, six round the farm a few days ago, he went on, leading us along a stream under tangles of secondary growth forest. We crossed the stream and climbed a near-vertical slope soft with mulch, at the top of which the ground, shadowed by birch trees with the bark peeling off, flattened into a confusion of odd little rock mesas.

'The road used to come up here,' said Yu Wuhe casually. He was the chatty one. His brother said not a word. It was hard to make sense of the contorted, dappled ground, but yes, I could see where a track might have run, past an overgrown outcrop about 5 metres high that might have been natural, or not.

There was a shout from further uphill, and a flurry of conversation. A man was on his knees scrabbling with his hands at the soft earth, and another over there in the shadows, and more – ten altogether.

They were collecting medicinal plants. They had walked in before dawn from their village 25 kilometres away, along one of the many paths over the mountains, and would work all day.

And so the wilderness revealed more of itself, as if gradually allowing me to understand what it was that made it so attractive over centuries to farmers, and hunters – and, for a few years perhaps, to nomadic warriors. This place was famous for its medicinal plants. I saw a list later: there were 39 of them. This particular one was called *chang-bo* around here. The local medical company bought *chang-bo* for 22 *yuan* (about $2.75 or £1.70) a kilo, and each of this party could collect 2–3 kilos a day. What the little onion-like root was for and how it was prepared, though, no-one had a clue. All they did was collect it and sell it.

Yu Wuhe waved an arm: 'This we call Genghis Khan's Medical Treatment Place.'

The dim light of partial understanding seeped from the dappled and overgrown confusion in front of me. This was an ever-changing ecosystem, all damp earth and teetering saplings and rampant bushes, so it was hard to tell natural from artificial. But if there had been a track, and the pinnacle was some sort of guard-tower, perhaps this, right here, had been some sort of a drug-store, where the sick and injured could come for special treatment with medicinal plants.

By mid-morning we were out of the woods, walking on carpets of grass, buttercups and blue gentians across an open ridge (though the mania for fir trees had spread even up there; in a few years, it would be entirely and unnaturally covered).

On the crest was the remains of a wall, which had once, I supposed, marked an all-round lookout over wave upon wave of forested mountain. From up there I could see no sign of humanity – no road, no building, no fire-smoke – only, below me, the valley along which we had come: the almost abandoned village, the tongue of pale green flax and, peeking from behind a coverlet of green, the three concrete domes of the tourist camp.

But a hilltop lookout was no base from which to watch army manoeuvres. I wanted to find the promised 'platform'. We descended, and struck thorn bushes. These were not ordinary brambles, but thick, gnarled, 3-metre trees, bristling with spearheads, a sub-forest tough and spiky enough to guard Sleeping Beauty. Somewhere near here, muttered Yu Wuhe as we made a wary circuit, there was the platform. Used to be, anyway. I was beginning to lose faith again when the ground levelled out. The four of us, scattered between more damned fir trees, regathered.

'Does he know where we are?' I asked Jorigt, despondently.

There was a brief exchange, then:

'This is it, the Sitting Place of Genghis Khan. He also called it the Lord's Place.'

There was to be no rock platform, I realized. It was of grass, or had been. I paced it out: the Sitting Place of Genghis Khan was about 250 metres long and 50 metres wide.

Well, frankly, no-one would bother to sit there now. When the Yus were children, it was open, and you could see stone equipment scattered across the grass, and you had a wonderful view down to the village. Now we were hemmed in by monoculture, and the rocks were buried. Some unthinking policy-maker had ordered brigades of planters up here, and ruined the very site that might have yielded intriguing artefacts and could then have been made into a viewing point that would have lured and rewarded and informed any semi-adventurous visitor wishing to commune with nature and history. Not that I believed Genghis himself used the spot. But his generals might have, because if you walk to the edge of the flat space, you can just see down the valley, and it is possible to imagine an immense parade ground, with tents and herds and formations of troops. And there were even a few rocks jutting up through the grass to inspire a vision of who may have stood or sat upon them, of what they may have seen.

We climbed down a steep and grassy path. The talk turned to bears. They were quite big, shoulder-height to the Yus, and came in several different shades of black, red and tawny, but they were not dangerous. 'Two days ago, those six bears? They come for the crops' – and indeed, I could see bear-scratched scars on the field past which we were now walking – 'and if you shout at them, they go away.'

Now we were almost back at the houses, and I tried to make sense of what I had seen. It was all a slurry of raw material, artefacts and folklore carrying me back 50 years, 100 years, 800 years, but with nothing to anchor the talk to history. My first excitement at the solid evidence – Mongol flag-holders! Drinking troughs! – gave way to a more sober assessment of possibilities. Campaigning Mongols didn't need to make stone drinking troughs. Perhaps these were just grain-rollers and millstones and pounding bowls left over from a century or two back, when there had been a temple and a large working community of farmers.

But that still left the legends, and the place itself: a secret valley with its medicinal plants, one them perhaps considered powerful enough to save the life of an ailing conqueror.

I was lucky. But if you, reader, go there, I'm afraid you will be too late. Those who remember what was once said about this place will be gone to villages and towns outside the valley. Eventually, as China's economy grows, there will be fewer who will take the long walk over the mountains to look for medicinal plants. The paths will become overgrown, the fields will vanish under saplings, the houses will fall, the blight of firs will claim the open spaces. All that visitors will experience will be the fenced road and a tourist camp where guides make claims that no-one can substantiate about a mountain without trails. Even if historians and archaeologists come, who will remember, who will show them where the Training Place, the Command Centre, the Medical Treatment Place and the Sitting Place once were?

13

TO A SECRET GRAVE

WE NOW ENTER UPON THE FEW DAYS IN THE HIGH SUMMER OF
1227 when the fate of Eurasia hung in the balance. The
murder of one emperor, the death of Genghis himself, the
destruction of a whole culture, the deaths of yet more
thousands of people – there is enough here to justify the
attention of historians, if only the details had been properly
recorded. But that 'if only' points to an element that gave
these events a significance of a different order. That element
is secrecy. It was the need for secrecy, foreseen by Genghis,
imposed by his entourage, that allowed his aims to be
fulfilled. Had news leaked out, all could have been lost –
enemies heartened, conquests lost, the half-formed Mongol
empire strangled almost at birth, the whole course of
Eurasian history turned in a different direction.

But how was an emperor on his deathbed, or his heirs in
obedience to his will, to arrange these matters? No-one can
know, of course, because of the deliberate veil of secrecy cast
over the drama. But scholars and archaeologists tinker with
the sound and lighting, and gradually, against a backdrop of

hills and mountains, we see ghosts go through motions and utter words that give an impression of what may have happened in and near the Liupan mountains almost 800 years ago.

To review where things stood in the second week of August 1227:

Genghis is on the verge of the final conquest of Xi Xia and has just occupied western Jin. This is to be a base from which to complete the conquest of all northern China, which will give him an empire running from the Pacific almost to Baghdad. The work of a lifetime is about to pay off, if all goes well. The emperor of Xi Xia is already on his way to capitulate. At this crucial moment Genghis falls ill, perhaps with the typhus brought by troops in their march southward. Historians generally agree that the illness struck some 100 kilometres south of the Liupan mountains, in the county of Qing Shui, in today's Gansu province; but there is room for doubt, because the county's name is the same as that of the river that flows north to the Yellow River. Some claim that he actually died in Qing Shui county, a suggestion rejected by two scholars who have immersed themselves in the evidence, Xu Cheng and Yu Jun of Ningxia University.[1] Their approach, based on historical sources and archaeological findings, acts as a sort of bedrock for the folk memories of the farmers in the Liupan Shan.

Wherever the illness strikes, it's serious, and everyone near him knows it. It is impossible to hide the fact that the khan is suffering a sickness of some kind; but no hint of its gravity must leak out. So, on the first day of the last week of his life, Genghis is rushed in a closed cart into the hidden valley in the

[1] Xu Cheng and Yu Jun, 'Genghis Khan's Palace in the Liupan Shan', *Journal of Ningxia University*, Yinchuan, 3, 1993.

Liupan mountains, where secrecy can be guaranteed, and where there are troops to take his orders and, if necessary, gallop out over the hidden mountain ways to attack Xi Xia and Jin. Here, too, he can be given whatever desperate remedies could be devised from the forest's medicinal plants.

Nothing works. Death approaches.

But for a few days, according to one Chinese source, the *Yuan-shi*, Genghis is still the strategist, planning for the future. His instructions were clear. In one version of these events, written by the Arabic historian Rashid ad-Din a couple of generations later, Genghis says: 'Do not let my death be known. Do not weep or lament in any way, so that the enemy shall not know anything about it. But when the ruler of the Tanguts and the population leave the city at the appointed hour, annihilate them all.'

And then, as Chinese sources record, Genghis lays out the strategy by which Jin must be defeated, as a prelude to the conquest of all China. But now, suddenly, the vision is blurred by approaching death. His entourage is face to face with possible catastrophe. The emperor of Xi Xia, on his way from Yinchuan, may well have no victor to surrender to. If he hears the news, he will at once turn round, and consider how to save himself and his kingdom. His best chance would be to turn instantly to Jin, join forces against a common enemy, destroy what has been achieved and kill Genghis's grand strategy for future conquest stone dead.

There is only one possible course of action. Everything must go forward as planned. No hint of the truth must leak out. It is vital, therefore, that the Xi Xia emperor arrive, capitulate, and then become the first of his treacherous people to die.

But the plot needs careful handling. These are a religious people. Whatever Xian's political role, he carries the aura of a great religious tradition, one that Genghis and his followers respect. In *The Secret History* Xian is called by a Mongol version of his religious title, Iluhu Burkhan, 'Exalted Holy

One', acknowledging his role as both temporal and spiritual leader. It would not be quite the thing to murder a living Buddha, any more than medieval kings undertook the murder of archbishops casually. Such an act needed dressing up. Henry II claimed Becket's death was all a terrible mis-understanding. Genghis was also capable of playing with words. To turn Xian from honoured prelate into an expend-able political figure, Genghis proclaimed that the Exalted Holy One would henceforth be known by the Buddhist title of Sidurgu (Faithful One). It seemed flattering, a due acknowledgement of his submission. In fact, it was a death sentence in disguise. A faithful vassal? A ruler who had led his people in resistance for the last six months? For such faith-fulness, death would be the only proper reward.

Where was this endgame to be played out? Not near Yinchuan, for Genghis was far to the south. Certainly not in the secret base hidden in the Liupan mountains. It so happens that there is a suitable site on open ground close by, which, I believe, had already been set up for an entirely different purpose.

Between Guyuan and the Liupan mountains, the road passes over low terraced hills and through a line of baked-earth houses, which is about all there is to Kaicheng, a village sustained by its wheat, barley, flax and vegetables. On nearby slopes, two-wheeled tractors putt-putt past haystacks that look like enormous loaves of brown bread. It was not always such a backwater, nor will it remain so. Just over the hill, a dam is being built to supply the whole region with power and fresh drinking water. But the dam is not the only thing that will restore Kaicheng to fame and glory.

A sign in English and Chinese pointed up a track to the right: 'Ancient Ruins of Kaicheng'. At first glance there was nothing there but wheat fields on their terraces and a field of tomatoes being weeded by a lone Hui woman in a white headscarf, against the Liupan mountains edging the horizon with a wavy line of green. The only sounds were a twittering skylark, a distant tractor and the scratch of hoe on earth.

Mr Yan explained what I was looking at. The vague shapes beneath the flowing wheat were once walls, making a square some 3–4 kilometres in circumference. In the thirteenth century Genghis's grandson, Khubilai, the khan whose conquests realized Genghis's dreams, built this into a provincial headquarters that must have rivalled Guyuan, 20 kilometres away. It was further developed by one of Khubilai's thirteen sons, Mangala the Prince of An-xi (in Shansi province), and Mangala's son in his turn was based here in 1297, in charge of the area's defences with 10,000 troops. But there are no records of what the town was like exactly, because in 1306 an earthquake destroyed it. Five thousand people died and the remainder fled; the baked-earth buildings were washed away, and Kaicheng vanished from sight and memory.

Now Chinese archaeologists are on the point of re-discovery, in what will be Ningxia's greatest work of excavation. The government had committed 100 million *yuan* ($12.5 million or £7.8 million) to the project. I wondered if they would be seeking international backing, imagining the place flooded with Japanese, American and European scientists. But China has experts enough, thank you very much. 'These are Chinese ancestors,' said Mr Yan, with no hint of any Mongolian connection. It should be up to the Chinese, working over the next ten years, to reveal the roots of the city and assess the objects that lie beneath the soil.

They are there all right. The Hui woman paused in her hoeing to answer my question. No, she had never come across anything, 'but two years ago an old man found a vase.'

'Where?'

'Right here, in this tomato field.'

Not only the odd vase; other workers had also found many

bits of tiles glazed in yellow, the imperial colour. Mr Yan had some in his museum in Guyuan, and was certain much more would be discovered about Khubilai's fortress.

Now to the point: Why would Khubilai build himself a headquarters in Kaicheng, when Guyuan was already there 20 kilometres away, with its walls and gatehouses? Possibly because Kaicheng was in effect a sacred site, chosen by his grandfather in the spring of 1227. There were sound reasons for Genghis's choice: it was safely away from Guyuan's intrusive inhabitants; within easy reach of the troops secluded in the Liupan mountains a day's ride away; and out in the open, where a vast army could gather without the hindrance of subjects, or buildings, or narrow gorges. Here, I suggest, Genghis decreed a temporary palace where the Mongols could receive the embassy that came from Jin seeking peace. And then, by happy chance, this new HQ, with its tent-palaces and garrison, found a second use, as a base for the meeting with the emperor of Xi Xia when he arrived to make his final capitulation, and meet his doom.

This whole charade would have been carefully orchestrated. The sources agree that five things happened in quick succession:

- the Xi Xia emperor submitted;
- he came for an audience with Genghis;
- he was granted a new title;
- Genghis had him killed;
- Genghis himself died.

The sources do not, however, make equally clear the order in which these things happened; so what follows is only the most likely of several possible scenarios.

Xian, the Xi Xia emperor, arrives at the tent-palace in Kaicheng, and is greeted with a strange circumstance: during his audience with the khan he is made to remain 'outside the door of the tent'. And during the audience, *The Secret History* relates, Genghis 'felt sick'. This is very odd. Surely the khan, the creator of what was already an empire larger than Rome's, would not willingly deal with his vanquished foe in such a fashion, when by doing so he must have raised suspicions in the emperor's mind, and in the minds of his entourage? There is only one plausible conclusion to be drawn. Neither Genghis nor his aides and counsellors had any choice, because Genghis was simply not fit enough to hold an audience. Of course, the Tangut emperor was going to be killed anyway; but it was important that he make his submission and offer his gifts, completing the ritual of formal surrender that would hand his kingdom to Genghis. And it was important that the impression remain in the minds of those whose lives were spared – and in the minds of ordinary Mongols – that Genghis was still in control.

In fact, this extraordinary drama – the doomed emperor with his horsemen and laden carts, the surrounding screen of generals and family members, the great imperial tent with its closed flaps – only makes sense if we assume that behind the curtain Genghis is so near death that he cannot be seen—

—*or is already dead*. This is the possibility that strikes me as the more likely. Genghis survived only a week after the onset of his illness. It would have taken the Xi Xia emperor, with his entourage and laden carts, some two weeks to cover the 300 kilometres from his capital to Kaicheng. Meanwhile, Genghis has fallen ill and been taken into the Liupan base for treatment. Surely only his death would have brought his treatment to an end? And only in the security of that valley would his grieving entourage be able to make the arrangements to keep his death secret, and then spirit their 'sick' lord out for the showdown in Kaicheng.

Xian, puzzled but compliant, lays out his offerings, the first being a set of golden Buddhas, followed by a cornucopia of other gifts, each one in a group of nine, the propitious number: nine golden bowls, nine silver ones, nine boys, nine girls, nine geldings, nine camels and much more, all in nines, and all laid out according to 'kind and colour'.

Then Tolun saw to the execution. The killing of rulers, like the killing of all nobles, demanded the observance of a ritual long recognized by the Mongols. No blood was to be shed. Death could be by the snapping of the neck, or by strangulation, or (as in this case, if we are to believe *The Secret History*) by suffocation. However it was done, it was done in secret, for no details leaked out of how or where the Xi Xia ruler died, or how many died with him.

It was only later, in the more formal Chinese sources, that a few facts were recorded. Genghis apparently died after a week of illness, in the Year of the Pig (1227), on the twelfth day of the seventh lunar month: 25 August. But a certain scepticism is in order. Those Chinese accounts that seem most reliable date from a decade later, at best, after the Mongol conquest of Jin was complete, and not all others agree on the exact day. And, of course, since no-one knows when Genghis was born, estimates of his age vary from 62 to 72; 65 is the most widely accepted, giving 1162 as the year of his birth. *The Secret History*, the most intimate source and the one that might have been expected to mark such a momentous event with some special statement, says nothing at all on this subject, except that 'he ascended to Heaven' – proof enough, I think, that the time and manner of the khan's demise were to remain a state secret.

Secrecy cast the field open to rumour. Stories multiplied that Genghis died besieging some city or other; or survived until the surrender of Xia. And later – decades later, centuries later – poets marked the great man's passing, turning rumour and folk tales into verse. Four hundred years later an Ordos prince, Sagang Tsetsen,[2] Sagang the Wise, turned the stories

[2] Or Ssanang or Sagan Ssetsen: transliterations vary.

into his *Jewelled Chronicle*, a 'History of the Eastern Mongols and their Royal House'. Another anonymous work, the *Golden Summary*, was compiled a few decades earlier and covers much the same ground. Both are no more histories than are Arthurian legends. The few facts are invisible beneath a tangle of post-Genghis lore, much of it Buddhist.

In Sagang's account, for instance, the Xi Xia king reveals his power by turning himself into a snake in the morning, a tiger at midday and a child at night. Genghis out-transforms his enemy – becoming bird, lion and sky-ruler – and captures him. But, when the Tangut king is stabbed by Genghis's followers, he proves to be invulnerable. 'You cannot harm me with ordinary weapons,' he says, going on, in one of those amazingly stupid admissions that are the hallmark of fairytales: 'But in the soles of my boots I have a weapon of fine thrice-beaten steel, with which I can be killed.' With these words, he pulls out the sword and speaks again: 'Now you can kill me. If milk runs from my body, it will be a bad sign for you. If blood, then it's bad for your descendants.' And one more thing: if Genghis takes his wife, he had better 'search her whole body carefully'.

So Genghis kills him and takes his wife, Gurbelchin. She is of a beauty that astounds all. But, she says, she was once much more beautiful, before she was sullied by the dust of Genghis's troops. So she bathes in the Yellow River, during which she is visited by a bird from her father's house to whom she predicts her own death by drowning. She emerges as beautiful as before her dusty encounter with Mongol soldiers. That night, having not apparently been searched very thoroughly, she 'did his body damage, from which he became weak and giddy', then duly drowned herself. Khan and followers deliver great speeches, after which Genghis 'ascends to his father in Heaven'.

There are many other versions. Here is one that was told to Owen Lattimore, traveller and Mongolist extraordinary. A brief word is due here about the legendary Lattimore, a man unrivalled in his experience and expertise, famous among Mongols, who nicknamed him Solitary Glass because he wore a monocle. I met him only a couple of times, when in the 1960s he addressed the newly founded Anglo-Mongolian Society, a rather small group of scholars, travellers and students. I was awed by him, because I knew that he had been driven from the United States, victimized in the most brutal way by Joe McCarthy for having 'lost China' to the communists. He had come to see us from Leeds, where he had set up a department of Mongolian studies. I don't recall a monocle. He was small, I remember, intense, generous of spirit towards a callow youth; the best possible inspiration. This is the story told to him by his Mongol companion Arash, from the Ordos:

Where is Genghis Khan? He is not dead. What happened was this. Genghis Khan had a dream of red blood on white snow, the reddest red and the whitest white. He called his wise men and asked them the meaning of the dream. They said it meant the fairest of all maidens. Then he summoned all the tributary nations and asked them where was the fairest of all maidens. They said: there is such a maiden. She is the daughter of the King of the City of the Red Wall, in the country of Tangut. Then Genghis sent a messenger and asked for the maiden. The king of the red-walled city said to the messenger: Certainly if Holy Genghis asks for my daughter, I shall give her. But secretly he said to his daughter: Here is a knife, very small and very sharp. Hide it in your clothes, and when the time comes you know what to do. Then they brought the girl to Genghis, and he went in to sleep with her, but as he lay with her she took out the knife and castrated him. Genghis cried out when he felt the cut, and people came in, but he only said to them: Take this girl away; I wish to sleep. He slept and from that sleep he has never wakened – but that was six hundred or seven hundred years ago, and would not Holy Genghis heal himself? When he is healed he will awake and save his people.

From this morass of Tibetan, Chinese, Buddhist and Mongolian lore, the only firm information to be gleaned is the enormity of the loss. Apparently, as time went by, people had been unwilling to accept their god–king's death as natural, and turned it into a story of revenge and tragedy with their hero undone, like Samson, by a woman and a foreigner. For the Mongols, the stories supplied a psychological need, still faintly felt, to explain the loss of power. Everyone knows the tale, now embellished in many ways, of how the evil queen did something terrible to Genghis and then cast herself into the Yellow River, which the Mongols still call the Queen's River to this day.

So died one of the most remarkable leaders in history. He differed from most others in this: the closer you were to him, the more admirable he seemed.

One way to understand him is to look at the experiences of his youth. He had been flotsam on an ocean of grass, a louse on a mountainside, and found that the key to survival lay in what he lacked: power. Power to befriend, to command, to fight, to win, to rule, to rebuild what had been lost, and then to go on to build a security in this uncertain universe that could never, ever be threatened.

But this is hindsight talking, and modern psychology. A therapist, working on his case up in Eternal Heaven, might explain that his drive all came from a deprived childhood, but I doubt if Genghis's spirit would agree, for that would be to deny the force that, in his view, lay outside himself. His personality was infused with the certainty of being divinely ordained for world leadership. Though help was needed to decide the means – through the reading of a sheep's fire-cracked shoulder-bone, Buddhist astrology, prayer on the sacred mountain on which he had been granted insight – the predestined end was clear: to achieve unprecedented power, an earthly power that would do justice to the heavenly one.

Power was the key. To win power, to hold power, to increase power: this was his purpose. He was not the first, nor the last, to win a following by a combination of charisma and faith, able to inspire in others the same certainty that the will of Khökh Tenger, the Blue Heaven – the Eternal Heaven, as it became – was equated with his own. What was extraordinary was the maintenance over 50 years of a balance between evolving personality, changing conditions and growing power – holding three variables in constant tension, never over-balancing into corruption or paranoia, never losing hold of the reins of power, never allowing events to dictate an agenda. This was something new, and fortunately unique, in human history. Call it Eternal Heaven leadership, to which the following is a quick guide.

The Ten Rules of Eternal Heaven Leadership

1 Reward loyalty

In dealing with his people, Genghis never forgot a generous act. When he came to power, he told the man who had shielded him when he escaped captivity: 'In my dreams in the black of night and in my breast in the bright day, I recalled the good that you had done me.' As part of his revolution he honoured the brave and loyal, whatever their status. The bonds of loyalty were not easily forged, and had to be main-tained by every means possible (including blackmail; his bodyguard, the sons of his officers, were in effect hostages). But once convinced of a man's loyalty, he delegated brilliantly; leaving, for instance, the rule of conquered territories in northern China and the conquest of the rest to his viceroy Mukhali. Under his leadership, taxes were raised to support poverty-stricken followers. This was not down to any foreshadowings of socialist or democratic impulses, or even humanitarian feelings, but on the contrary embodied a supreme traditionalism, the basic duties of the successful tribal leader carried to a logical conclusion.

2   Be austere

He remained the tough nomad, despising luxury for himself, honouring simplicity. It was said of him that he would give his own clothes to a Mongol in need. He was a hard man all his life, fit for the hunt until well into his sixties, rooted in the mountains and grasslands of his youth.

3   Exercise self-control

One of his most extraordinary characteristics was his ability to control his anger, and allow others their say. When an uncle defected to a rival tribe, he angrily ordered his death, but when his two brothers-in-arms Boorchu and Mukhali joined with his adopted brother Shigi to reprimand him – to kill your uncle would be to extinguish your own fire, he's the only reminder of your father, he didn't understand, give him a chance, and on and on – Genghis began to sob. 'Let it be,' he said, and fell silent.

4   Find talent where you can, and use it

Under Genghis, herdsmen became generals, enemies became officials. To non-Mongols who served him, he was just as generous as to his own kind. He admired and rewarded talent without prejudice, given only that it was exercised with loyalty. One of those who 'drank the muddy waters of the Baljuna' with Genghis was a Muslim merchant, Jafar, later an ambassador and a regent in northern China. As well as Muslims, Chinese (Chu-tsai, of course being the prime example), Nestorians and Buddhists were all to be found in his service.

5 Kill enemies without compunction

To those who were not bound to him or who opposed him, Genghis was merciless. Once convinced of disloyalty, even in a relative or former friend, he was a ruthless executioner. If he never forgot a favour, he never forgave an insult; and resistance insulted not only him, but Heaven above. The Merkits who abducted his wife, Börte, were 'divided until they were no more'. The Taychiuts, who had captured him, were made to blow in the wind like ashes. Of the Tatars, blamed for the death of his father, he decreed, 'We must seek revenge for our ancestors. Let them be killed!' Vengeance was a Heaven-sent duty, and, as his power increased, so did his retributions – against the Jin, against those Muslim leaders and cities that resisted, and against the Tanguts of Xi Xia. There was none of the magnanimity that military leaders in urban cultures often showed to their opposites, acknowledging that they shared the same traditions and might, in future, be allies. For Genghis, an enemy that did not at once defer was alien, hardly human, fit for destruction without second thought. Naturally, those on the receiving end judged him only in these terms, as a bloodthirsty barbarian.

The Arabic historian Rashid ad-Din summarizes his attitude in a famous anecdote. Once when Genghis was out riding with Boorchu and other comrades, he asked what they considered man's greatest happiness. After some debate, they replied that it lay in falconry – a sturdy gelding in spring, a falcon on the wrist, what could be more wonderful? 'You are wrong,' replied Genghis. 'Man's greatest good fortune is to chase and defeat his enemy, seize all his possessions, leave his married women weeping and wailing, ride his gelding, use the bodies of his women as night-shirts and supports, gazing upon and kissing their rosy breasts, sucking their lips which are as sweet as the berries of the breasts.' Famous words, because they capture a truth . . .

6   *Oppose cruelty*

... but only a partial truth. Those words were written 50 years after Genghis's death, when authenticity was already muddied by folklore. And it also suggests something else: a joy in the suffering of others. Yet no-one accused him of wanton cruelty. Mohammed, the Shah of Khwarezm, tortured, as did his son Jalal; but Genghis did not. Indeed, on several occasions he specifically ordered restraint. There may be no trace of those virtues we derive from Christian suffering – tolerance, forgiveness, loving one's enemies – but there was no trace of inquisitorial sadism either.

7   *Adapt, and be open to new ways of ruling*

Genghis had rather more subtlety to him than an image of mere barbarity suggests. If a leader is judged by the men he employs and the decisions he makes, then Genghis deserves some credit for seeing the benefits of writing and bureaucracy, and briefing the men he needed to take records and conduct administration – quite   remarkable   for   an   illiterate warrior–herdsman. In brief, he matured. With each leap in power, from clan, to tribe, to nation, to empire, he grew in stature – a progress that is the more astonishing given that he was the first of his people to make this jump and that his only mentors were his enemies.

8   *Know that you have divine backing*

And at every stage he never doubted Heaven's support; for every stage in his development, from louse to emperor, gave him further proof of it. During the campaign against Khwarezm, before the attack on one city, he sent envoys with a written message quoting the very words of Heaven: 'Let the emirs and the great ones and the common people know this: that all the face of the earth from the going up of the sun to his going down, I have given it unto thee.' It is an ideology with a simple and incontrovertible assumption: that all nations were already subject to Mongol rule by the will of Heaven before their conquest. Foreign rulers just had to acknowledge this simple truth, and all would be well.

9   Make your followers and heirs believe it too

Yeh-lü Chu-tsai joined Genghis because he thought the khan possessed the Mandate of Heaven. Success proved it: the conquest of Jin was a feat 'no human power could have achieved', and therefore released Chu-tsai from his previous obligations. Güyük, Ogedei's son and successor as khan (1246–8), wrote to Pope Innocent IV: 'Eternal Heaven has slain and annihilated those lands and peoples because they have adhered neither to Genghis Khan nor to the *khagan* [i.e. the khan of khans, Güyük himself], both of whom have been sent to make known Heaven's command . . . How could anybody seize or kill by his own power contrary to Heaven's command?'

10   Respect freedom of belief

Why Genghis had been chosen was a mystery to him, as was the nature of the godhead that had chosen him. With no clear way to understand Heaven and Heaven's will, respect was due to all who sought that understanding (unless this con-flicted with Rules Nos 8 and 9, the ones concerning divine backing; in which case Rule No. 5 – extermination – applied).

From Alexander to Stalin, the greatest leaders and the vilest dictators have had some of these traits. Did any have all of them? Pick a few, and consider. Jesus's kingdom was not of this earth. Napoleon was more brilliant in military and political leadership, but made no claims to divine backing; and he ended in defeat, with no empire. Mohammed balanced religion with military genius, but the briefly unified empire of Islam was less his creation than that of his heirs. Alexander comes close, though he never matched Genghis in ruthlessness. Perhaps his tutor Aristotle constrained him with lectures on ethics; or perhaps, since he died at half Genghis's age, he just never had a proper chance.

Leaderless and with most of their cities in Mongol hands, the Tanguts fell easy prey to their conquerors. Yinchuan was looted, tiles torn from the roofs of the royal tombs, the bones of Tangut kings dug up, the people scattered, Genghis's will meticulously fulfilled. Information on the level of destruction is scanty. *The Secret History* offers only a terse sentence: 'Because the Tangut people failed to keep their promises, Genghis Khan hunted them down a second time.' Chinese accounts are virtually non-existent, for neither the Mongols nor any later Chinese dynasty would have mourned the disappearance of a rival empire. The Tanguts almost vanished from history, along with most of their records, leaving only a few isolated pockets that failed, in the end, to save the script and language. Though this culture has now begun to re-emerge, with the decipherment of Tangut script, it is unlikely anyone will unearth an account of the carnage, because there was no-one left to write it.

What of Genghis's body? The question has no final answer, because there is no grave. Instead there are two separate traditions, which underlie respectively two competing claims by China and Mongolia, each determined to be the true heir of Genghis. The tradition in China focuses mainly on Genghis's accoutrements. It is in direct conflict with the second tradition, which deals mainly with his body, claiming that the corpse was brought back across the Gobi to the homeland of the Mongols and buried in a secret grave.

But there is nothing certain about any of this. It was high summer. Bodies decay fast in August. Irrespective of the need for secrecy, the return would need to be accomplished as quickly as possible. The cortège had 1,600 kilometres to cover, which for a cart travelling with a degree of care and attention would take some three weeks. The body would have been preserved as much as possible with herbs, but the Mongols knew nothing of mummification. It would have been a hurried trip.

The Secret History says nothing about the funeral cortège or the burial, jumping straight over the year following the death to the great meeting on the Kherlen which confirmed Ogedei as Genghis's heir. It is inconceivable that such an emotional event as the transport and burial of their khan would somehow slip the minds of those who compiled *The Secret History*. The only possible explanation is that the whole matter was deliberately omitted; and the only possible explanation for such a taboo is twofold: first, to preserve what had originally been a state secret, namely the death and progress of the cortège; and second, to hide the knowledge of the burial-site from all but the most inner of innermost circles.

Again, this strategy allowed legend to flourish. Soon, as with the death, folklore began to fill the information gap with stories, one of which was that the route of the cortège was marked by slaughter. This tale was related by two historians, the Arabic writer Rashid ad-Din and Marco Polo. Rashid says bluntly: 'On the way they killed every living being they met.' Here is what Marco Polo writes, in his intimate, persuasive style:

Let me tell you a strange thing too. When they are carrying the body of any emperor to be buried with the others, the convoy that goes with the body doth put to the sword all whom they fall in with on the road, saying, 'Go and wait upon your Lord in the other world!' For they do in sooth believe that all such as they slay in this manner do go to serve their Lord in the other world. They do the same with the horses . . . And I tell you as a certain truth, that when Mangou Kaan [Mönkhe Khan, Genghis's grandson] died, more than 20,000 persons, who chanced to meet the body on its way, were slain in the manner I have told.

The stature of these two writers and the prejudices of their readers ensured that countless histories since, both popular and academic, would take the story as gospel, without further comment. It is so *right*, somehow, that the final journey of the barbarian chief who had slain so many hundreds of thousands should involve more deaths. The authors who have accepted the idea include Ralph Fox, Leo de Hartog, Paul Ratchnevsky and Michael Prawdin, some injecting even more drama into the image. Prawdin, in his highly imaginative *The Mongol Empire*, wrote: 'All living creatures that were so unlucky as to be spied by these horsemen, whether man or beast, bird or snake, were ruthlessly hunted down and slaughtered.'

I don't believe it. It is not in any of the Mongol or Chinese sources. Friar William of Rubrouck, who was at Mönkhe's court in Karakorum in 1253–5, doesn't mention the story. Nor does Juvaini, who was in Karakorum at the same time as Friar William. Burial of treasure, of slain slaves and concubines, etc., yes; even live burials, possibly. But killing every living thing along the route of the funeral cortège?

Look first at the foundation of the story. Both Rashid and Polo were writing 50 years or more after the event. Rashid, though he had access to Mongol sources, did not speak Mongolian; he relied on the help of his master, Ghazan (r.1295–1304, five generations removed from Genghis), and the ambassador from the Mongol court in Beijing. Perhaps it was from one of them that he heard the story, which he relates in a mere ten words (in translation). And Polo did not attribute the murders specifically to Genghis's cortège, only to 'any emperor' and specifically to Mönkhe (who died fourteen years before Polo arrived in China; he did not see the funeral). What he wrote of them was hearsay, with not a little hype.

One justification for this alleged act was that it kept the secret of Genghis's death. But the argument is nonsensical. A secret was certainly to be kept, as we can deduce from the sources' silence on the subject. But it defies belief that killing people, let alone 'every living thing', would preserve secrecy. Did this supposedly apply to Chinese and Tanguts? Well, possibly; since they were considered inferior, and if you assume a suitably deserted route. But what happened in Mongolia? Are we to assume that the guards killed the very people of whom their lord had been so solicitous? On the steppe news travels fast, and everyone knows everyone else. On a clear day you can see for ever. Nothing would be more obvious than an immense cortège, and nothing would better advertise the fact that the cortège had something to hide than a mass of murders. Who, witnessing aggression on this scale, would stay around to be caught? How on earth could the guards guarantee to capture and kill every eye-witness? And the bodies: they could not be left to mystify and terrify the next passers-by. Would a royal cortège load itself with corpses? I think not.

The best way to preserve secrecy is to travel fast, travel small and not advertise the fact that you have something to hide. There would not, of course, be any vast, four-wheeled, 22-ox, tent-bearing wagon (remember the ravines crossing the Qing Shui, and the Yellow River itself). Far more likely was the two-wheeled camel-drawn hearse mentioned in the folklore gathered by Sagang the Wise and in the *Golden Summary*.

The route of the cortège is unknown, of course. It must have headed up the Qing Shui to the Yellow River. Then where?

There is a clue in one of the incidents Sagang relates. The

wagon sinks up to its axles in mud, and a Mongol general sings to his holy lord, lion among men, born by the will of Eternal Heaven, about how everything he holds dear lies ahead of him. Palaces, queens, children, people, nobles, subjects, water, comrades-in-arms, place of birth – 'They are all there, my lord!' And lo – for this dirge, one of the most emotional of Mongol poems, is quasi-biblical in its style – the lord heard, and granted his blessing, and the groaning wagon moved, and the people rejoiced, and accompanied the khan's body onward to the great homeland.

This incident happened, if it happened at all, in the 'Mona' or 'Muna' mountains. These are the two ranges now known as the Yin mountains that hem the Yellow River's great bend north of the Ordos. To the west, between mountains and desert, is a low-lying area where marshes and meandering side-streams make a sort of midriver delta, just the sort of ground in which a two-wheeled covered wagon might stick.

If the incident did happen, then the cortège would probably have been heading east, to join the route covered so many times by Genghis in his campaigns against Jin. This eastern route, through a region where the gravel plains of the Gobi give way to grassland, had become a sort of royal road. Today, part of it is crossed by the railway line that runs up to Ulaanbaatar from the border crossing points of Erenhot (Erlian in Chinese) and Zamyn Uud ('Door of the Road'). It is still a main road, though paved on the Chinese side only to the border and a few kilometres beyond. At Zamyn Uud the tarmac and cement stop and tracks fan out over the Gobi. Trailer-trucks from China, absurdly overladen, break away from the long queue at customs and heave themselves off at walking pace, belching their smoky way over the undulating Gobi to Ulaanbaatar, Irkutsk, Almaty and beyond.

A funeral cortège following this route would not head for Ulaanbaatar. It might perhaps make a dog's-leg via Karakorum, now beginning its transformation into imperial capital. Most likely, given the commitment to secrecy, it would strike out over hard-packed gravel, heading almost due north for three more days, until, on grassland now, it crossed the shallow and firm-bedded Kherlen to old Avraga. Then onwards for the final journey northwards along the Kherlen, skirting the hills of Countryside Island, to the Khenti's sacred heart, the forests and bare uplands of Burkhan Khaldun.

14

THE OUTER REACHES
OF EMPIRE

AT THE TIME OF HIS DEATH, GENGHIS RULED FROM THE PACIFIC TO
the Caspian – an empire four times the size of Alexander's,
twice the size of Rome's, larger than any nation today except
Russia. And it was only half complete. By 1300 the Mongols
would double Genghis's conquests, adding what is now the
rest of China, Korea, Tibet, Pakistan, Iran, most of Turkey,
the Caucasus (Georgia, Armenia, Azerbaijan), most of habitable Russia, Ukraine and half of Poland. They would reach
beyond, with campaigns into western Europe, Egypt and Japan.
A Mongol warrior who scouted the Vienna woods as a youth
in 1241 could in theory have travelled almost 10,000 kilometres to survive the storms that saved Japan from Mongol
ships in 1274 and 1281; and perhaps even have heard tales of
the sack of Burma and the landing on Java a decade later.

Twenty-eight million square kilometres; one-fifth of the
world's land area. Considering that no-one in Eurasia knew
of the Americas or Australia, and very few of Africa, it must
have seemed quite possible that the whole known world
would soon be under Mongol sway, just as Genghis had

THE RIGHT STUFF, MONGOL-STYLE

Child-jockeys near the end of a 20-kilometre National Day race. Such races ensure that Mongolia remains a nation of horsemen, as it was in the days of Genghis Khan. The winning riders will get prizes and be widely honoured, while the horses will become treasures for stock-breeders.

IMAGES OF HOLINESS

Everywhere Genghis went on his campaigns, he saw enduring religious images, like the great rock-carved buddhas of Xumi Shan (*below left and above*) and the 53-metre one in Bamyan, Afghanistan (*below right*, now a heap of rubble, thanks to the Taleban). In old age, Genghis (or perhaps his Chinese advisers) proclaimed his love of spirituality and wisdom. He summoned the Taoist adept, Ch'ang-ch'un, who travelled by carriage from China to Afghanistan to see him (*top left*). The only known thirteenth-century portrait of Genghis (*bottom left*), done some 30 years after his death, idealizes him as a simple sage.

IN THE HIDDEN VALLEY

The entrance to the Liupan Shan (*above*) leads
over a pass (*left*) to the valley that contains the
deserted village and 'Genghis Khan's Command
Centre' (*below*).

The deserted village

Mongol trough – or recent mortar?

Li Bocheng …

… and Yu Wuhe

Medicinal plant gatherer and his find (*inset*)

TWO LEGENDS RECALLED

A modern Mongol Chinese painting (*above*) shows Genghis's bier stuck in the mud, an incident that may reflect a real event in the Ordos near China's Yellow River. The incident later became attached to the legend that Genghis chose the Ordos for his place of burial.

An Indian Mughal painting of about 1600 (*left*) recalls the legend, popularized by Marco Polo, that Genghis's funeral procession was marked by the murder of all those who observed it. The legend is as spurious as the picture. The clothing, the guns and the horse-armour are all as Indian as the elephant, and all very sixteenth century.

The Almsgiver's Wall,
not far from several
sites associated with
Genghis, has been
claimed as his burial-
place. In fact, it
almost certainly
predates him, perhaps
by centuries.

A MOBILE PALACE

Travelling tent-palaces like this were seen by the first European travellers to arrive in Mongolia in the mid-thirteenth century. The one *above* is a drawing done for the Yule–Cordier edition of Marco Polo's travels. Several modern reconstructions stand in Ulaanbaatar today. The one shown *below*, 10 metres wide, was built for *Genghis Khan*, the Mongolian feature film.

THE EMPIRE SUPREME

Genghis's heirs built the new capital of Karakorum, of which the only surviving relic is the stone tortoise which was the base of a pillar. The Erdene Dzu monastery in the background was built 300 years later, using Karakorum's stones. In 1241–2, Mongol soldiers shattered the Polish army at Liegnitz (Legnica) (*above left),* and went on to destroy the Hungarians at Mohi, an event recalled by the grim 1992 monument (*above centre*), raised to mark the 750th anniversary of the catastrophe. In 1281, a Mongol invasion fleet was attacked by Japanese (*above right*) and then destroyed by the *kamikaze*, the 'divine wind'.

WORSHIPPING THE KHAN

The main building of the Mausoleum of Genghis Khan in the Ordos, Inner Mongolia (*below*), includes domes that suggest both Mongolian *gers* and Chinese pagodas. Before it was built in 1956, Mongolians worshipped Genghis's supposed relics in a mobile shrine photographed by Owen Lattimore in the 1930s (*left*). Today, they can offer incense and prayers at the Mausoleum's huge marble statue of Genghis (*right*). Photography is banned. I had to take the picture outside the door. The rituals have been recorded by the engagingly cheerful Sainjirgal (*bottom*).

Baatar

Goyo

Khishig

On the Holy Mountain

The bald ridge of Khan Khenti – Burkhan Khaldun, as almost everyone agrees – rears up from surrounding forests. A dot of snow has survived the summer,

Bogged down

On the Threshold

Threshold from far side

Tumen and Erdene, fresh

Tumen, still game

Site of Kamala's temple

Valley of the Bogd

Ovoo overlooking Bogd

Stony circle, on low-lying
ground near the Kherlen

Stony circles – or graves?
– near the summit

Stuck for the ninth time
on Threshold, prior to exit

THE MEMORY LIVES ON

In China: Genghis's rise is commemorated in a children's comic book. Here Temujin (young Genghis) and Boorchu rescue stolen horses – though the artist has never used a bow: it takes three fingers, not finger and thumb, to draw one.

In Mongolia: A Genghis banner above a National Day crowd in Sukhbaatar Square, central Ulaanbaatar, flanks the other great hero, Sukhbaatar himself, who restored Mongolia's independence in 1924.

planned, and Heaven ordained. The fact that one man, Genghis's grandson Khubilai, was nominal master of this vast estate is one of history's most astonishing facts.

How the empire arose and declined is a subject that has absorbed lifetimes and filled libraries. It is reason enough to make anyone wary of claiming to be a Mongolist, because to have access to primary sources alone such a person would need to read Mongol in both Cyrillic and vertical scripts, Chinese, Arabic, Persian, Korean, Japanese, Russian, Tibetan and Georgian – and Latin, of course, in which most reports by Europeans were written. So this survey of Genghis's legacy is a gallop, slowing to a trot to look more closely at the two opposite ends of the empire he founded.

Genghis had allocated his domain to his sons, by tradition granting Jochi, the eldest, the section furthest from home, beyond the Aral Sea. But by the time the inheritance fell due Jochi was already dead, so his estates were further divided between two other sons, Orda and Batu. Central Asia, from the Aral Sea to Tibet, went to Chagadai. To Tolui, the youngest, were given his father's local pastures, again as tradition dictated – which in this case was most of Mongolia. Ogedei, now *khagan*, khan of khans, also ruled most of northern China and newly conquered Xi Xia as his personal domains; the as yet unsubdued part of Jin and, with luck, southern China would follow.

In northern China, as Genghis had foreseen, administration would be the key, once conquest was complete. The campaign had been put on hold by the war against Khwarezm, by the death of the great general Mukhali in 1223, and by Genghis's own death in 1227. Much ground had been lost. After a failed campaign in 1230–1, Ogedei followed his father's deathbed advice, made a deal with the Song, swept into Jin with the help of his younger brother Tolui and the great general Subedei, and started to besiege Kaifeng. Leaving the siege to Subedei, the two brother khans camped for the summer in hills near Beijing. Here Tolui died in unexplained circumstances, leaving Mongolia to Ogedei. In 1234 Kaifeng fell, all male members of the Jin were executed, and the Mongols were supreme in northern China.

What was to be done with this new estate? The Mongol leaders had been arguing among themselves since Ogedei's succession. The place was devastated, in ways comparable to the wreck of Khwarezm, on a scale hardly comprehensible today. A population of 40 million or so in the early thirteenth century, as recorded by the Jin, had dropped to about 10 million by 1234, when the Mongols made their first detailed records.[1] Mongol princes had torn communities apart for slaves; the temples were crowded with escaped prisoners, deserters and refugees. Several at the new court in Karakorum suggested that the simplest solution, in these chaotic circumstances, was genocide. What use were farmers? Their work was pointless, they owned nothing of worth and they were a source of opposition. They were of less value than cattle and horses; let them be replaced by cattle and horses. Best kill the lot, however many millions of them there were, and turn the land to pasture. It wouldn't take long for 10,000 warriors to slaughter 1,000 people each. Could have the whole country empty in no time.

It was Yeh-lü Chu-tsai who stopped this lunatic talk. Chu-tsai had for some years been deputy to Genghis's brother-in-law in the Chinese section of the khan's rudimentary secretariat, working with a team of scholars drafting decrees in Mongol, Chinese and, more lately, Tangut. He was

---

[1] It was bad, but perhaps not quite that bad. The numbers derived from the numbers of households: 7.6 million dropping to 1.7 million. But what was the size of a household? Perhaps, with the disruption of war, individuals survived the destruction of their households. Perhaps a Mongol Chinese household, swollen by refugees, was larger than a peacetime Jin Chinese household. Perhaps northern China was reduced not by 75% but only – only! – 50%, by migration as much as killing.

advancing in his life's work – to help Heaven along in its odd choice of ruler by transforming barbarity and ignorance into virtue and wisdom. His dream was both revolutionary and utopian, his raw material a shattered northern China. He sought to apply Confucius's rules for good government while at the same time promoting Buddhism to cultivate the mind, his ultimate goal being the creation of a society that transcended Confucianism, rather as idealistic communists foresaw a society that would evolve through socialism to perfect communism. He had made a good start. His people, acting as scribes, interpreters, envoys, astrologers and tax experts, had proved increasingly vital in governing what had been won. He had been on hand in several cities – Samarkand, Ling-wu, Kaifeng – to save libraries, treasures and scholars.

He proposed a plan to Ogedei. Well aware that Mongols had no use for Chinese civilization unless it offered material gain, he pointed out that if the peasants prospered, they could be taxed, and thus contribute to the economy. To this end, he drew up a plan for renewal and government such as China, let alone Mongolia, had never seen before. First, civil authority should be separated from the military, with its self-seeking and arbitrary brutalities. Jin would be divided into ten districts, each with its tax collection office to administer a land tax for peasants and a poll tax for city-dwellers, all to be paid in silk, silver or grain, all flowing to the government. The Taoist priesthood, puffed up in wealth and numbers by Genghis's personal tax exemptions, was reined in by taxes on temple businesses and by laws against further appropriations of Buddhist temples.

To all this, Mongol military leaders objected bitterly. But Chu-tsai, with Ogedei's backing, held firm, and in 1231 his first taxes came in, right on budget, to the value of 10,000 ingots of silver. Ogedei made him head of the secretariat's Chinese section on the spot, directly responsible to the

Mongol–Uighur section's boss, the same Chinqai who had guided the monk Ch'ang-ch'un to Genghis.

Taxes involved records, which were also vital for the allocation of land to the Mongol elite; hence the census of 1234–6, recorded in the Blue Book held by Genghis's adoptive brother Shigi, the one who may have supervised the editing of *The Secret History*. And administration demanded educated people. In 1233 Chu-tsai rescued from captivity scores of scholars and other notables, including a direct descendant of Confucius who was restored to office as magistrate in Confucius's birthplace in Shantung. He set up a government publishing house and a college for the sons of Chinese and Mongolian officials to build the next generation of scholars and administrators. He arranged for former Jin officials who had been enslaved to take qualifying examinations, with punishments for slave-owners who did not comply; 4,000 entered, 1,000 regained their freedom through employment.

Chu-tsai did not have things his own way for long. By the late 1230s Ogedei, a notorious drunkard, was increasingly incapable, authority being wielded by his ambitious and shrewd second wife, Toregene. Anti-Chinese factions at court objected to Chu-tsai's alien methods. Muslim merchants promised faster returns by becoming loan sharks, battening on the hapless Chinese, charging 100 per cent annual interest and seizing assets in lieu of payment. In 1239 a businessman, Abd al-Rahman, was put in charge of 'tax farming' in all former Jin territories, and the following year Chu-tsai was effectively booted sideways. He retained some influence at court as Ogedei's astrologer, but even here his advice fell on deaf ears. In December 1241 the ailing emperor planned a great hunt, ignoring Chu-tsai's warning not to take part. After the hunt, he drank through the night, plied with liquor by his new favourite Abd al-Rahman; and at dawn he died.

Chu-tsai himself died, some say of a broken heart, two years later, aged 54, after almost 30 years of devoted service to an impossible ideal. Yet he had accomplished much. It's impossible to say whether the Mongols would really have exterminated the entire population of northern China, but it was thanks to Chu-tsai that we shall never know. If Genghis did one good thing, it was to employ this able, brilliant and idealistic man.

In death, Chu-tsai was duly honoured, with posthumous titles and a tomb beside Beijing's Kunming lake. Later, the tomb was moved – twice, ending up in the gardens of the Summer Palace. If you follow Kunming lake, with its mass of boaters, go past the Hall of Jade Billows, and turn through a high red-painted wall into a little courtyard shaded by cypresses, you will find 'Long Beard', all 6 feet 8 inches of him, in an eighteenth-century remake of his statue. Alongside him is a poem by the emperor Ch'ien-lung, also of the eighteenth century: 'Although we were born in different dynasties, I respect him for his honesty to his emperor. As emperor myself, I hope my ministers take him as an example.'

Meanwhile, the west remained only partially conquered. Indeed, with Genghis's withdrawal and death, old conquests had been lost; the caliph still ruled in Baghdad, and the call of the Hungarian grasslands had still to be answered. Those distant grasslands were clearly part of the Mongol manifest destiny, a sort of Mongolian equivalent of California. Their acquisition would, by pure chance, be brief; but it would last long enough to express Genghis's ambitions in their most brutal form.

Jochi's share of the empire was now divided, north and south, between his two elder sons, Orda and Batu. In 1235, as soon as Jin had fallen, Ogedei hosted a great national gathering of leaders at Karakorum, the new capital rising where once the Turks had ruled, on the steppes in the valley of the Orkhon river. In size, it was hardly more than a village, about 2 square kilometres. But it was all walled, with a second compound for Ogedei's palace, a church-like structure some 80 metres long. Eventually the town would have twelve smaller shamanic shrines, two mosques, a Christian church, many houses and a mass of tents. But the Mongols were not very good at architecture, and there was always something rather artificial about it – a Brasilia or a Canberra rather than a London or a Paris. Friar William of Rubrouck, who saw it in 1254, wrote disdainfully that 'the monastery of Saint Denis is worth ten times that palace.' Today it is Mongolia's main tourist site, but there is nothing of the old capital to see, except for a huge stone tortoise, once the base of a pillar. The stones of Karakorum were buried, or re-used in the seventeenth-century monastery that stands nearby.

It was in this embryonic capital that Ogedei and his generals gathered in 1235 to decide on future strategy, which meant in particular committing an army to the seizure of the Russian steppes and the Hungarian plains, and in due course the little-known but wealthy regions beyond.

Under the great Subedei and his lord, Jochi's son Batu, an army of 150,000 struck west in 1236, revisiting the regions familiar from the Great Raid over ten years before. This advance sent echoes bouncing ahead, like a yell in a canyon. News came to France and Britain from an unlikely source. The Assassins, a Shiite Islamic sect based in Persia and Syria, wanted help. The Assassins were as notorious as you would imagine. Fortified by hashish, from which they derived their name, they were the fundamentalists of their day, having adopted terrorism (though not suicide) as a sacred duty in opposing any Muslim, and in due course any Christian, who refused to acknowledge them. Now messengers arrived from the Assassins, of all people, in London and Paris, begging for a Muslim–Christian coalition against this new and dreadful enemy. They were given short shrift. As the Bishop of Winchester said, 'Let us leave these dogs to devour one another.'

The Bulgars, who had driven off Subedei on their first encounter, stood no chance. Nor did the Polovtsy, who fled westward; nor did a series of Russian cities. In late 1237 the Mongols crossed the Volga. The Russian princes had learned nothing from the Battle of the Kalka River fourteen years before. Forests so dense that not even a serpent could penetrate, as one source put it, were no defence. The Mongols cut roads wide enough for three carts to pass abreast, and rolled forward with their siege engines. After one unidentified victory, the Mongols tallied the slain by cutting off the right ears of the dead, producing a harvest of 270,000 ears. Divided, cities tumbled like dominoes: Riazan, Moscow, Suzdal, Vladimir, Yaroslav, Tver. In early 1238 one Mongol army defeated Grand Duke Vladimir 200 kilometres north of Moscow, while another headed for Novgorod.

Europe had warning enough of impending catastrophe. A Hungarian friar, Julian, journeyed to Batu's camp in southern Russia in the late 1230s and brought back a letter from Batu to the pope demanding instant capitulation: 'I know that you are a rich and powerful king . . . [but] it would be better for you personally if you submitted to me of your own volition.' In England, the chronicler Matthew Paris in St Albans recorded how 'the detestable people of Satan, to wit, an infinite number of Tatars . . . poured forth like Devils loosed from Hell, or Tartarus' – reflecting the enduring confusion in Europe between Tatars and 'Tartars'. The Mongol advance on Novgorod even had consequences for some English, namely the fishing folk in Norfolk. Every spring, the merchants of Novgorod sailed down their section of the 'river road' that linked the Baltic to Byzantium, and went to Yarmouth to buy North Sea herrings. In 1238 they stayed at home to guard their city, leaving the herrings to glut the Yarmouth quays or sell inland for a pittance. No European leader could claim ignorance of the menace.

In the event, the spring thaw turned the flat lands round Novgorod to bogs, and the Mongols retired southward for eighteen quiet months. In 1240 they turned instead on Kiev: the Russian capital, the mother-city of Slavs and the seat of Orthodoxy, its 400 churches gathered like a halo round the glory of St Sophia's Cathedral. As a Russian chronicler put it: 'Like dense clouds the Tatars pushed themselves forward towards Kiev, investing the city on all sides. The rattling of their innumerable carts, the bellowing of camels and cattle' – camels! The citizens must have been amazed – 'the neighing of horses and the wild battle-cries were so overwhelming as to render inaudible conversation inside the city.' Kiev burned and its princes fled – to Moscow, which from that time grew as Kiev declined.

And now, at last, the grasslands of the Ukraine were open, with Hungary beyond. In the west, the danger, though clear and present, was simply not taken seriously. These were primitive barbarians fighting in unknown regions, were they not, and Europe a land of knights and cities defending home ground? Not so; the Mongols were familiar with what lay before them from spies and deserters – the countryside, the towns, the distances, the rivers, even the utter disarray of the opposition in Hungary and neighbouring Poland.

To secure Hungary, Poland would first be neutralized, over winter, when rivers were highways of ice and the lowlands like concrete. In northern Ukraine the army divided, one arm striking into Poland, the other into Hungary. In early 1241 Lublin, Sandomir and Krakow died in flames. In Krakow, so it was said, a watchman in the tower of the new Mariacki Church, the Church of St Mary, had been sounding the alarm on his horn when a Mongol arrow pierced him through the throat. Today, a recording of the mournful bugle call known as the *hejna* sounds every hour from St Mary's, breaking off on the very note on which the watchman supposedly died. Tourists are told that this story is true and that his death saved the city. It isn't and it didn't. On Palm Sunday, 24 March, according to local records, the Mongols set the city ablaze and 'dragged away an uncounted mass of people'.

They drove on to the Oder, where the citizens of Wroclaw set their own town on fire and retreated to an island in the river. From this quick and easy victory, the Mongols raced on 40 kilometres to Liegnitz (Legnica today, though historians still prefer the German form). Here, at last, on the borders of the Holy Roman Empire, Duke Henry the Pious of Silesia confronted them, with an army of 100,000 (though all figures are highly unreliable). But this newly Christianized frontier country was a slurry of Poles, Germans and Czechs, where place names came (and still come) in linguistic multiples. The defenders were a mixed bag of local worthies, Hospitallers, Templars, Teutonic Knights keen to defend their possessions on the Baltic, rough-and-ready units of German and Czech settlers, and even a contingent of Silesian gold-miners. A Czech army of 50,000 was en route, but still a few days' march away when Henry headed south to join up with them.

On 9 April 1241, 10 kilometres outside Liegnitz, he met the Mongols instead. It is fair to say he had no idea what he was up against. His forces were superior in number only. In every other respect – weapons, tactics, strategy, morale, ruthlessness – the Mongols utterly outclassed the western knights, with their heavy armour, cumbersome horses and squabbling leaders. The Mongols performed their old trick, creating a smoke-screen with burning reeds, milling about as if in confusion, then pretending to flee. The Polish cavalry galloped in pursuit, until suddenly the little horsemen vanished and arrows zipped in from both sides. Duke Henry fled, fell, tottered onwards in his shell of armour; was overtaken, stripped, beheaded and cast aside. The Mongols paraded his head on a spear around the walls of Liegnitz to terrorize the inhabitants. According to a letter written by the Templars' Master to King Louis IX, the Templars alone lost 500 of their number. Something like 40,000 died. King Wenceslas and his 50,000 Czechs, still a day's march away, turned for the safety of the Carpathians, leaving all southern Poland to the Mongols.

Two days later, Duke Henry's headless and naked body was recognized by his wife, Jadwiga; she knew him because his left foot had six toes. Proof of this odd detail came 600 years later. Henry's corpse was taken along with several others to Wroclaw and buried in the church he had founded, now St Vincent's. When his tomb was opened in 1832 researchers found a headless skeleton with a six-toed left foot.[3] (I wonder about the right foot; polydactyly is not usually selective.)

In a month, the Mongols had covered 650 kilometres, seized four great cities and taken a nation. The battle of Liegnitz was a disaster that scarred the soul of eastern Europe. A church arose on the spot where Henry was found, which in the eighteenth century acquired a Benedictine monastery. Now doubling as a museum of the battle, the church was repaired for the disaster's 750th anniversary in 1991, and is today a popular visitor attraction.

To the south, Hungary awaited its nemesis. This was a country in chaos. Hordes of Kumans (Polovtsy), displaced from the Russian steppes by the Mongol assault, demanded residence. Hungarian barons, who would rather die than surrender their hard-won independence, were at odds with their king, Bela IV. Bela welcomed the Kumans as a potential private army; the barons hated them. The Mongols seized their chance. The southern army, now in Galicia, divided into three. Two columns circled across the Carpathians in a pincer

[3] Gustav Strakosch-Grassmann, *Der Einfall der Mongolen in Mitteleuropa*, p. 47, n. 2. This book is the main source for this chapter.

movement, while Subedei himself delayed before racing across the centre, so that all three columns would meet up near the Danube. It took just three days for the advance guard to cover 280 kilometres, through enemy country covered in snow. In early April the three columns snapped together on the Danube, ready to attack the Hungarian capital, Esztergom (Gran in German).

Bela had managed at last to raise an army at Pest, on the Danube's east bank (not yet linked to Buda opposite). The usual chance to submit had been offered, and rejected (strangely, the Mongol envoy was a Hungarian-speaking Englishman, who will reappear shortly). Batu and Subedei held back. They faced a strong army, backed by the Danube and a capital city, with its possible reinforcements, and no news yet from Poland. But Subedei was a genius, and part of his genius was that he fought only when certain of victory. So he withdrew his whole army eastward, a slow, skirmishing retreat across the grasslands for six days, luring Bela away from the Danube and from help.

On 10 April the Mongols backed across the river Sajo towards the gentle, vine-rich slopes of Tokaj, just up from the Sajo's confluence with the Tisza. It was a good spot, marginally higher than the surrounding plain, protected in the front by a stream. The Hungarians settled opposite near the village of Mohi, making a fort by chaining their wagons into a circle, confident in their superior numbers.

The generals took stock. Batu told his troops to take heart, for the Hungarians were 'crammed together and shut in as if in a pen'.[4] That very night, Batu and Subedei made their move.

---

[4] Chinese sources claim Batu saw the Hungarian laager from a hill. This cannot be true. There is no hill anywhere near Mohi. Driving around the battle-ground, I looked in vain for an overview. Even if there were one, Batu could hardly have seen the Hungarian army in detail, because he was 5 kilometres from it. He must have used spies. The nearest high ground is the Zemplen Hills, a good 30 kilometres to the north-east.

Now, this was just one day after the Poles had been shattered at Liegnitz. Was this a coincidence? I think not. The Mongols did not base victory on coincidences. It is fair to assume that each of the two armies knew exactly what the other was doing and where it was all the time. The two must have been in almost daily communication, across 450 kilometres of hostile territory, 200 of which were through the Tatra mountains of today's Slovakia, at a time when snow still covered the slopes. This implies a regular line of messenger posts, with spare horses, linking the two separated forces, an adventure for the few dozen post-riders so astonishing that it beggars the imagination; yet so obvious and so routine for the Mongols that no-one thought to record it, and so secret that European sources make no mention of it.[5] To explain the timing of Subedei's move, we have to imagine that a message from Liegnitz covered the intervening 450 kilometres in 36 hours.

That night, then, Subedei knew there would be no re-inforcements for his enemy and plenty for him if needed. The long-term risks had practically vanished. He ordered troops back across the river Sajo, seizing the only bridge with catapults and gunpowder, the first recorded use of this devastating weapon in Europe. The Mongols crossed by means of what became known in the First World War as a rolling barrage, with artillery lobbing shells just ahead of the advancing troops.

Meanwhile, 10 kilometres downriver, Subedei himself led a second column that built a pontoon of logs, an operation that might at any moment have been discovered by Hungarian scouts. But there were none. All the Hungarians were focused on the noisy battle at the bridge. By dawn both crossings were secure, and by 7 a.m. the Hungarians were driven back into

[5] Nor, as far as I know, have any modern historians analysed the logistics of Mongol communications.

their laager, now less of a defence than a trap. For the whole morning, arrows, rocks and fire took a terrible toll. At midday the encircling Mongols drew back, allowing an enticing gap to emerge through which the survivors fled, turning themselves from desperate defenders into easy game, stumbling across the spring bogs to ever more certain death. Some took refuge in a nearby church, only to perish when the flaming roof collapsed on them. Three archbishops, four bishops and two archdeacons, the leading lights of local Christianity, all died, having trusted that God would grant them victory over the heathen barbarians. With them died ordinary Hungarians, Germans, even French, by the tens of thousands – some 65,000 according to the Abbot of Marienberg in western Hungary, writing the following January.

Bela fled north, into mountain forests, then around in a circle that took him into Austria, and on south, through Croatia, where he found sanctuary on a succession of off-shore islands. In pursuit came Kadan, one of the heroes of Liegnitz, who thus brought Mongols to the shores of the Adriatic. Here he lost either track of or interest in his prey, and continued on southward into Albania, before turning inland again. Bela went to ground on the island of Krk – Veglia, as its Venetian owners called it – to await better times.

Meanwhile, another Mongol contingent had galloped west, burning, destroying, raping and killing in a campaign of deliberate terror rivalling their actions in Muslim lands. Their rationale was exactly the same: these Christians, like the Muslims, had dared resist, and had therefore doomed themselves to the vengeance of Eternal Heaven. In the Danube port of Pest, taken in three days, they burned the Dominican monastery, slew the 10,000 who had sought refuge within it, and 'heaped the bodies of the butchered multitudes on the river banks' in order to terrify those on the opposite shore. The author of this vivid scene was Thomas of Split (Spolato), a major source for the invasion. Some Mongols, Thomas wrote, 'skewered small children on their spears and carried them on their backs like fish on spits up and down the embankments'.

Terror worked – and so did a show of consideration. For the summer of 1242 the Mongols established a rudimentary administration, even minted some coins, encouraging peasants to plant and tend crops; but after the harvest the same peasants were slaughtered as of no further use. There was no Chu-tsai here to suggest taxation, no-one to counter the Mongols' traditional view that farm workers would be only a drain on an economy best served by horses and pasture, the seizure of which had been a central plank of their policy ever since Genghis had first heard news of the Hungarian grasslands 20 years previously.

Beyond Hungary, of course, there was another world, as rich as China. Batu had ordered scouting raids into Austria. One of these penetrated into the Vienna woods, almost within sight of the city, where they were chased off by Austrian troops, who caught up with them near Wiener Neustadt ('Vienna New Town'), 40 kilometres south of Vienna. The Austrians captured eight of the raiders – one of whom, to the astonishment of all, was found to be English.

The Englishman's story was recorded by a heretical French priest, Yvo, from Narbonne, who had been in Wiener Neustadt to escape the attention of papal inquisitors. The Englishman was the same man who had been sent by Batu to offer Bela peace in exchange for capitulation. His was an odd tale. His name was almost certainly Robert,[6] and he had been the chaplain of Robert Fitzwalter, leader of the barons' rebellion against King John in 1215, the rebellion that ended with the signing of Magna Carta. Banished from England,

---

[6] Robert's story, and the search for his identity, is told brilliantly by Gabriel Ronay in *The Tartar Khan's Englishman*.

Robert fled to the Holy Land, gambled, lost everything and became a beggar, but held body and soul together by talking his way into hospitality; for in extremity he discovered he had a gift for languages. It was this skill that brought him to the attention of Muslim merchants acting as intelligence gatherers for the Mongols in the 1220s, during Genghis's advance westward. The Mongols needed interpreters. They made Robert – never mind that he was a down-and-out ex-priest – an offer it would have been unwise to refuse, and he was taken east, along caravan routes now made safe by Mongol troops, to Batu's HQ on the Volga, and perhaps further. He had since served his khans well for almost 20 years. Now he was eager to tell all to save himself from trial as a traitor. This time, however, charm and fluency didn't work, and he ended in an unknown grave.

In just four months, the Mongols had routed the forces of central Europe. All Christendom trembled. 'Hear, ye islands, and all ye people of Christianity, who profess our Lord's Cross, howl in ashes and sackcloth, in fasting tears and mourning.' So wrote the Landgrave of Thuringia to the Duke of Boulogne, urging united retaliation. But unity was not much in evidence. Europe proved, if not its own worst enemy, at least its second worst. The Venetians, whose merchants had allied themselves to the Mongols in the Crimea, refused to send aid. The Holy Roman Emperor, Frederick, took advantage of Bela's collapse to extort bits of western Hungary from him on his flight through Austria. The pope's main enemy was not the Mongols but the very same Frederick. The emperor in despair begged Henry III of England for help, sending copies of his appeal to France, Spain, Denmark, Italy, Greece, Ireland, Scotland and Norway. Nobody took the slightest notice, assuming that what he really wanted was a united front against the pope. Proposals for crusades from both Pope Gregory and Frederick withered on the vine. Anyway, Pope Gregory died in August 1241.

So it is as certain as anything can be that western Europe, or large parts of it, would have fallen prey to the Mongols if they had followed up their dreadful successes in Hungary and Poland. It seems likely, however, that they would never have tried it. Hungary had been the goal. Poland had been taken not for its own sake but to guard the flanks of an invasion of Hungary. The only strategic purpose of carrying the invasion further would have been to secure the German border as well. Of course, there is no telling what power politics might have dictated. Neither the pope nor any western European monarch would have complied with the inevitable Mongol order to kowtow, which might conceivably have brought armies streaming towards Rome and Paris, as Attila's Hunnish armies had done seven centuries before, taking on the challenge of forests and heavily defended cities that were, after all, no tougher than China's.

In fact, by 1242 Europe was safe, without knowing it. Ogedei had died the previous December. It would have taken only six weeks for the news to arrive in Europe, but disputes about the succession delayed its passage. Only in June did Batu hear of his uncle's death and the rivalries that put the fate of the whole empire in the balance. As Genghis's grandson, ruler of his own portion of the empire, with a vast army, his presence back in the Mongol heartlands could be decisive. In the midst of securing his new domains, right on the brink, perhaps, of invading western Europe, he pulled out. That summer, when Bela returned from his Adriatic island, he found a wilderness of burned towns and decomposing bodies, a population reduced to cannibalism – and not a Mongol in sight.

The threat simply vanished, leaving Europe stunned by its inexplicable salvation.

For ten years after Ogedei's death, family strife threatened Genghis's aims and ambitions. Widow rivalled widow over his heritage, grandson fought with grandson. Only in 1251 did the empire settle under Mönkhe, Tolui's son, ably assisted by his two brothers, Hulegu and Khubilai. It was these two who took the empire to its fullest extent. Hulegu destroyed the Assassins, seized Baghdad and drove on towards Egypt, where at last the Mongols were thrown back, the myth of their invincibility destroyed. It was Khubilai who undertook the conquest of southern China after Mönkhe's death in 1260.

This was the turning-point at which the Mongol empire began to grow away from its roots. The new khan, Khubilai, had been with Genghis on his last campaign; yet he moved the capital from Karakorum to Beijing, creating a new glory owing little to Mongol antecedents while preserving a feel for his origins at his summer palace Shang-du, on the Inner Mongolian grasslands. When all southern China finally fell to the Mongols in 1279, he proclaimed the start of a new dynasty, the Yuan, of which his grandfather became the posthumous founder. Khubilai was a giant among rulers, by far the world's most powerful man of his time; but not all-powerful. He tried and failed to seize Japan, his fleet twice scattered by storms. His rule over the rest of his pan-Eurasian empire was nominal, its various subsections seeking their own limits, and evolving into independent entities.

In southern Russia, Batu ruled what would become the Golden Horde, from the Mongol *ordon*, a tent-palace (and thus by extension the throngs it ruled, which became its meaning when European languages adopted the term in the sixteenth century). Russians recall the two centuries of rule by the Golden Horde as the 'Tartar [or Tatar] Yoke'. In fact, it was less of a yoke, more of an accommodation, achieved when Alexander Nevsky, Prince of Novgorod, decided to fight the Lithuanians, the Germans and the Swedes rather than the Mongols. They were soon, moreover, ex-Mongols – turning to Islam, working closely with the rulers of Egypt, exchanging

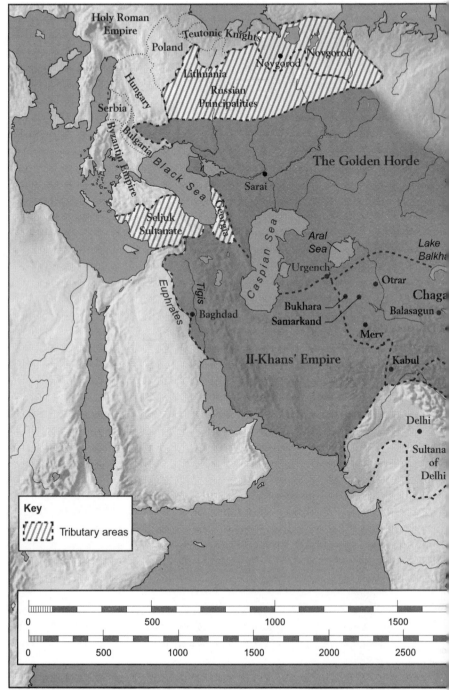

The height of empire, 1290.

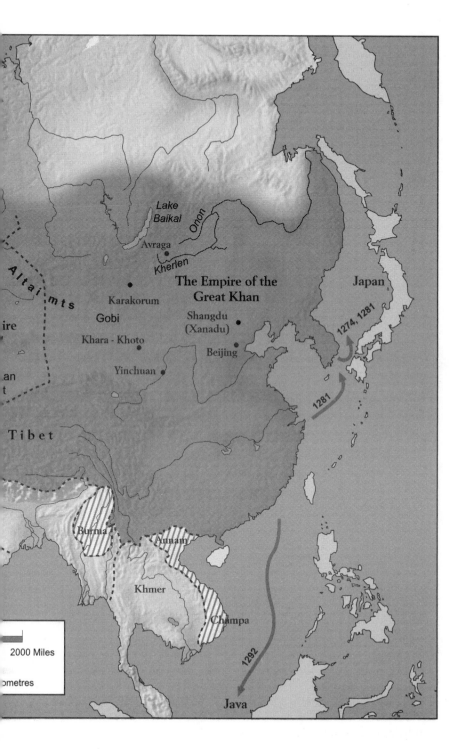

Lake
Baikal

Onon

Avraga

Kherlen

**The Empire of the
Great Khan**

Japan

Karakorum

Gobi

Shangdu
(Xanadu)

Khara - Khoto

Beijing

Yinchuan

1274, 1281

Altai mts

ire

an
t

1281

Tibet

Burma

Annam

Khmer

Champa

1292

2000 Miles

ometres

Java

diplomats whose correspondence, complete with gold lettering and elaborate salutations, was all conducted in Turkish. Supposedly every khan had to be one of the Golden Kin, a descendant of Genghis, but pretty soon almost any would-be ruler could make that claim. When the Horde broke into half a dozen separate khanates in the fifteenth century, everyone claimed Genghis as an ancestor. When a resurgent Russia under Catherine the Great annexed the Crimea in 1783, its ruler still forlornly insisted that he was Genghisid.

In Persia, Mongol rule sucked blood from stones. The Il-Khans (subordinate khans), as they called themselves, enslaved, plundered and taxed to the limit, exacting a land tax, tithes, a poll tax and a tax on all commercial transactions, including prostitution. Beyond the ravaged countryside and its bitter peasantry, trade favoured the cities, allowing the Mongols to amass enough wealth to keep a precarious hold, even as they lost contact with their roots. Hulegu's great-grandson turned Muslim; his failure to drive the Egyptian Mameluks out of Syria in 1304 marked the end of expansion, with Egypt and the Mediterranean forever beyond reach. In 1307 a Mongol embassy reached Edward II in England, but it was the last effort at self-promotion. Thirty years later, the last of the Mongols died with no heir, and Mongol rule vanished.

In Central Asia, Chagadai's heirs ruled over a vague expanse constantly riven by religious dissension and wars, some of them with family members to west and east. Here nomadic traditions remained strong, as did the urge to conquer. Constrained by Mongol rivals east and west, Chagadai's heirs looked south to Afghanistan and India, invading several times, and inspiring a tradition that endured when Mongol rule fell into the Turkish hands of the bloody Tamerlane.

In China, Khubilai and his heirs did what the Romans did for northern Europe: roads, canals, trade, efficient taxation, a postal relay system unrivalled for efficiency until the coming of the telegraph. Paper money underpinned a booming economy. Spices arrived from south-east Asia, Chinese silks and porcelains filled warehouses in the Persian Gulf. In brief, they protected and harvested all the benefits of unity and size that Chinese rulers had always sought, and they did it by abandoning their Mongol roots. Yeh-lü Chu-tsai would have been gratified.

For 150 years after Genghis's death, his scattered descendants linked east and west, sharing in the free flow of trade, diplomats and experts. In the 1280s a Chinese Nestorian monk, Rabban bar Sauma, visited the pope, and saw the King of England in Gascony. The pope, in response, sent several monks to Mongolia and China. Chinese engineers supervised irrigation projects in Iraq. There were Chinese communities in Novgorod and Moscow, Chinese merchants in Cambodia. The use of paper for books and money spread westwards, first to Samarkand, thence to Europe, where, once treated in just the right way, it became one of the technical improvements that underpinned the invention of printing.[7]

But the Mongols were never *liked*. Nomads no longer, they never became truly Chinese. The new rulers despised and feared their subjects, forbade them to bear arms, excluded them from their own government, employed foreigners to administer them. Marco Polo was a city governor, the minister of finance came from Tashkent, a Muslim father and son ruled Yenan. Mongol rule depended on power, and power seeped away. Many Mongol chiefs fawned on courtly fashion, took the royal coins, forgot the simplicity and toughness of their nation's founder. Others remembered; and mutual

---

[7] It should have been Mongol rule that allowed for the spread of the idea of movable type, but no-one has yet found evidence of idea diffusion. Gutenberg developed his great invention with no help from the east. On this much debated issue, see my own *The Gutenberg Revolution*, London, 2002 (*Gutenberg* in the US).

suspicions grew. Hatred on one side and corruption on the other inspired rebels, one of whom at last succeeded. In 1368 a former monk, Zhu Yuanzhang, drove the last Mongol emperor, Toghon Temur, back to the steppes of Mongolia, making himself the founding emperor of the Ming dynasty.

There remained the memories of a golden age, of the glory that had been, of the giants who had lived in those days. And the magic lasted, drifting across Eurasia and down the centuries. Every ruler wanted his handful of Genghis's magic dust. Long after Russian victory over the Golden Horde in 1480, members of the Golden Kin commanded noble status, right into the nineteenth century. The dreadful Tamerlane – Timur-i-Leng, the tyrant from Uzbekistan – claimed to be a Genghisid, which he wasn't (though his wife was). That was why Timur's descendant Babur called himself 'Mughal' when he seized power in India in the early sixteenth century, establishing a dynasty that ended only when the British shuffled the last Mughal off the throne in 1857. His name, by the way, was Bahadur, a distant echo of the Mongol *baatar*, hero, the second element in the name of Mongolia's capital Ulaanbaatar (Red Hero), and the epithet that had honoured Genghis's father. Even today, we remember: a 'mogul', originally a wealthy Indian, then a wealthy Anglo-Indian, is now a media tycoon. To an etymologist, Rupert Murdoch is the Genghis Khan of the tabloids.

And so, against a slow but steady dissipation, the wisps of smoke drifting away from the great explosion preserved the evidence of their origins. Genghis remained a hero to the rulers who ruled in his name, a monster to his victims – Muslims, Christians, Russians and finally the Soviets. Russians recall the 'Tartar Yoke' as the worst of times, and blame the Mongols for many ills, including grim aspects of their national character; scratch a Russian and you'll find a Tartar. Western Europe breathed a *phew!* of relief, and returned to pre-national, post-Roman scrapping, except in

Hungary, where the brief and brutal conquest reminded a once nomadic people of the benefits of a settled lifestyle. Hungarian schoolchildren learn of Mohi as a defining moment in their history, recalled at last by a memorial set up there to mark the battle's 750th anniversary in 1992; it's a 10-metre hillock covered with crosses set every which way, like a huge corpse stuck with swords, and will shortly be a weird punctuation mark beside a new section of the motorway across the Great Plain.

IV

RESURRECTION

15

THE MAKING OF
A DEMI-GOD

EAST OF YINCHUAN AND THE YELLOW RIVER, WE DROVE INTO THE
Ordos through a wasteland of factories and blue trucks, a fog
of chemicals, a wilderness of rock, sand and tussocky grass.
Jorigt and I were in good hands. Driver Chog was as burly as
a wrestler, with neck muscles that looked like an anaconda, a
sinister image modified by snappy shorts and carpet slippers.
The carpet slippers were a reassurance. Carpet slippers would
not be quite the thing if we broke down in a toxic smog or on
the high, arid and desolate heartland of the Ordos. Clearly
Driver Chog had confidence in his ability and his car. With
good reason. Even when the road gave out and we found ourselves weaving between trailer-trucks full of coal that loomed
at us through their own dust-storms, and edging past a fallen
monster that had spilled its overladen innards across the
desert like a dead diplodocus, even then I had no scintilla of
doubt that Driver Chog, with his carpet slippers and his
anaconda neck muscles, would get us through.

We were heading for the area where, according to some
legends, Genghis Khan was *really* buried. Or might have

been, depending on whom you talk to, though no-one can say exactly where. Anyway, put the mountains of Mongolia out of mind for this chapter. We are dealing now with a totally separate tradition, which takes as its starting-point the story of how Genghis's 'soul-cart' stuck in the mud. In one version, his entourage had recalled a previous incident, when Genghis had admired this precise spot and declared it 'a desirable resting-place for an old man'. Perhaps that was why the cart stuck: because he had chosen it as his burial-place. The notion took root, and sprang different versions in different settings, all painting a romantic scene of an old man struck by the beauty of a pasture fit for golden deer to graze and hoopoes to nest and the aged to find eternal repose.

Here's another variation on the same theme, explaining why no-one knows exactly where the burial site is:

Once the Lord came to a beautiful pasture in the Ordos region, south of the great bend of the Yellow River. It was so beautiful that he said, 'This is where I wish to be buried when I die.' So it came to be. And those who buried him there wished his remains to be undisturbed. But they also wanted to remember the spot. How was this to be done? They knew that female camels have excellent memories. So they found a camel with a baby to which she was giving milk. They slew the baby camel and buried it next to the Lord's grave. Then, each spring, they released the mother camel, and it returned to the spot where the baby camel was buried. Every year this happened, and every year people were able to honour their khan, until the camel grew old and died, and all knowledge was lost of the place where the Lord was buried.

But the high Ordos was a plateau of ravines and mangy pasture. Surely Mongols did not consider this beautiful?

'Conditions change,' said Jorigt. 'When you take the bus from Hohhot to the Mongolian border today, you cross sand. But ten years ago, it was very good, and it is now worse than this,' he continued, waving at the grim surroundings. 'Besides, this is high Ordos. They do not say he was buried up here.'

Thanks to Driver Chog, we were able to celebrate our survival with a sheep's-foot stew in a cement mock-*ger*, a faint reminder that this had once been all Mongolian, until the Chinese settlers came. We dropped from the semi-desert to Dongsheng, the Ordos capital, and struck south through a savannah of scattered trees and pastures. After an hour, a wall running up a hill enclosed firs, through which we caught glimpses of three red-and-blue domes, topped by little pillars, like nipples on strangely tattooed breasts. The road ran through a small town, at the end of which we turned left through a gateway into a giant courtyard lined with single-storey buildings. A long flight of stairs led through a triple archway up the hill, over the crest of which lay the multi-coloured domes.

We had arrived at the Mausoleum of Genghis Khan – Edsen Khoroo, as it is in Mongolian: the Lord's Enclosure – where Genghis has undergone the final and strangest part of his metamorphosis from barbarian chief to divinity. This is the story of the evolution of a religious sect from historical roots, through legend, to ritual, which fed back to make new legends, creating along the way a self-sustaining entity – with community, temple, rites, belief-system – that is beginning to show signs of developing a universal theology. It is an astonishing example of how a new religion can spring from an old one, branch out, and flourish.

Though buried obscurely in the mountains of Mongolia, Genghis had to be honoured, his possessions preserved, provision made for worship. In the west and in China, there would have been a temple nearby, but in the early thirteenth century the Mongols had hardly built anything much except old Avraga. The new imperial capital, Karakorum, was only just begun. His heir Ogedei decreed a solution that was original and appropriate for nomads. In the words of Sagang Tsetsen in the seventeenth century, 'eight white tents were raised for the purpose of veneration.' To protect the tents, a few families of Mongols were granted freedom from all other duties so that their members could act as guardians in perpetuity, caring for the Lord's possessions – his bow, his saddle, his clothing, his yak-tail standards – and supervising the rituals by which he was venerated. In this way, Genghis would watch over his people for ever.

At first, the focal point of veneration was, of course, the probable grave-site on Burkhan Khaldun. The perimeter of the Forbidden Precinct, as it was called, was well guarded and well served with offerings and rituals. But there was an impermanence about these arrangements, with the secret central location trodden and overgrown. After 70 years or so, one of Genghis's descendants felt a need to give the area, if not the exact site, something permanent, as told by Rashid ad-Din in his account of what happened after Khubilai's death in 1294.

An assembly was called to decide which of two of Khubilai's grandsons would succeed him, Kamala or Temür (the heir designate, Khubilai's son Chen-chin, having died ten years before). There was a dispute. A matriarch suggested a solution: Khubilai had said that whoever knew the sayings of Genghis best was best suited to rule. It was agreed that the two claimants would compete. Temür, the younger, being eloquent and a good reciter, declaimed well, while Kamala, who stammered, could not match him. All cried out: 'Temür knows them better! . . . It is he that is worthy of crown and throne!' So it was.

Kamala (1263–1302) was generously treated in his defeat, being given command of Genghis's *ordos*, his tent-palaces – in other words, his home estates. In a significant passage, Rashid says that the estates included 'the great Khorig [Forbidden Precinct] of Genghis Khan, which they call

Burkhan Kaldun, and where the great *ordos* of Genghis Khan are still situated. These latter are guarded by Kamala. There are four great *ordos* and five others there, nine in all,[1] and no one is admitted to them. They have made portraits of them [the family] there and constantly burn perfumes and incense. Kamala too has built himself a temple there.'

At some point, perhaps during a time of unrest after the collapse of the Yuan dynasty, the focus of veneration shifted south. Perhaps there had always been a dual focus, with a separate shrine at Khubilai's summer headquarters, Shang-du (Xanadu). Or perhaps the guardians of Genghis's memory commuted between the two sites, and perhaps others, with their tents and relics. In any event, the main shrine became not any one place, but the tents.

These tents were not of the usual *ger* shape, but had a roof supported by a pole, which stuck out of the top like a little spire – 'a *ger* with a neck', the Mongols called it. At times of worship, the main tent, which contained Genghis's relics, was covered with yellow canvas, making it a 'golden palace'. After the collapse of the Yuan dynasty in 1368 the tents followed the Mongols out of China, back to the ancestral grasslands, roaming with their guardians. Of course, Genghis was venerated in other shrines, like the Imperial Ancestral Temple in Beijing, completed in 1266, and at Kamala's temple on Burkhan Khaldun itself, as well as at three other shrines across the Mongol empire. But the White Tents were the heart of what soon became the cult that turned Genghis from hero and lost leader into a divinity.

A body unseen, a secret grave, a forbidden area, a shrine of movable tents: the evidence for what happened to Genghis's body was shifty from the start. Soon – perhaps because the main focus of worship was now provided by the White Tents

---

[1] The number varies. Sagang, writing in the seventeenth century, has eight. Perhaps there were nine originally, which had become eight by Sagang's time.

and because Kamala's temple was abandoned – stories arose that Genghis was not on Burkhan Khaldun at all, had never been taken there in the first place. Since the *ordos*, the golden palace-tents, had now given their name to a whole region south of the Yellow River, legends arose to claim he was actually buried there, in the Ordos.

Years passed. The White Tents moved from place to place as a travelling shrine, wandering back and forth across the Gobi, to the Altai mountains of the west, to the eastern grasslands, to the semi-desert of the Ordos, until some of them settled and became a site for special acts of worship. The site was a well-watered spot on the eastern edge of the Ordos, a place of wonderful pastures, with deer grazing among the scattered trees. Then the descendants of those set to guard the White Tents improvised the tales and modified the names until, with the passing of the generations, it seemed to them that this must have been the place where Genghis's soul-cart stuck and where he wished to be buried – where he *was* buried, though no-one knew the exact spot. Beliefs and rituals became encrusted with Tibetan and Chinese lore. When the remainder of the White Tents, now formally designated as eight in number, were eventually brought to the spot in the seventeenth century, it acquired its present name – Edsen Khoroo,[2] the Lord's Enclosure.

By then, reading back from nineteenth-century accounts, it's a fair guess that each tent had its own purpose. There was one for Genghis and his first wife, Börte, with a black shrine table, a casket and various artefacts – a butter-lamp stand, a little pot with jewels and grains to symbolize wealth, a mirror for perception, coloured ribbons for the regions and peoples of the empire, an arrow-shaft of thirteen joints (Genghis, the thirteenth generation of his family, became a hero at thirteen).

---

[2] As always there are several transliterations of this from the Mongol. The Chinese version transcribes roughly as Yijin-huoluo.

Another tent was for his second wife; the third for the divine white horse, an incarnation of which was chosen every year to be tied to the 'Golden Pole [hitching-post]' at the main ceremony of worship. Number four, rather weirdly, was for Gurbelchin, the queen who, in one version of events, dealt Genghis a fatal cut and threw herself into the Yellow River, though in another version they loved each other, and she drowned herself in grief; the fifth tent was for a mare's-milk bucket made of red sandalwood, from the original of which Genghis gathered the milk of 99 heavenly mares before setting out on campaign. Tents six to eight were for his bows, his saddle, and for gold, silverware and jewels.

The temple and its rituals were, and still are, controlled by a special clan, known as Darkhats. They claim descent from the 500 families designated as guardians of the White Tents after Genghis's death. The claim, more folklore than history, lives side by side with others – that the families are all descended from Genghis's generals, sometimes two, some-times nine in number. In the words of one Darkhat, Surihu:[3]

> When Genghis Khan was about to pass away, our ancestor, Boorchu, was at his bedside. He was very sad and crying as he said: 'What will happen after the Great Khan passes away? What will happen to my descendants?' Finally, Genghis said, 'After my death, your descendants will live with me, gener-ation after generation.' So this task was assigned to Boorchu. After Genghis Khan died, we, the descendants of Boorchu, have been engaged in making offerings and guarding the maus-oleum. And the duties have never been stopped. I am the 39th generation of Boorchu's family.

[3] Rihu Su, 'The Chinggis Khan Mausoleum and its Guardian Tribe', University of Pennsylvania dissertation, 2000. This excellent monograph was thought-fully placed on the internet by the author, whom I have totally failed to trace. If he reads this, would he please get in touch?

Whatever the truth of their origins, the Darkhats became an elite, exempt from taxes and military duty, free to raise cash all over Mongol lands, which they did with a combination of emotional blackmail and sincerity, rather like pardoners and sellers of indulgences in medieval Christendom. So things remained for some 700 years.

Over the centuries these functionaries, following the law that bureaucratic groups always tend towards complexity, broke into subgroups and evolved specialized tasks as arcane and trivial and as jealously defended as medieval guilds, or dyed-in-the-wool trade unions, with the difference that these tasks were far more ancient and far more sacred. These were all men, of course, and all the jobs were inherited from father to senior son. It's hard to imagine an equivalent. Imagine an old-fashioned family of inbred typesetter–printers, except that they can look back *centuries*, reeling off genealogies preserved by oral tradition, and know in their bones that they are performing a duty imposed by their god-king-ancestor.

There are two main divisions, which spring from two of Genghis's generals, Boorchu and Mukhali (best not to enquire too closely how this claim squares with the nine generals and 500 families). According to this explanation, Boorchu's descendants were among those who looked after the Mausoleum and its ceremonies. The second group were descendants of Mukhali, and their job was to care for the war standards – spears with shaggy circlets of yak-tail attached just below the point – and the ceremonies that honoured those. Both spawned subgroups and individuals responsible for the minutest points of ritual, such as caring for the horse-headed clappers, etiquette, chanting, reading decrees, arranging offerings, supervising liquor ceremonies, boiling sheep, carrying lanterns, butchering horses and monitoring lookouts.

From the sixteenth century onwards, original shamanistic rituals gave way to Buddhist ones. Genghis became a

reincarnation of the bodhisattva (or 'Buddha-to-be')
Vajrapani, the Thunderbolt-Bearer, who in Tibetan
mythology fights demons to protect Buddhism. Rites settled
into a series of 30 annual ceremonies, with four great
seasonal observances, of which the greatest occurs in the
spring, each with its songs, prayers and incantations, many
beginning with words which, if the names were changed,
could just as well be used by a priest invoking Christ:

> Heaven-born Genghis Khan,
> Born by the will of sublime Heaven,
> Your body provided with heavenly rank and name,
> You who took overlordship of the world's peoples . . .

Attributes, possessions, actions, looks, wives, children,
horses, pastures: all are invoked as a means of assuring the
Lord's blessing in the overcoming of obstacles, demons,
illnesses, errors and discord.

Take one ceremony among many. This one happens once a
year outside in front of the temple's main *ovoo*, the sacred
pile of rocks that marks the top of the hill. It is held in
memory of the Golden Pole to which Genghis tied his horse,
a horse of pure white, such as the ones allowed to wander
around the temple today. It is said that a thief took the horse
and as a punishment was made to represent the Golden Pole,
standing all night holding the horse with his feet buried in the
ground. After that, it became the task of one particular man
to be the Golden Pole for a night. People would come and
throw money in front of him. Then milk would be brought
from the temple and scattered 99 times on the ground, using
a special spoon with holes in it. Priests would observe how
the milk ran – a pattern known as the 'Flower of the Gods' –
and foretell how good the pastures would be, and how
healthy the cattle. Then after the ceremony the man would
be released, hand over the horse, quickly gather the cash

and run off, with people yelling 'Stop thief!' in ritual protest.

Parts of this practice derive directly from a tradition recorded by Marco Polo in Khubilai's time:

> You must know that the Kaan keeps an immense stud of white horses and mares; in fact more than 10,000 of them, and all pure white, without a speck . . . Well, when the Lord sets out from the Park [in Shang-du] on the 28th of August, as I told you, the milk of all these mares is taken and sprinkled on the ground. And this is done on the injunction of the Idolators and Idol-priests, who say that it is an excellent thing to sprinkle that milk on the ground every 28th of August, so that the Earth and the Air and the False Gods shall have their share of it, and the spirits likewise that inhabit the Air and the Earth. And thus those beings will protect and bless the Kaan and his children and his wives and his folk and his gear, and his cattle and his horses, his corn, and all that is his.

This ritual, like all the others, has changed with time. No man today stands out all night with his legs half buried. His place was taken by a real pole 50 years ago. So there is no throwing of cash, no shouting of 'Stop thief!' Nowadays children and adults run back and forth between the pole and the *ovoo*, throwing the milk on the pole, recalling the old pre-Buddhist rite.

The Mausoleum and its web of ritual practice remained for Mongols a sort of *cosa nostra*, from which Chinese and other foreigners were excluded. This was an exclusiveness for which its guardians were prepared to die. In a story told by two historians of the Mausoleum,[4] when the Manchu emperor Shunzhi died in 1661 the Mongols refused an official decree to mourn. Summoned to Beijing to explain their

[4] Sainjirgal and Sharaldai, quoted in Rihu Su, who feature respectively later in this chapter and in chapter 18.

recalcitrance, a group of Darkhats said they had been ordered to remain in mourning for one emperor only, Genghis Khan, all their lives: 'If we were in double mourning we would make a serious mistake regarding the Sacred Lord's brave soul . . . we would rather die obeying our late Emperor's order than live violating [it].' The Manchu officials knew when they were beaten, and granted the Mongols freedom to follow their own ways, pretty much unmolested, for the next 300 years.

Owen Lattimore was one of the very few outsiders to observe at first hand the Lord's Enclosure and its ceremonies until recently, and certainly the first to cast a critical eye on them. He came to Edsen Khoroo in April 1935, in time for the spring festival. Arriving for this 'Audience with Jenghis Khan' as he called his vivid account, he found five tents (not eight) flanked by two dozen *gers*, ox-carts, tethered horses and lines of poorer tents belonging to traders and servants, with a spread of cloth, buckets, hoes, shovels, whips, saddles 'and all kinds of pathetic extravagances, an illusion of luxury for a miserable people'.

The ceremony started with a humble approach to Genghis's tent from 30 paces away, battered by an icy wind and stung by flying sand. Inside the tent was a low silver-plated table, which was the altar, and a silver-plated wooden chest, the 'coffin'. This was supposed to contain the bones or ashes of Genghis himself, but Lattimore, with his excellent Mongol, noticed an inscription in the silver which suggested it was Manchu, no more than 300 years old. He had his doubts about the other items as well, given the frequency of rebellions and bandit raids.

There followed an offering of silk scarves, a ninefold prostration, a retreat back the 30 paces, the drinking of milk-wine from silver cups, another six advances and retreats, all followed by the offering of a sacrificial sheep, more prostrations, the gift of another silk scarf, and the receipt in exchange of a smaller scarf, which was rubbed against the 'coffin'. Then came a circumambulation of the other four tents, three of them dedicated respectively to the empress, the eastern empress (one taken in the invasion of Manchuria), and the Bows and Quivers of Genghis, with a final White Tent for prayers. Lattimore noted how much of a Mongol business this was; the Buddhist lamas performed only an insignificant role, their main task being to blow curved Tibetan trumpets, producing a sound like 'the splitting of gigantic trousers'. At the end of the ceremonies the following day, all five tents were lifted in their entirety onto carts drawn by two sacred white camels, and taken back to a walled enclosure.

It was clear to Lattimore that the origins of the cult were back to front. Normally, rituals are designed to sanctify traditional beliefs; you would expect a body, a burial, then the rituals. But there had been no body, this was no true mausoleum, the 'relics' were of dubious authenticity, and 'as for the tradition that the body of Jenghis is at Ejen Horo [*sic*], or his ashes, this is neither clear nor specific.' Somehow the rituals seemed to have come first, the beliefs following along later as rationalizations. The practices were apparently based on a combination of thirteenth-century court observances and even older ancestor-worship. Once, in these newly conquered lands, imperial subjects, envoys and tributaries had brought tribute to the khan in his *ordos*. After his death, his spirit was honoured in the same way, with gifts; then, since the ancestral spirit partakes of divinity, the rituals acquired their religious content; and perhaps only then did the 'relics' appear, to provide a physical focus for worship.

War, which Lattimore just managed to avoid, changed everything. So far, the only contest to possess the soul of

Genghis had been between shaman and Buddhist, a rivalry hidden by the slow-motion nature of the Buddhist takeover. Now the story shifts gear. Since the turn of the century Chinese officials had been encouraging Chinese peasants to colonize traditional Mongol lands, turning pasture into farmland, and to pay a high rent for the privilege. By the 1930s Mongols had been effectively squeezed out of the Yellow River valley into marginal pastures. At this point, three new elements intruded: Japan, expanding into Inner Asia from its colony in Manchuria, challenged by two Chinese rivals, the nationalists under Chiang Kai-shek and Mao's communists.

Japan sprang upon China rather as Genghis had done, but from the opposite side. In 1931–2 Manchuria became a Japanese puppet state, a prelude to the planned conquest of Mongolia, China and Siberia. The first step was to take eastern and central Inner Mongolia, which acquired its own puppet regime, the Mongolian Autonomous Government, complete with a revolutionary calendar which had as its founding date the year of Genghis's birth. Held back briefly by the nationalist army, the Guomindang, Japanese troops advanced to the Yellow River in 1937, and remained in control for the next eight years.[5]

In the autumn of 1937 an unexpected guest arrived at the Lord's Enclosure. He announced himself as a representative of the Royal Japanese Army based in Baotou, 100 kilometres to the north. Local officials were gathered. Demands were made. The officials were to declare themselves against both Chinese parties, and for the Japanese; and to move the Eight White Tents and their contents into Japanese custody. The Japanese had realized that whoever ruled the Lord's Enclosure held the key to Mongolia and this part of China;

---

[5] In 1941–4 the Japanese backed the construction of a Genghis Khan temple in Ulanhot. Its three white buildings, in a 6-hectare enclosure, were redeveloped in the 1980s, with a 3-tonne copper statue of the hero at its heart.

and that whoever ruled Mongol lands had a fine base from which to secure the rest of China and Siberia. Suddenly Genghis's relics, Genghis's very soul, had become the key to empire in Asia.

A tricky position for the provincial chief, Shakhe. The relics had been there for 700 years, give or take, and the local Mongols were guarding them 'as if protecting their own eyes'. Besides, close by on the other three sides were nationalist troops. Shakhe pointed out that if the Mausoleum were moved there would be riots, which would not benefit the Japanese cause. The invaders saw the point, and backed off.

But the damage was done. Many Mongols in China turned to their own independence movement, while others approached the nationalists for help in moving the relics to a place of safety, far from the reach of the enemy. The Guomindang government agreed, planning to move everything by truck and camel to the mountains south of Lanzhou on the Yellow River, 600 kilometres to the south-west. The area was chosen because it was safe, though the argument was also made that it was not far (well, only 150 kilometres) beyond the Liupan mountains, where Genghis had spent his last summer.

On 17 May 1939 200 nationalist soldiers arrived unannounced at the Mausoleum, to the astonishment of the confused locals, who blocked the way. A nationalist official explained the need to protect the place against the 'East Ocean devils'. Panic gave way to negotiations. The nationalists promised that all expenses would be paid, that some of the Darkhats could go along, and that all the ceremonies would be allowed to continue. The news spread fast. Hundreds, then thousands, came, spending the night in lantern-lit ceremonies, weeping and praying as the tents were struck and the carts loaded. At dawn the train of vehicles moved off, with a brief pause when an old man prostrated himself in front of one of them. One nationalist soldier reportedly muttered to another,

'Given such loyalty, no wonder Genghis Khan won wars.' Across a 'sea of tears', in the words of a journalist, the carts slowly pulled out, heading south at walking pace towards Yenan, almost 400 kilometres away.

Yenan (Yan'an in pinyin) was the HQ of the Communist Party's Central Committee. By some unrecorded negotiation the communists allowed the convoy, with its nationalist contingent, to enter their territory. Because Genghis was, of course, a Chinese emperor and the whole Mausoleum a Chinese relic, both sides in what would soon be a vicious civil war united in competing to praise Genghis as a symbol of Chinese resistance to the invader, seeing him not as the founder of the Mongol nation and empire, but as the founder of the Yuan dynasty. There was, therefore, a political subtext to this apparently altruistic gesture: the Mongols had better not forget that Genghis's conquests were not conquests at all, but a little difficulty that led to the Chinese majority being ruled, for a short while, not by foreigners but by a Chinese minority; in brief, they had better remember that Mongolia was actually part of China.

So, in mid-June, the communists did Genghis proud. Camel-carts gave way to an eight-car convoy, one vehicle for each tent, the lead car bearing the coffin being draped in yellow satin. On the roadside at the town of Shilipu, 8 kilometres east of Yenan, a crowd of 20,000 watched the convoy draw up at a room designated as a funeral hall. Here a huge scroll proclaiming Genghis 'The Giant of the World' was flanked by a couplet:

The Mongolian and Chinese nations are more closely united
Continuing the spirit of Genghis Khan to fight to the end.

An arch hung with a sign – 'Welcome to Genghis Khan's coffin!' – led to a shrine laid with wreaths, one from Mao himself. A dozen senior party and army officials paid tribute to the convoy in a four-hour ceremony, the high point of which was a 'vehement and passionate' funeral oration by Secretary-General Cao Liru.[6] 'It praised Yuan Taizu [the Yuan dynasty's first emperor] as the world's hero,' and instantly linked him to the Communist Party's cause, urging 'Mongolian and Chinese people to unite and resist to the end!' Next day, the convoy moved on southward, past another huge crowd of spectators. (That wasn't the end of the matter for Yenan. The following spring, the town opened its own Genghis Khan memorial hall, complete with statue, dancing dragon and murals.) This was how to deal with a barbarian conqueror: confer upon him a retrospective change of nationality and turn him into a symbol of Chinese culture, fortitude and unity.

Three days later, the convoy again passed into nationalist hands. In Xi'an, the nationalists gave a reception that far out-did their rivals. Here, 200,000 people packed the streets to greet the convoy. A cow and 27 sheep were sacrificed in welcome. It was an astonishing display, given that this was the Chinese heartland, with few Mongols in evidence. Genghis had devastated the area. Yet ordinary people fell for his magic, because he had become a Chinese emperor, albeit posthumously; also, they were ancestor-worshippers, and Genghis was certainly a great ancestor, even if not theirs. So they knelt and kowtowed with joss-sticks in their hands as the convoy passed.

On 1 July, another 500 kilometres to the west, safe in the Xinglong mountains south of Lanzhou, the convoy arrived at Dongshan Dafo Dian, the Buddhist temple that was to be the Mausoleum's home for the next ten years.

*

[6] Ju Naijun, 'The Coffin of Genghis Khan Passes Yenan', *National Unity*, vol. 6, 1986, quoted in Rihu Su.

In 1949, as communist troops approached to wrap up the civil war, the nationalists shepherded the Mausoleum away again, 200 kilometres further west to the great sixteenth-century Tibetan monastery of Ta'er Shi, where monks welcomed it with chants and prayers. To no avail: a month later the communists won anyway. The nationalists fled to Taiwan. The Japanese were gone, along with their puppet regimes in Manchuria and Mongolia. Heaven, it seemed, had granted a new mandate – to Mao.

For the next five years, the Communist Party had its hands full with land reforms and other such revolutionary matters. Inner Mongolia was in the hands of its own communist warlord, Ulanhu. Once, before the war, the communists had agreed that minority areas could secede from China if they wished. Not any more; not in the new China. But the communists did recognize the right to some local autonomy, and Ulanhu pushed Mongolian claims to the limit. Mongolians made up only 15 per cent of the population – in a region that had once been theirs alone! – of the new Mongolian Autonomous Region, but dominated its administration. This mitigated the revolutionary zeal to root out collaborators, herd-lords, lamas and nobles. There were some executions; some fearful herdsmen slaughtered their livestock rather than have them redistributed; but overall Ulanhu's softly-softly policies – 'Be favourable to the hired herdsmen! Be favourable to the herd-owner!' – brought a slow return to normality. This was to be a measured step towards a more 'advanced' socialism.

With a pro-Mongol leadership and a need to prepare people for further change, local and national officials turned at last to the Mausoleum. For Mongols and Chinese alike, Genghis deserved some prestigious and enduring memorial, something better than a few tents. A brand new Mausoleum was commissioned, costing 1.2 million *yuan*, to be built on the original site.

In spring 1954, by truck and train, the hero's bier and his relics returned to the Lord's Enclosure, in time for the laying of the foundation stone on 20 April. Ulanhu himself did the honours. On 15 May, an auspicious day, the day of the most important observance, with *gers* crowding the surrounding pastures and sacrificial sheep piled in mounds, a memorial rite marked the Mausoleum's renaissance. An official condemned the Guomindang 'reactionaries' for removing the relics in the first place, and claimed credit for their return.

In 1956 the new temple was complete.

It seemed right, in the first instance, to enter as an outsider should enter any place of worship, with humility in the face of one's ignorance. Jorigt knew the form. We should be prepared to offer something to the spirit of Genghis. From one of the gift shops that lined the entrance courtyard we bought a length of blue silk – a *khatag* – a bottle of vodka and a brick of tea. Passing a lumpish statue of a mounted Genghis, we climbed the auspicious flight of 99 steps – 99 being the number of minor spirits subordinate to the overarching deity – through pines and cypresses to the temple's gateway, a protective screen of exhibition rooms topped by white crenellations. Beyond was a huge paved courtyard, 100 metres square, spilling across to the temple itself, a central dome flanked by two domed wings.

In hindsight, it's easy to withhold admiration. Yes, those three tiled domes, with their blue anchor-shaped patterns set against gold, were obviously inspired by Mongolian *gers*. But the Mongolians have no indigenous architecture to speak of; it all derives from Tibetan Buddhism, which inspired its own architectural traditions in China. So this is a 1950s attempt to do justice to all three elements. The domes jut from pagoda-style roofs with curled-up eaves, like ballet skirts, the three of them linked by bland corridors, as if the designers had run out of ideas.

No prizes for the design, then. What Ulanhu's men did get right was the setting – the scale, the dramatic potential of this grand site. The temple is a jewel in a clasp of greenery, displayed on its hilltop like an offering to the Blue Heaven. After all those sweaty stairs, and the entrance gateway, which acts like the iconostasis in an Orthodox church, concealing then revealing the mystery within, and the huge courtyard, I felt myself drawn towards something greater than the merely mortal.

And inside there was the divinity himself, as a vast and shadowy marble statue, a Buddha figure 4 metres high, beneath a frieze of dragons. Darkhat Mongols in suits and brown trilbies stood watch, dour as guard dogs. A sign warned against photography. They tore the film from your camera if you dared disobey (which I saw them do with a hapless Mongolian tourist). I felt the last of my scepticism retreating in the face of their seriousness. Perhaps it is the show of faith in others, not the literal truth of that faith, that induces a sense of the sacred.

A young Darkhat, Bulag, guided us past the looming marble presence, which, now that my eyes were accustomed to the shadows, I saw was set against a huge map showing the extent of the Mongol empire. Humbly we trooped into a back room, where three tents stood beneath an array of banners, like rather tatty Christmas decorations. This was the Mourning Hall, the three tents being for Genghis himself, for his senior wife Börte and for Gurbelchin, the Tangut princess, reviled elsewhere as a murderess but here adored for her loyalty. We laid our *khatags* and our bottle down. We knelt. We lit incense. Bulag muttered a prayer, in Mongol: 'Holy Genghis Khan, John and Jorigt have come here today to pray at your tomb. We beg you to grant them good luck in their work.'

And then, thanks to the spirit of Genghis answering our prayer, I regained my scepticism. That was, after all, what was needed for this work. I was amid relics as daft as any Splinter of the True Cross. Here were the Sacred Bow and Quiver, the Chamber of the Miraculous Milk Bucket, and the Holy Saddle, one of two on display, with pommels of chased silver. The one on the right, said Bulag – that was Genghis's. The one on the left was given in the seventeenth century by the last Mongol emperor, Ligdan Khan. Both looked in suspiciously good condition.

Ligdan Khan's saddle is worth a small detour in our story. A twin of Genghis's, it represents a claim to his imperial heritage. Ligdan made a doomed attempt to re-establish Mongol independence and unity in the face of imminent Manchu conquest. But by then Mongol independence had been fatally compromised by internal squabbling and by Buddhism's links with China. Ligdan tried to grasp the complexities by claiming to be a bit of everything: a Chinese emperor, an heir to the Yuan (Mongol) dynasty, a Genghisid and a Buddhist saint, with a bit of Mongol shamanism thrown in. The saddle is a symbol of his attempt to match Genghis object for object and cause for cause, and at the same time to juggle religion and politics into a new whole. It didn't work. He spread himself too thinly, ruined his own plans with greed and arrogance, and died of smallpox in 1634. Mongolia fell to the Manchus two years later.

Murals display the glories of Genghis's rule in figures that reminded me of 1930s fashion plates, all suave elegance and fabrics falling in neat folds. Nothing mars the perfection of the costumes, the good looks of the men and women. Here Genghis presides over his united empire, there Khubilai confers the title of dynastic founder upon his grandfather, who hovers, dragon-flanked, in the Blue Heaven. Musicians have never been happier to sing, maidens never prouder to present silk scarves. Foreigners cannot wait to offer tributes and products, for Genghis was the man who bridged east and west, stimulated a transfer of art, scholarship and trade, and assured the well-being of all.

Of dead bodies there is no trace.

For a decade, the temple served its purpose with increasing success, reaching a high point in the 1960s. In 1962 Mongolia declared the 800th anniversary of Genghis's birth, and proposed a great celebration. In Mongolia itself, this proved a disaster. Mongolia was a Soviet satellite. To Russians, Genghis was a reactionary, a destroyer of culture. The celebrations came to a sudden halt; their instigator was banished. But China knew very well the benefits to be had from the cult of Genghis, and in the same year the Lord's Enclosure hosted its largest rite ever: 30,000 people, mostly Mongols, participated in an excess of adoration that suited the official line perfectly. With the Mongols firmly behind the Party, Inner Mongolia would be a stable bastion against the Soviet threat rolling its way across the Gobi.

But when Mao unleashed the Cultural Revolution in 1967, Genghis suddenly fell from grace. There could be no challenge from the past to the new ruler, who was about to usher in an era that would eclipse Genghis. 'The hero!' wrote Mao in a sneering poem. 'The one Heaven is proud of for one generation! What he knew was no more than hunting eagles.' With the Cultural Revolution, Mao released a wave of xenophobia. In Mongolian lands the Mongols became victims, the prime political target being the so-called Inner Mongolian People's Revolutionary Party, which had, it was claimed, wanted total independence for Inner Mongolia, with the long-term aim of reuniting with Mongolia itself and establishing, presumably, a new Mongol empire. Now the masses must unite against the threat of pan-Mongolism.

This was a hard time for Mongols, as Jorigt recalled. His

father had a job as a small-town official, the job that had moved the family from their grassland *ger* into a house. There came a time when he was arrested.

'Because he was an official?' I asked.

'Because he was a Mongolian!'

'Was he badly treated?'

'Of course badly treated! He could walk, but his hands had been broken. And he had been branded with words on his skin. He was a "dog", because he was educated, and if I had talked about this they would have called me a "young dog". We had to become "red", not "white", which meant educated.' He paused, lost in memory. 'This is a long story. So many dangerous things happened.'

'What is your strongest memory?'

'Too many strongest memories! Let us not talk about these things.'

A prime symbol of Mongol nationalist and religious feeling was, naturally, the Mausoleum; but in Cultural Revolutionary eyes it was a symbol of reactionary fervour, the seething heart of treason, the headquarters of pan-Mongolist plotters. In 1968 the Red Guards tore the place apart, destroying almost everything of value – the Bow, the Quiver, the Miraculous Milk Bucket, the standards, the tents: all gone.

All these objects had a certain eminence, being at least a century, some perhaps several centuries old; but their destruction leaves the tantalizing thought that something among them might actually have dated right back to Genghis himself. Nachug, the head of the Mausoleum's Institute of Genghis Khan Studies, certainly believed this to be so. What, for instance, of the contents of the silver coffin, which Lattimore had been told held the Lord's body, or ashes? Well, Nachug didn't know about the body. How could there be a body if it had been buried out on the steppe, its position remembered only by a mother-camel? All he knew was that it supposedly held 'the last breath of the Lord'.

'You mean – just . . .' I struggled. 'Just *air*?'

'No, no. Inside the box was a clump of hair from a white camel. And it was this hair that held the last breath of Genghis Khan.'

I couldn't follow. It still sounded like nothing but air.

'You see, the hair had a little blood on it.'

Somehow by the 1960s the legend about the body had slipped away, leaving a mere trace, the stain of a bloody cough caught on a twist of camel-hair used as cotton-wool to clean the royal lip.

'And there was also the umbilical cord. That was what was in the coffin that we worshipped here.'

'Were they really in there?'

'Well, the box was never opened. Only worshipped.'

We were back to hearsay, legend, rumour, almost certainly myth. But here would have been something that could have been checked. Imagine opening this coffin, never mind that it was only two or three centuries old, and finding nothing at all but a little wisp of white camel-hair with its faint rusty stain and a shrivelled scrap of dried flesh – what tests might have been made, what theories spun. But now, as the result of revolutionary zeal, there would be no chance of DNA analysis and carbon-dating tests, no way of checking whether there was any truth in Nachug's words. Almost certainly not; but one cannot help wondering.

So the temple itself dates from the mid-1950s, the 'relics' were remade in the 1970s, the great marble statue finished in 1989 (as attested by the signature of the artist, Jiang Hun). It seemed that the only 'genuine' elements were the prayers, the songs, the rituals of the ceremonies themselves. Even these might have been lost, had it not been for the efforts of a few dedicated men like Guriljab, a Darkhat who had made it his life's work to collect the songs associated with the Genghis Khan rituals. He recalled to Rihu Su how his work survived:

In 1968, I was locked up for more than 70 days. Some people were gone even longer, four or five months. My songs were almost finished. Suddenly one day, some Red Guards came to search my home. They took me and all my writings to their headquarters. I was very much worried because my written record of the songs was also among them. When they left to have their meal and locked the room in which I and all my materials were, I quickly took it out from the rest and put it in my pocket. Since they had already searched me, I thought they would not do it again. Fortunately, they didn't. After I was locked up for three days, my wife came to bring me some food. Eventually they allowed her to enter the room, but we were not allowed to speak in Mongolian, only in Chinese. They were afraid we would exchange information in Mongolian. As soon as I saw that the Red Guards standing outside did not notice us, I quickly put my songs into her bag and told her to keep it in a less important place, like a storage hut, which those people would overlook in case of a second search, and in a dry place ... No sooner had I come home than I asked my wife where she had put that thing. She told me it was kept between the rafters and the roof of our storage hut. It was wrapped in a piece of cloth and inserted into the gap. After I took it out, I had to make another copy of it right away ... Thus I have saved the songs, which would otherwise have been gone for ever.

Did nothing else remain?

'The saddle is genuine,' said Nachug. 'It alone was saved.'

But he didn't know how exactly. He was only forty-something and a relative newcomer. It was all so long ago. If I wanted to know more, I should speak to Sainjirgal, once the chief researcher at the temple, now retired.

Sainjirgal was living in a nearby town, in a neat little house set round a tiny courtyard down a side street. He made a charming contrast to the grim Darkhats at the temple, with twinkling eyes and a ready smile beneath a trilby which he wore permanently, even indoors. In his mid-seventies, he had the strength and looks of a man 20 years younger. No, he wasn't from this area at all, he was from Shilingol and had come as a teacher, but had become intrigued by the worship of Genghis Khan – 'I am not a Darkhat, but I am a Mongolian. He was my ancestor' – and had found his life's work as a local historian.

'Of the Eight White Tents,' I nodded.

'Not necessarily eight!' he corrected. 'Traditionally we go hunting with eight yellow dogs, but that means maybe six or ten. Our numbers are often more or less. They have a deeper significance. If we say a number, that means we confer on the subject the characteristics of that number. The tents only became eight under the Manchus [in the seventeenth century]. Who can say how many there were to start with?'

He seemed to radiate virtues that owed little to Genghis or the Mausoleum, and everything to his own generosity, dignity, intelligence and intellectual rigour. His world was not one of ritual and incense, but of evidence, gathered in the books that lined his shelves. His directness and clarity made the temple seem all dogma and cloying self-righteousness. Yet it was precisely that dogma in which he had chosen to immerse himself, spending his professional life collecting details of rites, prayers, songs and beliefs.

It had not clouded his objectivity. 'Most people round here see Genghis as a god. They do not see him as a man. I respect him only as a man who unified his people. Yes, I take part in ceremonies, I worship him. But I use worship as a form of respect for a human being, as Mongolian children pray to their father and mother and to their ancestors.'

Sainjirgal's work was well under way when Mao unleashed the Red Guards. He saw the kids – young Mongolians, of all people – turn on the temple, destroying whatever they could, all the artefacts, tents, relics, the lot, all except the saddles. Ah, yes, the saddles. How were they saved?

'I think someone hid them in the top of the dome,' he said, but he had not been there at the time.

'What happened to you?'

'During the Cultural Revolution, I was arrested.' He said this as if he were describing a holiday, twinkling and smiling. 'I was in prison for over a year, then sent to do manual labour, and that was sometimes worse than prison. They tied me with arms outstretched, and beat me with canes. They made me stand close to fires and burned me.'

'But why?'

'Because I worshipped Genghis Khan, and this had become a crime! They also said I was a spy for Mongolian independence fighters, and for the Russians. That was when things were very bad with Russia.'

Jorigt added bitterly: 'At that time anyone could be accused of anything!'

'The Chinese said every Mongolian was an enemy,' said Sainjirgal. 'But it was just an excuse.'

'You seem very relaxed about it. Do you feel no bitterness?'

He laughed. 'My experience during the Cultural Revolution was good for me.' I had a sudden presentiment that I had got him all wrong, that he was about to spin an old Party line about the benefits of re-education. Not a bit. When he was finally freed in 1974, after six grim years, he was not broken, but inspired. 'Before we had trusted that smaller nationalities would always have the same rights as everyone else. Now I saw the truth. What truth? That big nationalities can oppress little ones. That encouraged me. I knew I had to fight for our culture. I had to publish the history of my ancestor.'

It was an extraordinary commitment, given the state of the Mausoleum in the 1970s, for it had been turned into a store for salt. He saw my incredulous look. 'Yes, a salt-preserving place! For the next ten years! It was to prepare for war.'

'For war,' I repeated, flatly. I couldn't make sense of what he was saying.

'Salt for war! To store salt in case of war with Russia!'

I had forgotten the madness of the times, the bitterness of the Sino-Soviet split, the frontier clashes between armies on the Ussuri river, the legacy of fear stoked by government propaganda. Now I remembered distant echoes of that fear in the West, remembered buying Harrison Salisbury's *The Coming War between Russia and China* to prepare myself for an apocalypse that never came.

But when Sainjirgal's book, *The Worship of the Golden Chamber*, finally appeared, he had already decided that he had done his subject less than justice. So he ditched it and began again, gathering yet more material, which had just been published in the book he now reached down from a shelf and signed for me. *Mongolian Worship* is his life's work, distilled between golden covers in 600 pages, beautifully printed in the old, vertical Mongolian script that is still used in Inner Mongolia. He was justly proud of it, of its depth, of his 30 years of effort, of his integrity. 'After 1949, writers accepted Marxism, and everything to do with Buddhism and old customs was seen as bad. But to study Mongolian worship and customs, you must study the Mongolian documents from before the foundation of the People's Republic. This is what I did in this book.'

Mongolian Worship is further evidence of just how far today's Genghis, venerated in prayer and ritual, has been removed from the historical Genghis of conquest and genocide. But it is far more than that. It is a tribute to one man's determination to preserve and assert a major strand of his people's identity; and also a symbol of hope, in that a culture so overwhelming as China's can publish such a statement from a subculture so precariously balanced as Mongol. Forty years ago, Sainjirgal would have been lucky to survive if he had tried to publish this book. Some things do improve with time.

*

Most worshippers are content to make offerings and pray to Holy Genghis as if he were a god himself. But Genghisid theology is not that easy, as Nachug revealed on our return to the Mausoleum. Strolling round the immense courtyard in front of the temple, we came to a platform on which fluttered yak-tail war standards, the symbol of Mongol military prowess. Nachug told the story of how Genghis came by them, adding a whole new element to this strange set of beliefs:

'Once, when Holy Genghis was fighting to unite the Mongol tribes, he despaired, and addressed Heaven. "People call me the Son of God, but yet I fail! I beg Khökh Tenger, the Blue Sky, to give me the power to win!" At once, the heavens thundered, and something fell among some trees. He was unable to reach the object. So he commanded his generals to cut the trees and get it. It turned out to be a yak-tail standard. In thanks, Genghis sacrificed 81 sheep, leaving the remains for the "sky dogs" [wolves]. So the standard – the *sult* – became like a flag, a sign from the Blue Heaven uniting the Mongols, going before them in battle. That is why we worship the *sult* today.'

Then he added a conclusion that put the whole Mausoleum and its ceremonies in a new light: 'This is a form of worship even higher than that of Genghis Khan. If Genghis Khan himself worshipped the standard, then it must be higher than him. It is a symbol of Heaven itself.' As such, it has a power of its own. Some people say that birds flying over it fall dead.

I had thought until this moment that Genghis was a god. Now I saw that in the pantheon he inhabited he was not at the pinnacle, only near it, a demi-god; not a Zeus but an Alexander, who is worshipped by some Hindu sects. And perhaps with a hint of something even more mystical, a sort of Mongolian Trinity, with God the Father, Son and Holy Spirit mirrored by Blue Heaven, Genghis and Standard. Now we were all out of our depth. This was a subject for the temple's resident theologian, Sharaldai, who would be able to explain the next level of complexity. Sharaldai was in Ulaanbaatar. Perhaps, with luck, I could track him down there and quiz him on the subject of the Mongolian trinity.

Like a cathedral, the Mausoleum is more than a focus for rituals and legends. It is also a tourist attraction, one of China's finest according to the tourist literature. Though too far off the beaten track for the masses, its annual tally of 200,000 visitors provides its financial life-blood, now that China has embraced capitalism and privatization. Most of the visitors were Chinese, the investment was Chinese; but the beneficiaries were all Mongol. This was another strand in the problematical matter of Mongol national identity.

Half a mile from the Mausoleum, down a track and out on open pasture, is a village of *gers* where tourists can stay and eat and ride horses. Over a long lunch and too many toasts, Nachug spoke of the tensions and the changes the Mausoleum faced. It received 3 million *yuan* a year from grants and ticket sales, hardly enough to support its upkeep and the town's 3,000 people, in particular the 500 or so Darkhats who still depend on and serve the temple. There are plans afoot. In a few years, there would be a big hotel. It would cost 200 million *yuan*, to be raised from government funds and private investors.

But development needs space, and the available space is pasture, and the pasture belongs to the herders. So, to ensure stability and prosperity for this most Mongolian of sites, pasture would have to be acquired from the herders and money from the Chinese. And how, having done this, were the spiritual purposes of the place to be balanced with the repercussions of an invasion of Chinese tourists? 'If we continue with this plan, it has to be built in the Mongolian fashion. We will have horse racing, and show Mongolian songs and dances. A Mongolian city, with Mongolian-style buildings and Mongolian street names.'

Nachug saw the paradox clearly enough. Yet to him it seemed appropriate to take the risk. After all, this place was inspired by Genghis, and Genghis himself had moved towards the very people he had assaulted, by employing Chinese administrators. He had himself bridged cultures. With luck and good leadership, this community could emerge as a true reflection of its hero, minus the dead bodies.

Does the spirit of Genghis still have power? Well, this is not a place of miracles, where the blind are made to see and the lame to walk. Nor do people pray with the certainty that their prayers will be answered. But most people have a shrewd suspicion that Genghis mediates between earth and heaven, and will, on occasion, intervene if asked in the right way.

I asked Nachug directly whether people believe Genghis's spirit is a help.

'*Bain, bain, bain!* [It is! It is! It is!] People believe that the spirit of Genghis will bless them. This place is not rich, but every family sacrifices, and they benefit by the worship of Genghis Khan.'

And if they fall short in their devotions, they suffer. The Darkhat Guriljab recalled in 1993: 'All those who offended against Genghis Khan and were activists in damaging the Mausoleum during the Cultural Revolution are now dead. They were all about my age. I saw them die one after another. They all died abnormal deaths. One suffered a kind of stroke. He couldn't move for eight or ten years before his death. Another one, his head swelled up three times the size of his normal head, and he died. Yes, this is retribution. Our former banner magistrate, he was the leader of this rebel team. Later he was accused of being a member of the Inner Mongolian People's Revolutionary Party, and he was beaten and killed by a long nail being driven into his head. His wife

and daughter died, and his son has gone mad. Another one
. . . he fell into a manure pit and drowned.'

Everyone has their own stories proving Genghis's power. A
group of soldiers break a taboo by killing two snakes in the
Mausoleum; their car crashes, killing six. A young man gets
drunk at a liquor ceremony, and urinates against a wall; that
night his wife dies. A ceremony was omitted in error after the
Cultural Revolution; sheep fall ill and die. Such stories carry
a message: Have respect! Take care! Genghis is as powerful in
death as in life!

And in the end he is not, as he was in life, an avenger, but
a power for good. In Guriljab's words, 'To us Darkhat
Mongols, if there is any problem or crisis or the like, as long
as Genghis Khan is given an offering, it is so effective that
everything turns out right.'

16

THE GRAVE-HUNTERS

ON THE SUBJECT OF GENGHIS'S TOMB, ABOUT THE ONLY
certainty is that little is certain.

The *Yuan-shi*, the history of the Yuan dynasty, records how
imperial burials were made. When the retinue reached the
place of burial, 'the earth removed to dig the pit was made
into lumps which were disposed in order. Once the coffin had
been lowered, [the pit] was filled and covered in the order [of
the lumps]. If there was earth in excess, it was carried to other
places far away.' A European observer, Friar John of Plano
Carpini, who visited Karakorum in the 1240s, wrote, 'They
fill up the pit . . . and place over it the grass as it was before,
so that the place should be impossible to find afterwards.'

Where this may have happened in Genghis's case is, of
course, the big question. It seems likely that the burial took
place on or near the natural temple of the deity that had saved
Genghis from his enemies: Burkhan Khaldun, the mountain
that almost everyone now agrees is Khan Khenti, the King of
the Khenti. *The Secret History* doesn't say, but several other
sources mention Burkhan Khaldun as the burial-site. The only

near-contemporary record is infuriatingly vague. In 1235–6 the Song court sent an embassy to Genghis's successor. The two ambassadors, P'eng Tah-ya and Xu T'ing, claimed they saw where the conqueror was buried. 'Mongolian graves have no tumuli,' wrote P'eng. 'Horses are allowed to trample the area until it is as flat as its surroundings. Only at Temujin's grave-site have posts [or arrows] been erected in a circle of 30 *li* [16 kilometres; whether in circumference or diameter is not clear] and horsemen set on guard.' His colleague added: 'I saw that Temujin's grave was to one side of the river Lu-kou, surrounded by mountains and rivers. According to tradition, Temujin was born here and for that reason was also buried here, but I do not know whether this is true.'

Two eye-witnesses, only nine years after the burial; but what did they actually see? A symbolic enclosure and watchmen? Did the two together define the 16-kilometre circle? How do a 16-kilometre circle and trampling horses and water square with a mountain burial? And, most tantalizing of all, what on earth was the Lu-kou river? Some major rivers have Chinese as well as Mongol names, and this one is very close to Lu-chu, which was one version of what the Chinese called the Kherlen. But, as all Mongols knew, Genghis was born on the Onon, not the Kherlen, so the visitors cannot have been exactly rigorous in their research.

My guess is that these two diplomats asked to see Genghis's grave, without realizing that they were asking for something that could not possibly be granted. The site of the grave was to be kept secret, closely guarded until such a time as no-one would be able to identify its position. On the other hand, it would be bad form to deny such officials their request outright. So, from Karakorum, they ride for a few days to the Khenti mountains. They are taken roughly to the right area, get the name of the river slightly wrong, pick up some distorted information – official disinformation, more like –

see a few distant horsemen and are told that to enter the
sacred site is taboo; not that there would be anything to see
anyway, because it was all trodden flat and is now covered
with saplings.

But soon even soft information like this began to slip away
into hearsay and rumour. Marco Polo, writing 50 years later,
said that 'all the great kings descended from the line of
Genghis Khan are taken for burial to a great mountain called
Altai.' The same name crops up again almost four centuries
later in Sagang's history. He writes that the corpse was buried
'between the shady side of the Altai and the sunny side of the
Khenti mountains', a description so vague as to be almost
useless. Modern historians had to start virtually from scratch.

Where the grave might be is one problem. Another is what,
if anything, it might have contained. Again the evidence is not
much help. Juvaini, who began writing his history at the new
Mongol capital of Karakorum only 25 years after Genghis's
death, says that upon his election by the Mongol princes,
Genghis's son and successor Ogedei ordered that 'from moonlike virgins, delightful of aspect and fair of character, sweet in
their beauty and beautiful in their glances . . . they should select
40 maidens . . . to be decked out with jewels, ornaments and
fine robes, clad in precious garments and dispatched together
with choice horses to join his spirit.'

It is not totally impossible, because it was an ancient
custom in China and across Central Asia before the spread of
Buddhism that ordinary soldiers, servants, wives, concubines
and animals were killed to accompany the ruler in the after-
life. In Anyang, the capital of the Shang dynasty in the
fourteenth century BC, tourists can see a whole mausoleum of
graves filled with the skeletons of slaves and horses and the
remains of chariots. Sometimes victims were buried alive, a
practice not formally banned until the late seventeenth
century. It was certainly stated and widely believed that
before the arrival of Buddhism Mongol khans were buried

with their armour, items of clothing, concubines and other possessions.[1]

But the evidence is shifty. These practices had never been universally observed, with the living often being replaced by replicas (as in Xian's famous terracotta army and the much smaller version to be seen in Guyuan's museum). No Mongol tomb containing sacrificial victims and treasure has ever been found. And Sagang does not claim that the 40 moonlike maidens were actually interred with their khan, which would have meant unearthing the coffin buried at least a year before, with all the risks to security that would have involved.

Despite the lack of tradition and evidence, it remains a tenet among tomb-hunters that Genghis 'must have' been buried with a full panoply of weapons, women, slaves, horses and the riches of half Eurasia. The tomb has become a Holy Grail for treasure-seekers and historians. Surely, it is widely assumed, the grave of the ruler of half Eurasia should rival that of Tutankhamun. In fact, the search is not just for one grave but for a whole necropolis, a Mongolian Valley of the Kings, where Genghis's family and heirs, including Khubilai, must lie buried, along with wives, concubines, slaves, horses and Eternal Heaven knows what else of gold, jewellery, costumes and weapons the imagination can conjure up. In Mongolia, Genghis is good business. Every year, visitors are sold adventure tours that promise a taste of him, with trips to his birthplace, and even a few on horseback to his burial-site, never mind that no-one knows where it is or what might be in it.

It is a search with huge potential significance. If the grave exists, and if it were ever found, it would create a revolution in archaeology, scholarship, cash-flow and – since China

---

[1] A major source for this information is the Ming writer Xiao Ta-heng, commander of Chinese troops on the Mongol frontier, in his *Customs of the Northern Barbarians*.

claims Genghis as its own – international relations. There are already a Genghis Khan University and a centre for Genghis Khan Studies. The discovery of the grave would signal the start of a feeding frenzy, attracting funds, most of them probably in dollars, to the delight of both the institutions that already exist and many more that would spring up overnight. Universities would rival tour companies for control of access, with the government acting as umpire, trying to seize a share of the inflow for the nation, and probably failing, given the current passion for privatization and prevalence of bribery. Even now, occasional efforts are made by the Mongolian government to assert control over the search; a hard task, since regulation would mean spending money and limiting tourism. And the tensions are wound ever tighter by those who argue that the search itself is a sacrilege, that what was intended to be secret should remain secret, and that anyway foreigners should be excluded from something so intimately connected with the nation's roots.

All these passions swirl around a site the very existence of which, let alone its position, is still in dispute. The sources for the burial-place have been analysed by many eminent scholars,[2] and most agree that the original site lay on the 'sunny side' – the southern, auspicious side – of Burkhan Khaldun, today's Khan Khenti, as Sagang implies, but does not say explicitly. But some perfectly respectable Mongol researchers still doubt that Burkhan Khaldun is in fact today's Khan Khenti mountain. Even assuming it is, the mountain is actually a ridge, with two peaks (2,362 and 2,452 metres) linked by an immense shoulder 20 kilometres long. Our needle, always assuming it exists, could be anywhere on the southern slopes of this haystack: an area of something like 100 square kilometres of forested ridges and peaty plateaux

---

[2] The best summary is Paul Pelliot, *Notes on Marco Polo*, vol. 1, pp. 33–360.

and steep-sided valleys and bare uplands, all trackless, hard to get to, hard to leave. The nearest paved road is in the nearest town, Möngönmört, 70 kilometres away.

Given that few foreigners went to Mongolia before it became the world's second communist state in 1924; that it was then pretty much closed off until the next revolution of 1992; and that conditions are pretty horrendous – iced over in winter, boggy in summer: given all that, it is not surprising that so little work was done on the subject of Genghis's grave until recently.

First off the mark was an East German, Johannes Schubert, of Leipzig's Karl Marx University,[3] who explored the mountain in a week-long expedition with a Mongolian colleague, Perlee. The first European to climb it, he described it in an account that reveals just how hard it is to get to and how tough the journey can be. This was in 1961, but it sounds like something out of the middle ages.

Schubert started from Möngönmört, as expeditions must, with four local Mongols to manage a caravan of 13 horses, winding their way single file through the willow bushes, crossing and recrossing the Kherlen – a tough journey for a man approaching his 65th birthday. The second evening, while chasing a deer, one of the men, Damba, fell; he tottered back to camp hours later, in darkness, with a damaged arm. Next day they came upon an overgrown and collapsed tumulus, 95 paces by 65 and 8 metres high, which made

---

[3] The Mongol–East German connection has an odd origin. In the 1920s, when newly independent and communist Mongolia started to look outward, the government sent 50 children to be educated in Berlin. Back home, these children became a little elite, with great influence. After the Second World War, when East Germany became part of the communist world, the link came into its own. In Mongolia, German became the foreign language of choice after Russian, and East German universities the main channel for western contacts. This was a story I heard often from the children's mentor, a Russian émigré named Serge Wolff, who, having moved to London, was another inspiration for young members of the Anglo-Mongolian Society in the late 1960s.

Schubert wonder: mountains, water, thick forest, near Burkhan Khaldun – could this be Genghis's tomb? No, he decided, it was almost certainly a Hun grave, a reminder that the area had been a burial-site for centuries before Genghis.

Then onwards, over a ridge up the Bogd (Holy) river, with the guides exclaiming at bear droppings and distant views of moose (elk, as they are known in Europe). At the foot of Khan Khenti was an *ovoo* of trunks and brushwood, where the locals laid strips of material and bits of bread, sugar and curd. Communist disapproval, it seemed, had done little to curb reverence for Genghis. They camped here for the third night; the injured Damba insisted on hunting, fell again and this time broke a shoulder. Another man set off at a gallop back the 70 kilometres to Möngönmört to fetch a doctor (rider, doctor and assistant arrived three days later). Meanwhile, one of the other hunters had shot an elk, and arrived with bits of it dragging behind his horse. Cut up and skewered on sticks, it made wonderful kebab, strengthening everyone for the next day's climb.

It was hard going: dense forest, thick underbrush, fallen trees, loose stones, and only deer-paths through it all. They came to an overgrown terrace, with another *ovoo*, two big, three-legged iron cauldrons and a bronze container. Scattered about were semi-circular tiles, shards of pottery, bits of lacquered wooden bowls, nails and clasps. Schubert guessed these were the remains of the temple built by Kamala, Khubilai's grandson, in the late thirteenth century.

Higher up, as the trees became thinner, they came out onto a flat place 'scattered with holes, which are filled up with boulders and between which grow scanty mosses'. (Please note these holes; they will play a significant role later.) Here the Mongols dismounted, in reverence. And finally, on top, they came upon a field of *ovoos*, with a main one where bits of armour, arrow-points and various lama-istic objects had been laid. Undoubtedly, Schubert concluded, this had to be the historic Burkhan Khaldun; somewhere on these slopes, therefore, must be Genghis's tomb.

So the search is not for amateurs. Mongolians themselves are by no means amateurish in researching their own country, but they lack resources for high-tech archaeology. These became accessible only when the fall of communism in 1990 opened the country to outsiders.

The Japanese were the first to seize the opportunity, with the Three Rivers Project – the one that had done the radar survey of the old Mongol capital of Avraga. Since the backer of the four-year enterprise (1990–3), the newspaper *Yomiuri Shimbun*, wanted to recoup its investment in terms of publicity, there was no shortage of hype. According to the introduction of the report written by an eminent Japanese archaeologist, Namio Egami, the project's stated purpose – to find Genghis's tomb – was 'so significant it may mark the beginning of a new history of the world'. Named after the three rivers that rise in Genghis's ancestral homeland – Kherlen, Onon and Tuul – it was an immense undertaking, with almost 50 members, ground-penetrating radar, superb cameras, global positioning devices, many cars and a helicopter. In the face of such financial commitment, the Mongolian Academy of Sciences' Institute of Geography offered its support.

Work started in spring 1990, proceeding from the start in a strangely slipshod fashion. First call, of course, was Burkhan Khaldun/Khan Khenti. Approaching from below, the team re-discovered the ruins of Kamala's temple; landing by helicopter on the top for an hour, they recorded the existence of the 200–300 cairns described by Schubert (not that anyone on the expedition seems to have read his account). They found no trace of any ancient tomb up there, or indeed anywhere else – which was not surprising, given that the survey was so superficial. No-one ventured down from the top or up from the bottom, so no-one saw the 'holes' described by Schubert on the middle level of the mountain.

The project went on to find an astonishing range of graves and implements at sites other than on Burkhan Khaldun, without turning up a hint of anything from the early thirteenth century. From the point of view of archaeology as a whole, the four years of research performed a vital service by showing just how untouched Mongolia is. Judged by its original purpose, however, the project was a total failure. The huge expenditure could hardly be justified by reporting hundreds of minor Turkish graves and offering detailed but irrelevant descriptions of the countryside as observed by satellites, aerial cameras and radar. The Three Rivers team needed to produce 'underground relics' that were 'treasures of the world'. Luckily, two areas proved potentially reward-ing. One was Avraga, the pre-Genghis capital: an important site, which the Three Rivers report glorifies with a bald and totally unsupported conclusion: 'It is almost certain that Genghis Khan's tomb is in this area.' The second possible source of 'treasure' is truly a wonder – a vast stone wall enclosing a 3-kilometre section of a ridge in the neighbouring hills. It is known locally as the Almsgiver's Wall, and is almost certainly nothing to do with Genghis. Yet the Three Rivers report blithely says that, from geographical observations and interviews (neither detailed), 'it appears that Genghis Khan was buried somewhere in [the Almsgiver's Wall].' There are other signs of sloppy research: Johannes Schubert comes out as 'Y. Shubert', and Countryside Island is transformed from a slab of land into a prince who wrote *The Secret History* and 'organized Genghis Khan's funeral'. All that cash spent, two different sites claimed for the grave with equal vigour, the main site ignored, no new evidence at all for Genghis's burial – without denigrating the other findings, for amateur glibness it is, in my opinion, hard to beat.

The strangest omission was the failure properly to in-vestigate the place that is the most likely burial-site, Burkhan Khaldun/Khan Khenti itself. The omission passed without comment in the project's report. It is baffling: that the best-funded research project ever should ignore the most significant site in Mongol history seems perverse, in-competent or deliberate. In fact, several experts told me it was deliberate, on government orders. In the words of Badamdash, the old philologist we met on our way from Avraga, 'The authorities decided that the Three Rivers Project would not find any graves.' If so, the order reflects a well-known 'prophecy' that if Genghis's grave is found, the nation will fall. Some take this very seriously. I was told that a Mongolian project member was actually threatened with death if the team investigated Khan Khenti's southern slopes. No proof, of course; certainly never any formal admission. But a word here and a rumour there would have been enough. The whole thing was doomed from the start, planting a lin-gering suspicion that the Japanese had a hidden agenda, namely conducting a secret survey for minerals by satellite. Hearsay, folklore, foreign cash and national pride: this is a recipe for a murky brew that drives mad those who drink it.

So the Three Rivers team disbanded, leaving the way clear for the latest, the most determined and perhaps the most well-publicized grave-hunter: Maury Kravitz, financier, from Chicago. Kravitz has been passionate about Genghis and Mongolia ever since he read Harold Lamb's classic biography of Genghis 40 years ago, and now has one of the world's greatest libraries on the subject. He raised $5.5 million, set up an advisory board and signed a contract with the Institute of Geography – the same organization that had backed the Three Rivers Project – for exclusive rights to search for the grave, announced in a flurry of publicity in August 2001.

The place he chose to excavate, the Almsgiver's Wall, is a marvel in its own right. It is a beautifully chosen site, up a side valley just off the plain that sweeps northward from the old capital of Avraga into the Mongol heartland, with the main mass of the Khenti mountains off to the west. When I arrived with Khishig, Baatar and Goyo, we found a highly professional dig in full swing, based in a fenced compound of five smart one- and two-room wooden houses, four *gers* and a dozen vehicles.

Behind the compound was a 200-metre-high ridge loosely scattered with firs, with a rubble of boulders shouldering through on the higher and steeper flanks. The site's main feature is the immense wall that encloses a semicircle of the ridge 3 kilometres in length. I walked to the top of the ridge and marvelled: it is an exquisite example of dry-stone walling, 3 or 4 metres high, sheer on the outside, leaning back a few degrees for solidity against a sloping bank of lesser stones, making a bulwark roughly triangular in cross-section. In the section I walked, the stones forming the outside edge were rough-cut, as if levered straight from bedrock. Some could have been lifted by one man, most could be managed by two or three, but a few would have needed a team. At a rough estimate, the wall's main outer edge would have had a few hundred thousand large blocks, with some 10,000 cubic metres of smaller stones as backing. In fact, the quality is not continuous. At the top, the wall was little more than a bank of rubble filling the gaps between outcrops and monoliths. Still, the whole gigantic construction must have taken a small army, including some experts on dry-stone walling, several years to build.

What on earth was it for? It is not a fortress, for there are no gates or proper defences, and attackers would find it easy to pull out its loose stones; the weather alone has tumbled bits of it over the centuries. Without a gatehouse, it could hardly have been a town wall. Anyway, the position is wrong:

there have been many towns built by successive cultures in Mongolia, but they are built on plains, where the inhabitants can see around them. Here, horizons were closed in by crests and trees. According to one bizarre suggestion, it might have been a game reserve; but a flat-topped wall backed on the inside by a slope of rubble would hardly keep in an aged cow.

The on-site supremo was John Woods, Professor of Middle Eastern History at the University of Chicago. Woods, with the bulk of a light-heavyweight wrestler, was every inch the burly boss of his half-dozen colleagues and score of workers, all digging, scraping, sifting and dusting in four shallow pits. He stepped aside from a theodolite to tell me why this place was important: 'There are tombs all over this country, tombs of all periods, square, round, Scythian, bronze age. The place is an archaeological paradise. Untouched, totally untouched. Especially the medieval period. The Soviets were interested in prehistorical sites, but they did not do medieval research because for them that was a regressive period in the history of mankind. Even if we don't find anything, the fact that we generate interest in this place and get people working, that's extremely important.'

They had already found quite a bit. Some charcoal. A bit of a cranium, perhaps. Something black, human remains maybe, which should yield a carbon date. The four pits seemed to be floored with heavy stones, but it was hard to tell if they really formed floors because everything tends to drift downhill, and fallen boulders look much like foundation-stones.

There were no answers yet, but Woods had a working hypothesis: 'My major goal is to establish that this is a necropolis.'

The word carries implications of royal tombs. But whose? The few indications so far suggest that the wall is probably pre-Mongol, possibly Liao (dating from the kingdom of the Khitan, 947–1125), though what a Liao necropolis is doing in this most Mongol of places nobody has a clue. And a dry-stone wall on its own is virtually impossible to date. It could have been made by any one of half a dozen cultures, dating back to Hun times several centuries BC.

Which takes us to the nub of the matter, and the controversies surrounding the project. Kravitz, who uses Genghis as an icon to raise interest and money, had apparently hoped to dig on Burkhan Khaldun, but had been forbidden to do so. The Alsmgiver's Wall was the default site. Still, he made the best of it, expressing high hopes that Genghis himself was buried here. It is, after all, an easy 130 kilometres from Avraga, 30 from Genghis's probable birthplace, 90 from Burkhan Khaldun, just on the frontier between mountain hideaways and rich grasslands. But there are several objections. This immense structure took years to build; are we to assume that Genghis planned it years in advance as his final resting-place? And could it be that a secret tomb would be left in so obvious a place? And how does a rocky hillside equate with a grassland grave flattened by galloping horses?

So far, there is no evidence that the place has or had anything at all to do with Genghis. But because Genghis was on the agenda that raised the cash and generated all the publicity, he had somehow to be made a part of the operation. This certainly suited one Mongolian member of the expedition, Bazagur, who has built something of a career in marketing sites connected with Genghis, many of them of questionable authenticity. A wooden sign proclaimed this to be the 'Place of the Great Ones as specified in *The Secret History*. [Signed] Genghis Khan Expedition.' This was a blatant hype, because the phrase 'The Place of the Great Ones' is itself spurious.[4] It exists at all only as the result of an error committed in 1941 by a Russian translator of *The Secret History*, who interpreted an obscure phrase referring to a sacrifice as an

---

[4] Igor de Rachewiltz, 'Searching for Genghis Qan', *Rivista degli Studi Orientali*, 71, 1997, pp. 239–56.

ancestral cemetery. The misunderstanding was then re-incorporated in a popular Mongolian version in 1947, this being a time when Russian culture and language dominated scholarship. The mistake was never rectified, with the result that Genghis's burial-site – on Burkhan Khaldun, here at the Almsgiver's Wall or anywhere else – is commonly called 'The Place of the Great Ones' by people who should know better, and often do. There is no evidence that the Mongol leaders ever had a single ancestral burial site, let alone that Genghis was buried there.

Confusion and controversy blurred into outright hostility. The philologist Badamdash was incensed at what Kravitz's team was doing. 'He is one hundred per cent wrong!' – wrong in both senses, theoretically and morally – 'It's too soon to dig up Genghis's grave. He won't find it anyway. It's a state secret. Certainly it's not inside the Almsgiver's Wall, which is from Khitan times, long before Genghis.'

By an irony, it seemed to be precisely the publicity about Genghis that brought Kravitz's dig to a sudden end soon after I was there in summer 2002. Top people had become incensed that foreigners were meddling in Mongolia's most sacred places, even though there was no proof that the Almsgiver's Wall was sacred to anyone or anything to do with Genghis. Kravitz's team got their marching orders – at least, so the press reported, with some glee. 'Let's Respect Our Ancestors!' proclaimed the Mongol daily *Unen* (Truth), in an interview on 17 August with Woods, who was by then on his way home. The interview implied the existence of some real, if indeterminate, political opposition:

Reporter: Who stopped you?
Woods: I do not know exactly who. I think the *aimag* [regional] governor made a request to the local governor on July 22.

Listen to Kravitz, though, and the truth is the exact opposite. What about the supposed ban on digging on Burkhan Khaldun? Nonsense, he said. They had the rights to dig anywhere they wanted, including Burkhan Khaldun. They had just chosen the Almsgiver's Wall because it was the best place to look. The dig ended because it was the end of the season. Simple as that. All talk of political controversy and local opposition was untrue, or dealt with, or insignificant. Given Kravitz's drive and financial backing; given the undeniable importance of the site; and given the team's commitment to involve Mongolian archaeologists and institutions, I have a feeling that any opposition will fade, and that Kravitz's team will be back, with significant, indeed astonishing, revelations to follow.

But only from the Almsgiver's Wall. Not from Burkhan Khaldun. And not, I'll bet, about Genghis Khan.

17

ON THE HOLY MOUNTAIN

FROM A DISTANCE BURKHAN KHALDUN – KHAN KHENTI – SEEMED quite accessible: not too high, only 200 kilometres from Ulaanbaatar, a day's run by car. But when I talked over the idea of climbing it with people who knew, heads were shaken and lips pursed. There was a 30-kilometre approach road, over permafrost, which melted in spring, turning the track to mud. In summer, rain regularly made it impassable. I put the idea to the back of my mind.

But a chink of opportunity opened. The trip to Avraga, to Genghis's probable birthplace and to the Blue Lake where he was probably crowned left a day or two to spare. We were fording the Kherlen, 150 metres of fast-flowing, shallow water, when I saw how close I was to realizing a dream. The UAZ van was in the middle of the river, where the water ran a metre deep, when water splashed into the engine and stalled it. Khishig, the driver with neck and arms scarred by an exploding blow-torch, treated this typical countryside occurrence with typical phlegm. Either the engine would dry out or it wouldn't. If it didn't, another car or a horseman would appear, or Khishig would go for help, or something. Anyway, for the next few minutes, there would be peace, with no sound but that of the water lapping just below floor level.

Here was a chance to find out exactly where we were, in every sense. Goyo took a reading with her GPS scanner. I unfolded the map. Yes, the co-ordinates told us exactly which part of the river we were in the middle of. I followed the Kherlen's course on the map. There, 60 kilometres to the north, only a hop and a skip from the Kherlen itself, was Burkhan Kaldun. No distance at all. Besides, the last few days had been dry. It would be a crime not to see if we could at least get close.

The engine restarted after five minutes. On the other side of the Kherlen, upriver, was our destination for that night, a *ger* camp; here I could get more detailed advice from the camp's owner, Gansukh, who was expanding his travel business into the countryside. Instantly, a major deterrent became apparent: the flies. In the Khenti a wet summer breeds flies, and this one had been wet, making rich pastures for the pestering little midges and vicious horseflies that draw blood from the horses and force people to seek the protection of *gers* filled with dung-smoke. Outside, hands wave constantly. Gansukh and I might as well have been communicating in semaphore. If the mud didn't stop me, the flies would.

And besides, what was no distance for a vulture was an infinity for an inexperienced foreigner in a hurry. The approach track, if passable, led to a bog, which gave on to a shoulder between two hills, which dropped through another bog to a river, and then there was another 20 kilometres to cover before you even reached the bottom of the mountain. But people make it every year, I countered, they go to honour Genghis. Yes, but Mongolians go on horseback, slowly, in crowds. For me, it would be a logistical nightmare. This was all within the uninhabited Khan Khenti National Park. There were no herders nearby to provide food and lodging.

There was no guarantee a car would get there. If I opted for horses, they would have to be hired in Möngönmört, 70 kilometres from the mountain, which meant the approach alone would take a couple of days, which in turn meant the whole thing would have to be organized weeks in advance. I would need a guide, and someone for the horses, and food and tents, to be carried by a fourth horse. And this operation would be large and slow enough for the whole community to know about it, and since Burkhan Khaldun was part of a national park, I would need official permission. If I tried an approach with the UAZ and my three companions, I would be up against a local taboo. The shoulder of high ground over which I would have to travel guarded land sacred from long before the arrival of Buddhism. No lamas were supposed to cross it, *and no women either*. Goyo would have to remain on the ridge. Best forget the whole idea.

I couldn't. I had to try for a distant glimpse of Genghis's sacred mountain. We would do it simply, directly and quickly, and hope for the best.

Next morning we struck north, through the patchwork of car tracks and dark-brown houses and stockades of Möngönmört. It looked like the Old West before roads and fences, with a name to suit: it means 'At the Silver Horse'. Beyond this, for a few hours, was a happiness far beyond that offered by travel on horseback: the wind through the windows keeping the flies clear, the UAZ running easily through open savannah, the Kherlen winding prettily among aspens and birches a kilometre away, the mountains drawing us on.

We had stopped for tea at a *ger*, the last human habitation before the Khan Khenti National Park, when we received a small warning of trouble ahead. Sitting on a little stool on the left side of the central stove, as was proper for a guest, I noticed two pictures amid the photographs that today take the place of household gods in family *gers*. One was of Stalin, in his benign 'Uncle Joe' guise; the Russians had abandoned Mongolia so brutally fast in the early 1990s, and the rejection of communism had been so total, that it was a surprise to see any remnant of old respect. The other was a child's drawing of Genghis Khan, done by a twelve-year-old who was away at school. Was there some link between these two authority figures? The thought died at birth, swept aside by the noise of galloping hooves and a yell:

'A wolf! Attacking the goats!'

In seconds, someone had a gun and we were in the van, the four of us and two other men. No question this was our problem as well, because the van was all we had to offer in return for hospitality. We reached the herd, a few dozen sheep and goats, which scattered to a wary distance – all except a small bundle on the ground. There was, of course, no sign of the wolf. The bleating bundle was a kid, with blood pouring from a tear in its abdomen. The two men rolled it over. The wound was dire, intestines on the grass, half-eaten. Obviously, it would die soon.

'We will leave it here,' one of the men explained. 'Wolves return for their kill. Perhaps we can shoot it then.'

So I was half-expecting the gun. Instead, one of the men took out a penknife, slowly and steadily drove the blade into the chest cavity, forced a hand inside and grabbed the heart. The kid made no complaint, seeming to feel no additional pain, and the operation, surprisingly peaceful and surprisingly affecting for an outsider to watch, was over in seconds.

Ten minutes on across the grassy billows, a wooden watchtower marked the entry to 1,200 square kilometres of wilderness. Mountains rise only to about 2,500 metres, poking bare crests above the forest like the pates of tonsured monks, but tracks are few, visitors fewer, inhabitants nonexistent. This is the domain of deer, moose, bear and wolf, the same species that inhabit the Siberian taiga stretching away northward. It was not always so empty, of course, because this is part of the Mongol heartland, the source of the three rivers that were a part of Mongol identity. The hard-to-reach valleys, where willow beds and patches of poor grassland run up into fir forest and bare rock, were hideaways for Genghis's family when he was young, and had remained occasional pastures and good hunting grounds ever since. Only in 1992 was the area finally declared a park, and nature left to take its course. Our recent encounter made me wonder what our fate might be if we broke down in this unpeopled region.

The mountains crowded in, forcing the track to cross the Kherlen over a remarkably heavy-duty wooden bridge, its bulk an indication of the significance of this route. It was the only way to Burkhan Khaldun, the only way for government officials to make their occasional visits to the sacred slopes. We were in luck: the last rain had come and gone a few days before, and the track from the bridge was almost dry. It led on across beds of willow bushes sloping down gently to the river, punctuated with burned pines, the black and spiky remnants of forest fires three years before. Baatar burst into song in his high, accurate tenor, singing of the Khenti, and, as if in response to a shaman's chant, a stag bounded away through the supple willows. We were alone in pure wilderness, the only sign of human presence being the track, along which, judging from the crushed grasses, cars came once or twice a week. What on earth did they come for? To make lonely offerings to Genghis?

The track rose towards a low ridge.

'It is the place they call the Threshold,' said Baatar. 'But that is not its real name.'

'What's its real name?'

'We do not say it,' said Goyo in a low voice, for many sacred places, usually mountains, have a name taboo upon them. 'We do not even point to it.'

'You can tell me,' I said, crassly. 'I am a writer.'

Goyo hesitated, then muttered the name, a confidence it

would be churlish to break. The track levelled out briefly and then, as if punishing us for our temerity, ended in a chaos of wheel-marks where cars had plunged and spun themselves axle-deep. We were on the edge of a small bog, created by meltwater from the slope ahead. Khishig and Baatar squished about, assessing whether we could make it through to the wheel-tracks which picked up again 20 metres beyond. To our left, the Kherlen cut between two steep hills. Flies invaded the car. The heat rose.

'They say there is no way,' said Goyo.

'But who made these marks?' I was irritated with Khishig for not being ready to take a risk. '*They* got through.'

'It was government people, two months ago,' said Baatar. 'They come once every three or four years. Many cars, many ropes, winches, maybe a tractor.' Actually, they could well have been made by Kravitz and his team, who had also been this way earlier in the summer, before starting work at the Almsgiver's Wall.

'If we get stuck, we will be here for days,' Khishig added. 'Only the birds can do it.'

He was right. I could see where some cars had turned and given up. The best I could hope for was a view of my impossible goal from the top of the slope.

An easy walk led to the ridge, and to a shrine, an *ovoo* made of pine-trunks leaning against each other like a tepee, all strewn about with tattered bits of blue silk and vodka bottles. We made our ritual threefold circuit. This was the way – the only way – in: the way Genghis must have fled to safety, the way his coffin would have been brought, down to the valley which lay open and welcoming in the midday sun. There ran the Kherlen, making a sharp bend around a scree-covered hill known locally as Genghis's Nose.[1] And there, beyond, rose the mountains I so much wanted to

---

[1] According to Schubert, who relied on Perlee. I had no local to ask.

explore, one of them, I couldn't tell which, surely being Burkhan Khaldun. They were as breathtaking and remote as a mirage, because at our feet the ground fell away sharply in an appalling mess of wheel-torn peat. Even without Goyo, who was distinctly nervous about breaking the taboo on women going beyond this point; even if we had driven the impossible ascent this far; the headlong descent down the 200 metres of rutted peat into the valley beyond would have been madness, for then what? There would be no possibility of escape. Besides, a storm was moving in, rolling down over the mountains opposite. As we fled back to the car, valley and mountains vanished with my hopes under a curtain of cloud and driving rain.

Back in Ulaanbaatar, I became angry at my bad luck. To be so close, and yet so far! I had three days to spare. Inspired by frustration, an idea jumped into my mind, mildly crazy, but worth a try. I knew a car could get to the Threshold. From there, it was only 18 or 20 kilometres to Burkhan Khaldun. There was no need for horses. I could *walk* it. All I needed was a companion, a tent and a little food. A 20-kilometre hike, a night on Burkhan Khaldun, 20 kilometres back – why, it could be done in two days, three maximum. I put the idea to Graham Taylor, the Australian who had organized the trip so far. I valued both his advice – he's a traveller himself, fit, experienced, ambitious, straightforward – and his contacts, one of whom out of the blue became an inspiration.

Igor de Rachewiltz, in the Department of Pacific and Asian History at the Australian National University, Canberra, is supreme in his field. As Vice-President of the International Association for Mongol Studies, he had kept a critical eye on both the Three Rivers Project and Maury Kravitz's venture; moreover, he had climbed Burkhan Khaldun himself. Now he responded instantly to my enquiry, emailing two unpublished papers on Genghis's tomb and on his visit to the mountain five years previously. From a quick reading it seemed that the climb itself wasn't hard – if I could only get to the starting-point.

The guide Graham found for me had never been on the mountain, but he was an ex-tank-commander with spirit to match. A Tintin-in-Tibet T-shirt and a digger hat, given to him by an Australian tourist, endowed him with an air of jaunty optimism. His name alone was enough to inspire confidence: Tumen, 'Ten Thousand', the name of the largest of Genghis's military units. By another of those coincidences that mark life in Mongolia, I had almost met him once. On leaving the army he had been an oil-company worker at Zuunbayan in the southern Gobi, at a well once run by Russians and since taken over by a small American company, Nescor, which had put me up on a previous trip. We knew the same people, and had missed each other by only a few months. It was in Zuunbayan that he had learned English by being employed as an interpreter – in that order: the job first, then the language. Considering he hadn't started to learn until he was over 30, he had an astonishing facility. The third member of the party was the driver of our 4×4, Erdenebaatar ('Jewel Hero'): slim as a weasel, as expert with his Russian Jeep as a warrior with his horse. Both listened to my deeply suspect plan for a 40-kilometre, two-day walk with no hint of what they thought. With some pot-noodles and salami bought in a Korean supermarket and a tent from Graham's stores, we were all set.

As soon as we reached the Threshold and its dead-end bog, Erdene showed his expertise. He checked out the bog, remounted his Jeep, and spurred it in a wide, bouncing sweep across virgin willow bushes. With the whippy branches acting as matting over the quaking ground, an impassable obstacle was suddenly reduced to a minor hindrance.

At the top, having paid the *ovoo* due deference, we

explored the descent, a steep and forbidding combination of sun-hardened ruts and peaty subsoil. Erdene and Tumen agreed. It would be like crossing tank-traps in a cambered marsh. Tumen and I explored further, down to the Kherlen, and were returning to load up for our marathon walk when Tumen pointed in astonished silence. There, way off along the shoulder of the Threshold, was the Jeep bumping over the willow bushes, and then descending towards us, taking the slope in zigzags as if it were an alpine pass.

Erdene pulled up beside us on the flood plain and explained. When the government party came through a couple of months before, a few cars had taken this route. He had followed their tracks. 'It was easy,' he said. 'But boggy. There are two places which I cannot cross going back.'

I could hardly grasp what he had let us in for, or why. Obviously we couldn't take the direct, steep route back, straight up the Threshold. Now he had discovered there was no way up the gentler, indirect way either. We were trapped.

Equally unnerving was the reaction of the two men: total unconcern. What was done was done, what would be would be. There was nothing for it but to follow through what had been started, with the advantage to Tumen and myself that we had no need to walk the next 20 kilometres.

Where now? I looked at my map. Burkhan Khaldun was ahead somewhere, hidden by an intervening shoulder of hills. The Kherlen cut across our path running from right to left, east to west. Beyond, three tributaries led up valleys into the highlands. I peered at the names, written in print almost too small to read. Igor's account had mentioned heading straight up the 'Bogd', the Holy River, and yes, it seemed that the one on the right was the Bogd. I could just see the initial *B* and the *o*.

But once across the Kherlen, I became confused. If there were mountains ahead, they were in cloud. The track was still well worn by official cars, and there was a signpost pointing straight ahead over the plain to the Bogd river. But on the map this same river was clearly labelled 'Kherlen'. Both fell from the great shoulder of Khan Khenti ridge. But the ridge had two peaks, one 90 metres higher than the other. On the map the river labelled 'Bogd', which was not the one signposted, led right to this high point. Surely we should be following the map, proceeding up the 'Bogd' to the higher of the two peaks, which must be Khan Khenti itself?

Suddenly, in a fit of paranoia, I saw the light. Were we not heading for a location which Genghis himself had ordered to be kept secret, a place carefully preserved for the last 800 years from prying eyes? Was there not an enduring confusion about which mountain was Burkhan Khaldun? Why, if there was a big secret and historical confusion, were there tracks and signposts? *It was all too simple.* We were being horribly and deliberately deceived, the victims of a government dis-information plot.

'Tumen, we're in the wrong valley.'

'Where should we be?' He was so trusting he never even asked to check my map-reading, poor chap.

'Over there, not the next valley, the one after that.'

'What do we do?'

It was blindingly obvious to me what we had to do. We had to walk across several miles of willow bushes and through a bit of forest, then eventually turn left and head uphill to the higher peak, which just had to be Burkhan Khaldun itself. I proudly rediscovered long-hidden qualities of leadership. 'We'll eat,' I said. 'Then walk until dark. Camp. Follow the Bogd as far as we can, climb Burkhan Khaldun if possible, but anyway be back by Wednesday midday. Right?'

Erdene was left with strict instructions. He was to wait right there, unless it rained, in which case he was to head fast for the Threshold, cross it somehow, and wait for us the other side. If he got stuck, as he had predicted he would, we would find him easily enough and think again. Anyway, we would see him in a day or two.

Tumen and I took our packs and strode off as best we could, zig-zagging through waist-high bushes, wading across side streams of what my map said was the Kherlen and the signpost said was the Bogd. We sweated. My feet squelched in water-filled track-shoes. Flies milled above us. I tried to escape them by going uphill, through tongues of fir-forest. The flies were just as bad, and the forest was a litter of fallen trunks from the fire three years before. Tumen, carrying his pack and something of a beer belly, began to lag. Whenever I turned, I saw him up to his waist in willow bushes, flies round his head like a halo against the setting sun. It was hell.

After three hours we reached the river I was aiming for. In gathering gloom and irritation, we argued about where to make camp between the willow bushes and how best to raise a tent that was all whippy strutting and odd shapes. Then there was a fire to be lit. Oh, yes, I said, burning what exactly? Dung, said Tumen. And there was indeed much dried dung scattered between the bushes, from deer I supposed. But the willow-twig kindling was wet and wouldn't burn.

'I am an idiot,' muttered Tumen, as we took turns with the single box of matches. 'I forgot the gasoline.'

I didn't tell him what I had forgotten: the compass. So if we woke up in cloud, we would be seriously, seriously in deep deer-dung. By now there were only a dozen matches left. We became competitive about lighting the fire, grinding up damp twigs into ever finer tinder, until at last dung-smoke and darkness saved us from the flies.

I took out our food, the pot-noodles I had picked up in a Korean supermarket in Ulaanbaatar.

'What is this women's food?' sneered Tumen. 'Who bought this?'

'Goyo,' I lied.

'Why did she not ask me? I am a Mongolian! I need meat!'

In the end, shared adversity and women's food reconciled us, and we slept.

*

At six-thirty, I crawled out into sanity and clarity. There was a ribbon of mist along the valley below, but the flies were not up yet, and the sun bathed the firs above. If there was a mountain up the valley, I couldn't see it for the forest. I got out the map and started to cross-check it against Igor's account. He had headed for Khan Khenti, which meant going up the river labelled Bogd on *his* map. But Khan Khenti was off to the left, approached by what *my* map called the Kherlen. Now I was on the Bogd, so the peak ahead had to be the right one.

But it couldn't be. This was a trackless waste, utterly unmarked by cars or horses. I held the map out to the rising sun, peered more closely, and remembered a magnifying glass in the depths of my pack. Oh, God. The river below wasn't labelled Bogd at all. The tiny blue print read not *B-o* . . . but *B-a* . . . Baga something . . . Baga Ar, 'Little Back'.

I must say, when I broke the news to Tumen that we were in the wrong valley and had better head back to the car, he took it very well. We finished the damp bread, packed the dew-soaked tent and set off downhill. It was a relief, I suppose, to know that quite soon we would be back in the car heading up the right valley towards the right mountain.

We were following low-lying ground, where the willow bushes gave way to coarse grass, when I stumbled on a strange collection of stones, all roughly fist-sized, forming an irregular blob about a metre and a half across. Perhaps someone had been buried down here. But it seemed an odd place for a grave, away from the mountain, in the middle of a boggy plain, where no-one – that much was obvious now – had any reason to come; and an odd shape too, even assuming the effects of centuries of weather. Wouldn't a grave be overgrown? The stones were suspiciously clear of grass. It seemed to me that they had more likely been washed together by some natural process. I took a picture, and put the puzzle to the back of my mind, where it remained until I had cause to retrieve it later.

Away from the trees we followed the main river, which was obviously the Kherlen itself, whatever my map said, heading westwards, the sun drying our backs. Any moment, we would be able to see the car round the flanks of the forested slopes we had crossed the previous night.

Suddenly, now that we were back from the obscuring foothills, looking up the valley I saw straight ahead our unmistakable and unclouded goal. Burkhan Khaldun, the Khan of the Khentis, was a grey shoulder of rock rising clear above its surrounding forests, jutting out like a flexed muscle. It was incredibly bad luck that cloud, or hill, or forest had kept it hidden until now; the best luck of all that it was now revealed. Near the summit glistened a single white spot, which, from a distance of 15 kilometres, made me wonder if someone had built a *ger* up there or some sort of *ovoo*.

In the right conditions, we would have been well on our way. But the conditions were not right. The Khenti were brewing something extremely nasty. Although we were in bright sunlight, as was Burkhan Khaldun, the western sky was being swallowed by a grim, dark-purple cloud-bank, spreading out above the hills, flowing towards us with throaty rumbles, like a Harley-Davidson waiting at a red light. No wonder we couldn't see the car. Erdene would have seen and heard, and fled for the Threshold. We had better do the same.

We were ten minutes from the Threshold when the sun vanished, the growling motorbike turned to Western Front artillery and the heavens opened. My world contracted to a blur. I whipped a poncho over pack, camera, tape-recorder and notebook, and glanced at Tumen. He had no protection over his Tintin-in-Tibet T-shirt and track-suit but his Australian hat, which poured like a roof without guttering.

At the pass, there was no sign of Erdene or the car. He must have made it over to the other side somehow. This was good news in that we could get out; bad news in that it marked a depressing end to my ambitions, with a muddy exit still to come, assuming the road was passable.

We climbed the Threshold, while behind us the storm rumbled on up the valley, and descended the other side as far as the bog. Still no sign of the car. I checked again what Tumen had agreed with Erdene.

'I told you a thousand times!' he shouted. 'Either he would stay where he left us, or he would be here!'

Perhaps we had missed him. We plodded back up, and over, and down, and all the way to our drop-off point. No car. We looked for tracks; all had been washed away into mud and puddles.

Dreadful scenarios hovered before us as we recrossed the Threshold for the nth time. The car had developed a fault, and Erdene had taken off to get it fixed. A bear had got him (but where was the car?). He had simply abandoned us (but why?). Anyway, we were on our own. We would have to walk out along the 30-kilometre track, and then some, to get to the first *ger*, assuming the family with the wolf-problem was still there. And we were almost out of food.

Night was coming, and so was another storm. We pitched camp right in the middle of the track, by the bog, just in time to avoid the first heavy drops. In seconds, a waterfall turned the tent into a snare-drum. With the tent's thin fabric trembling under the assault, talk was impossible. I sank into a morass of bewilderment and depression, trying to rationalize our plight. We would never have made it far on foot in this weather. Some wild driving by Erdene had opened the way, only for me to blow it with a stupid mistake. Then again, without that mistake, we would have been halfway up Burkhan Khaldun by now, in *this*, without a compass. Bad luck and bad judgement seemed somehow to have either ruined us or saved us; perhaps both. I could make no sense of it.

'It's good you are patient,' shouted Tumen over the thrashing of the rain.

'There's no choice,' I yelled back.

'Other people would have blamed me and beaten me.'

'Don't be silly.' I couldn't imagine anyone taking against his determined optimism. Besides, it was all my fault.

'I am not silly. *They* beat me.' He shook his head at a memory.

'Who beat you?'

'The . . . the Italians! And you know the first thing that came out of their mouths? "But we paid! We pa-a-i-id!"' He brayed the word above the rain, as if his Italians were donkeys to think that payment guaranteed anything in this uncertain world.

I never got around to asking what happened. I was thinking what we had left to eat: two bits of salami, one pot of yoghurt and half a bar of chocolate. Just women's food; no meat for the 30-kilometre walk that might confront us the following day, rain or no rain.

So I would have to rely on the written accounts of others' experiences, principally those of Schubert and de Rachewiltz, who had followed in Schubert's steps 36 years after him. As the rain fell from a darkening sky I now read his words again, with greater care.

De Rachewiltz's expedition had not been quite so easy, after all. His team had consisted of ten people who were all on a two-week trip to several historic sites. The team included a woman. Since women were barred from Burkhan Khaldun, there was to be a special dispensation, supplied by a shaman hired for the purpose. They travelled in three vehicles, with several horses hired in Möngönmört following on behind for the final climb. With such good support they were able to cross the Threshold – 'a horrible ride,' he wrote to me later.

'We got bogged several times and spent hours extricating ourselves.'

As they set up camp at the lower *ovoo* a feast was prepared, while the shaman did his stuff – 'with dancing, chanting, drumming, trance, the lot'. At the end of the feast, 'we were informed by the shaman that the spirit of Genghis Khan had granted permission for all of us to climb the mountain in order to revere him.' It took 20 minutes to reach the first plateau, where Igor, like Schubert, found fragments of tiles and bricks, along with two large metal vases, all left over from the collapse of Kamala's temple.

On they went, through thickets to the next level, which sounded far more interesting than in Schubert's description, because it really looked to Igor like a vast burial-ground. 'We found ourselves on a flat, bare area a few hundred metres wide, the ground clearly pock-marked by ancient excavations, i.e. by holes dug and then refilled with earth, stone and debris, all clearly visible through the sparse cover of low grass.' After another steep rise, they found the *ovoo*-cairns. 'There were no traces of graves, but looking down over the mountain shoulder below, the work of man on the surface of the ground is clearly visible.' Igor's intriguing conclusion was that it seemed 'plausible, and indeed most likely [that] here, on the south and southeastern side of the mountain . . . the Mongol emperors lie buried'.

The fact that I had missed a chance to make a relatively simple two-hour climb to a cemetery that might include Genghis's grave was almost too much to bear. I switched off my torch and lay in miserable darkness. It was still raining. To cap it all, I had no foam mattress and no pillow. Exhausted by damp and disappointment, I escaped into a long sleep.

I awoke after a ten-hour limbo. The storms were past. It was a gorgeous morning, with a sky of eggshell blue, while all around over the willow bushes lay soft mist, veiling the lower slopes and the track along which we would soon have to walk.

I had been outside only a few minutes when I heard a sound from deep in the mist. For a second, my mind denied the evidence of my ears. I stared, blank as the mist itself through which, like a manifestation from the spirit world, emerged the Jeep, with Erdene nonchalant at the wheel.

Tumen murmured a soft greeting from inside the tent, and began to extract himself from his sleeping-bag while Erdene told a story of drama and coincidence. After dropping us, he had foreseen rain, and started back the way he had come, taking the dog's-leg with the easy climb. As he had guessed, he couldn't make it. He spun himself into a trench, and then had no option but to wait for us to dig him out. So he went to sleep. He was woken next morning, about the time I realized I had misread the map, by seven men. They were hunters, off to poach moose in the national park (so it was poachers who kept the approach track open, not lone worshippers). They were on foot because their car had got bogged down on the approach road, 7 or 8 kilometres back, in the previous day's rain. For them, Erdene's presence in his bog was a minor miracle, as their arrival was for him. They pulled him out, hitched a lift back to their car, and took him to their camp, where he slept the second night, receiving by way of thanks a marmot cooked in its own skin, wire-tied and blow-torched in the proper fashion. So here he was, right on schedule – and with meat into the bargain. We were saved. The mist was rolling away, revealing a true blue sky. It was going to be a fine, un-muddy day for the run back to Ulaanbaatar.

We were happily tearing our way through the marmot, slurping the rich juice, prising tough meat from between our teeth, when Tumen, who had been exchanging a few staccato comments with Erdene, said the most astonishing thing I had heard on a trip full of astonishments.

'So what do you think? We go to Burkhan Khaldun now?'

'*What!?*'

'Don't you listen? The hunters told him it is no big deal. You just go to the end of the road where we parked the car, and then we climb.'

This struck me as completely crazy. I didn't doubt we could get there. It was leaving that was the problem. With one exit too steep for the Jeep, the other an impassable bog, they both knew we couldn't possibly get out again without help. Tumen watched delight, disbelief and apprehension chase each other across my face.

'Once we're here,' he shrugged. 'The job's gotta be done.'

Well, when help was needed, help had come. Obviously, in the vaguest and least religious way possible, they expected Eternal Heaven to provide. Who was I, on whose behalf a prayer had been offered to Genghis himself, to gainsay them?

'OK. Let's go.'

I had to turn away briefly to hide my reaction, because I found their gesture too touching for words. I couldn't see why they would want to do such a mad and generous thing. Apparently whatever we had shared had inspired a commitment way beyond anything money could buy.

We repacked, we reloaded, we reclimbed the Threshold, and Erdene did not pause. The descent down the steep and wheel-rutted slope was a lurching helter-skelter of exhilaration and fear, and over in half a minute. We were committed, in fact trapped, as far as I could see, to the utter unconcern of Erdene, who was back now on the track he had covered two days before. This man was charging by the kilometre, with no thought that some kilometres were worse than others. God knows how much the last one was worth on the open market; a lot less than the return would be, in any event.

Forty minutes later, with the sunlit summit of Burkhan Khaldun drawing us on, the valley closed in, the track rose through trees and we reached its end, by a sign reading 'Protect our natural places!' Beneath firs stood the enormous *ovoo* of tree-trunks mentioned by Schubert and Igor, littered with tangles of blue silk and flags. One big *ovoo* on the Threshold, and now this, with more to come: we were on a pilgrim route marked by shrines, a sort of Mongolian Stations of the Cross. We circled slowly three times, flapping at flies, and filed onto a path leading up through the trees.

A 20-minute climb through cool, sweet-smelling firs brought us to a flat area of mossy hummocks. It looked suspiciously level, artificially so; this was obviously the spot where Kamala's temple had once stood. It was still a sort of a temple, for in among the slender firs was another *ovoo* of fir-trunks, in front of which stood two enormous metal pots for sacrificial offerings and an altar, also of tree-trunks, covered with empty bottles and saucers for incense. From the *ovoo*'s wigwam-like trunks dangled Tibetan prayer-flags. I wandered over the hummocks, wondering what they might conceal. What had become of the temple? Were its walls of stone or wood? Did it fall or was it pushed? Where had all the rubble gone since Igor saw it – stolen, pirated for other buildings or buried?

Right at the edge of the flat area, where footsteps had worn into the soft earth, were bits of tile. With a rush of excitement, I picked up a couple. I have them still, these two bits of grey-brown pottery: nothing special, coarsely made, smooth on one side, unglazed. As I write, they still smell faintly of damp peat. They would have formed half-cylinders of two sizes, one with a diameter of a dinner-plate (21.5 centimetres across), the other a saucer-sized 9 centimetres. From the tiny impressions on the inner surface, they were moulded or dried on some sort of sacking. Jessica Harrison-Hall, an expert in Chinese ceramics at the British Museum, tells me they are typical of Chinese roof tiles, and could easily be from 1300, probably made on the spot from clay brought in from elsewhere.

As we set off upwards again, more steeply now and through firs becoming stunted by altitude, I imagined wooden walls, a portico roofed with little tiles, leading to a simple room with an altar, an incense burner, and a portrait of Kamala's great-grandfather restored in spirit to the mountain that he had designated as holy. But that was just dreaming. What I had in my hand was hard evidence to back the theory – no, the *fact* – that this was Burkhan Khaldun, and that the grave must be here somewhere. Kamala would not have got the wrong place.

But if Genghis was buried nearby, where? Here, on this plateau? Surely not. If Kamala had genuinely wished to respect Genghis's wishes, he would have kept the grave secret; in which case, would he really have drawn attention to it by setting workmen to dig the place flat, cutting trees, importing clay, making a kiln, baking tiles, ensuring regular obser-vances? No: the second platform, where Igor's stone-filled holes were, would be more rewarding.

Again the path rose steeply through firs, twisting upward over roots. It is not a hard climb, which is – of course; how stupid of me not to have realized – as it should be for a sacred mountain. My conspiracy theories about official dis-information were ridiculous. The whole point of a sacred mountain is that it should be accessible – not too easy, of course, for that would invite over-use, but not forbidding either. For anyone prepared to make the long approach with horses and a tent or two and follow the signs, Burkhan Khaldun is no harder than a Pyrenean stage on the pilgrim route to Santiago de Compostela, though without the cheer of a pilgrim hostel.

'It looks a tough place to live,' I said to Tumen as we climbed on. Erdene was out of sight ahead, striding up a hill-side that was all pines and larches and rooty soil. 'What would Genghis have lived on?'

'Pine-nuts.' Tumen caught up, panting. 'They make good

eating in the autumn. And there are berries, too. And the deer, the moose, and antelope. Marmot and squirrels down below.'

'What about wolves?'

'No problem, I think. Wolves prefer domestic herds. Not many in these deserted places.'

So much for that worry. After climbing for another half-hour in silence, we emerged onto the second plateau, where a cool wind blew between stunted evergreens. Ahead and above loomed the bald shoulder of the summit, with its enigmatic white eye, which I could now see was a patch of snow. All around were the features mentioned by Igor – scores, perhaps hundreds, of irregular collections of stones, some of them just the right size for graves. There were also a few little *ovoos* and proto-*ovoos*, where pilgrims had thrown together loose rocks in passing. My mind had been set on graves by Igor's words: *Ancient excavations . . . holes dug and then refilled . . . the work of man clearly visible . . . here . . . the Mongol emperors lie buried.* Once the idea is implanted, you can see exactly how these graves could have been made: the pro-cession of coffin-bearers climbing the steep trail up the cathedral-mountain, the digging of shallow pits, the ceremonial deposition, the careful piling of fist-sized stones into low piles, the rituals consigning the dead to Eternal Heaven, the sad and reverential departures, the centuries of rain and frost and snow gradually flattening the piles into their present forms.

Except that I did not credit my own imagination, because now that I saw the stone-patches, I could not believe they were graves.

The suspicion had been planted in my mind by the 'grave' I had seen the day before, down in the boggy and trackless lowlands. It had seemed to me then that the features were probably natural. Having now seen both sets, I felt the suspicion harden. The piles of rock were the same in both places: some roughly circular, but most with twisted edges, irregular as puddles, and of no standard size, ranging from 1 metre to 3 or 4 metres across. If the features down below were not graves, neither were the ones on the mountain.

I was almost certain that there was an entirely different explanation for these 'graves', and later research all but confirmed it.[2] This is a region of permafrost, in which only the top few feet of the ground thaw in the summer. Permafrost of this type has a life of its own, because freezing soil expands, as ice does, in winter and contracts again in summer, with results that depend on the type of rock and soil, and the slope, and the amount of surface water. Natural forces combine with the raw materials in strange and complex ways, producing features alien to those who live in temperate regions but familiar enough to Eskimos and Lapps – and to geocryologists, a rare breed of specialists who deal in cold-climate geology. From gravels, stones and rocks, periglacial environments produce a wonderful variety of polygons, circles, rings and mounds that look artificial, as if nature has indulged in Zen gardening on a massive scale (indeed, some of the first scientists in the Arctic thought they really were artificial). The world of geocryology is sonorous with jargon terms – frost-heave and solifluction, pingos and palsas, thermokarsts and hydrolaccoliths – but they all come down to the annual cycle of freezing and thawing at work on the many forms of stone.

I believe the 'graves' on Burkhan Khaldun are 'stony earth circles'. To understand how they are made, imagine a stone covered by damp soil in autumn. The first frosts come. Since the rock conducts heat faster than the surrounding soil, the

---

[2] My main source for these paragraphs is Peter Williams and Michael Smith, *The Frozen Earth: Fundamentals of Geocryology*.

earth underneath the rock freezes faster than adjacent soil. The newly frozen soil expands, pushing the rock upwards. Gardeners see the effects of this force in spring, when flowerbeds are mysteriously dotted with stones. The same process is at work on telegraph poles all over Mongolia's grasslands: unless rooted deep into permanently frozen ground, they rise, lean and fall. Different-sized rocks move at different speeds, and in a rock population slight differences in temperature and expansion push rocks on the fringes inwards as well as upwards. Eventually rocks sort themselves into similarly sized groups. As they rise to the surface, wind and rain scoop away debris and seeds. The result is a sort of rock fountain surging upwards and outwards, infinitely slowly, evolving perhaps – *perhaps*, because no-one has yet observed these processes over decades – from one form into another.

Sorting happens on a larger scale as well. Beside the field of stone circles was another uniform field, a couple of hundred metres across, of reddish rocks, ranging from fist-sized stones to boulders. They were terrible to walk on, all edges and angles that threatened to twist my feet as I picked my way over them. Even these solid blocks were on the move, elbowing each other aside here and there, leaving a few little grassy circles, micro-ecologies that mirrored the stone circles where Tumen and Erdene were lounging, more concerned with the weather than the sanctity, or otherwise, of their surroundings.

At the far side of this field was an *ovoo* of the same sharp rocks, built where worshippers could overlook a heart-stopping view down the valley of the winding Bogd, along which we had come, the little river glinting through trees, running down towards the open flood plain and the Threshold 20 kilometres away. To my right, several hundred metres down, was a lake scooped out of scree and forest. This was no place for family life, but a lone individual who knew these flanks and kept watch on the valleys for enemies could hide for ever, and find food and water, and still be only an hour away from pasture.

Was this a place for a khan to be buried in a secret grave? It should be, but I couldn't see it. The few accounts speak of grassland flattened by galloping horses, and thick forests growing to make a secure and secret precinct. But this plateau was hard for horses to reach en masse, and with the scantiest of tree covering, and on a highway to the summit – as public a place as you could get within 1,000 square kilometres.

And above, the high altar of this natural cathedral was suddenly lost in a cloud-bank, its edge rolling ominously downhill.

'John, we go! Fog's coming!'

I hesitated, then followed. I would have to take for granted the view over the Onon's headwaters and the field of *ovoos*.

We fled, over the stone circles, from the plateau that was not a cemetery, down over the flattened area where Kamala's temple had once been, to the Jeep. I left with the certainty that Genghis's spirit was rendered ever-present by regular obser-vances, offerings and the creation of *ovoos*; but as for his remains, my feeling was that grave-seekers should look some-where else, on flatter, better-forested slopes. They should look, but they should not expect to find.

And yet I do not feel the overwhelming certainty I should, partly because of the persistent rumour that some people know exactly where the grave is on Burkhan Khaldun; and partly because Igor de Rachewiltz totally disagrees with me.

Let me quote his chastening words:

> They [the stone circles] are not geological formations, but man's work. There is a lot of debris too next to the diggings, as you would expect. If you had had more time to cover the area you would not have missed the telling details. It is possible of course that some of the graves are empty; therefore only probes like those used by the Three Rivers team and Mr

Kravitz can reveal the real contents. In the meantime, one is kept guessing. Behind their jolly mask, the Mongols are a very secretive people, and under [communist prime ministers] Choibalsan and Tsedenbal Genghis was taboo, but a few scholars managed to by-pass the system and pass on inform-ation. It must all be taken *cum grano salis*, but certain patterns emerge when you put this info together and test it against data coming from other sources . . . The exact spots where Genghis and the later emperors are buried may still elude us, and I am sure even the Mongol cognoscenti could not point their fingers at them, but I personally am certain that the general area of the imperial burial ground is the shoulder between the Kamala shrine at the bottom and the *ovoo*-covered area at the top.

Well, he is very certain; and I am left wondering if there is a way to reconcile graves and stony circles. Perhaps there is. What if, among several hundred natural stony circles, there is one that isn't natural? How better to hide a royal grave than to place it in full view, right en route to the sacred summit, yet impossible to recognize among so many look-alike false graves? I can imagine a scene that makes sense, a single, simple burial deep in the permafrost, a gentle covering of stones roughly shaped to resemble the other stony patches, the horses of the coffin-bearers and mourners milling about the site until even those present could hardly tell man-made from nature's work.

Of course, this is a mystery that would be cleared up with proper archaeological research. But it would be an immense undertaking, to explore every one of the hundreds of stony circles, excluding one after another, until at last, perhaps, the one true grave is found, its plug of weather-shuffled stones concealing a coffin at least, and who knows what else besides.

It would be even easier if there were those who knew which is the one true grave. Here, though, we come up against another and deeper mystery: the nature of the secrecy that surrounds the grave. It is said by many that someone somewhere knows the real location. As Igor puts it, 'They have carried out the probes and found the exact location of the graves on the mountain.' Mongolia's most eminent academic, Professor Rintchen, told Igor 'that the area had been positively identified before 1970'. You hear the same thing from many scholars. Baatamdash told me: 'The grave is in the foothills of Burkhan Khaldun. It is a state secret.' But what is the nature of this state secret? Who are 'they'? No-one names names; there is no legislation; nothing is public; all is hearsay. It is supposedly a state secret because the grave is sacred, which confers a particular sort of protection not only on the grave, not only on the information about the grave, but also on the question of *whether the information even exists*. We are in a hall of mirrors, discussing a secret about a secret.

I went to see one of Mongolia's most respected historians, Dalai. An old friend, another Erdenebaatar, an expert on animal husbandry who had accompanied me into the Gobi six years before, tracked him down to one of the grim apartment blocks that arose in Ulaanbaatar after the war. He was in his seventies when we met but looked older, an image of ageless wisdom. History, his life's work, was written on his lined face, sounded through his powerful bass voice, was apparent in shelf upon shelf of books in old Mongol, Cyrillic Mongol, Chinese, Russian, Japanese, Korean, English even – there was Owen Lattimore's *Mongol Journeys*, the book that had been one of my sources on the Genghis Khan Mausoleum. I asked to look at it. The dedication startled me: 'To Dalai. In token of 10 years of friendship. Owen.'

'You knew him, too?' he said, and added casually, pointing to a dusty corner: 'I have Lattimore's camera. He left it here in case he should return. And his projector. And a suit of his clothes.' Lattimore died in 1989, at the age of 89, and had not been in Mongolia since the 1970s. The camera, projector and suit had been sitting there for some 30 years, awaiting a collection that never came.

When I asked about the grave, Dalai said, 'Many people are now searching for Genghis's grave. But I have never tried to find it. My heart would not let me. I recall Genghis's orders: Don't touch my burial-ground! Since then, no-one has touched it. It is a holy place, and should not be touched.'

In a way, Dalai said, the grave was unimportant. The important point was that Genghis himself was as real as a father. 'Let me describe Genghis as a personality,' he said. 'He was very open-hearted, very clever, not simply a military hero. We Mongolians are not happy to see him just as a military leader. He was a man with links to the Blue Heaven. Our Genghis Khan is sleeping in sanctified land, and would dislike it if you described him only in military terms.'

Does the grave exist? Does the secret knowledge of his grave exist? To neither of these questions is there an answer, because although many claim that both do indeed exist, no-one seems to know who exactly has the knowledge. Perhaps only those who know it know that they know it, the knowledge being shared by the members of a secret society sworn never to break trust, always (like Dalai and Badamdash) protecting their nation's founder with a shroud of holy untouchability.

I will serve the cause of secrecy, by clinging to scepticism. I think the double secret is a product of wishful thinking and awe. It is like the twist of camel-hair that was said to have captured Genghis's final breath. The hard evidence – the body, the grave, the knowledge – has dissipated into thin air, where it will drift for ever, unless politics and archaeology combine in the attempt to give it substance.

An hour after we left the mountain, the Threshold rose in front of us like a barricade. Erdene knew, with utter certainty, that he could not make it the long way round over the bog. He had no choice but to try the steep, direct, equally impossible route, straight up from the river to the *ovoo* at the top. He walked it carefully, planning his assault over the muddle of ruts and tussocks and soft ground. I began to see a purpose in his apparently mad decision. Here and there, our predecessors' wheels had left soil untouched; and at the edge, behind a line of willow bushes, was some firm footing, once used as a foot-path perhaps, without wheel-tracks.

While Tumen and I watched from the slope, Erdene reversed the Jeep to a side channel, accelerated across the rough but level ground, drove hard up the lower slope, and stuck, all four wheels digging their own graves. He got out and checked the ground, getting the measure of the problem. Now the advantage of choosing this steep track became clear. He was not stuck after all, because he could use gravity to reverse out of his axle-deep trap. He retreated, like a long-jumper measuring his run-up, revved the engine and threw himself at the slope again. Again he stuck, a little higher this time; again he checked the ground here and there; again he reversed back to the very edge of the side channel. Now I understood the strategy he was exploring – to combine speed and direction so that he could bounce from one hard spot to the next, from this sun-baked tussock to this willow bush to this untouched sliver of grass, using each new base to maintain speed. But each spot had its own quirks, and every intervening metre was a chaos of boggy ruts. It was like trying to hit a target by ricochet, while riding the bullet. He had twice tried, and failed. Seven more times he drew back, fired himself, bounced this way and that, almost turned himself over, stuck with screaming wheels, and reversed. The only thing that gave me any hope was that through it all he remained impassive, and some of his attempts carried him a metre or two further up the slope.

The tenth try was pure magic. The Jeep hit hard tussock,

firm grass, willow bush and path, shot past me at a gallop, bucking like a wild thing, and disappeared over the crest above. Half a minute from bottom to top. It was a brilliant display of planning, confidence, skill and understated courage.

We ran to join him at the top. The last time I had felt so exhilarated was watching the first lunar landings. Maybe my reaction was a trifle extreme; but the last three days had been a roller-coaster of ecstasies and disappointments. It didn't seem to matter that the Jeep had broken a spring on that last insane charge. I stuttered my admiration like a groupie. 'Have you ever, ever done anything like that before?'

'Many times. I have been driving for twenty-three years.'

Why had my companions put themselves into these dire circumstances? Here's a theory: when the human genome researchers finally get around to Mongolian genes, they will discover something unique: a loyalty gene, the result of a mutation that allowed herdsmen to colonize the grasslands 4,000 years ago. This was the genetic heritage exploited by Genghis in life and in death, guaranteeing that he would be brought safely to a secret grave, that I had the right companions to come looking for it, and that his heirs, if they have the knowledge, will keep the secret of his burial safe for ever.

18

THE PROPHET OF
ETERNAL HEAVEN

IT IS A CONSTANT SURPRISE TO SEE WHAT POWER GENGHIS STILL
exerts today. It is, of course, particularly evident in Mongolia.
At a National Day celebration the parade round
Ulaanbaatar's stadium is led by Genghis – in fact the opera
singer Enkhbayar, who played the lead in an epic film about
Genghis. Horsemen bear Genghis's yak-tail standards, black
ones for war, white ones for peace. The great imperial tent-
on-wheels, a wagon 10 metres wide, makes its cumbersome
way round the track, drawn by a team of oxen. A grandstand
of troops display lettered placards that spell out a vast
'Genghis!' A helicopter drops a fluttering 'Genghis' banner.
The face and name are everywhere, on the grandest hotel, a
(German-made) beer, vodka, colleges, institutes – and babies
by the hundred: one day, Mongolia is going to be led by
another Genghis. In 1962 there was that fuss over his 800th
anniversary. Now the anniversaries are crowding in. In 2002
his official 840th was celebrated. It will be a wonder if the
nation can bear to wait for the 850th. Perhaps he will acquire
a birthday, and inspire an annual holiday.

Much of this is nothing more than 'heritage', with no more genuine link to its origins than the Beefeaters at the Tower of London. But Genghis also symbolizes several living aspects of his land and its people: the nation as an independent political entity; the nomadic, herding lifestyle; the spirit of rugged individuality; the feel of the landscape. And that is just in Mongolia. In China, Genghis is also a symbol, but of very different values – those of Chinese unity and imperial grandeur. The two attitudes, the two symbols, the two cultures seem at loggerheads, with worse, perhaps, to come; for Mongolia is poor and empty and struggling, China bursting with people and capitalist ambition. But there is the possibility of resolution, to be found beyond politics, beyond economics, beyond the differences between two powers of vastly disparate scale, in the strangest of Genghis's manifestations.

In Mongolia, Genghis-as-symbol is alive and well right now. Will he remain so? *Should* he remain so? Oyun is well qualified to address the matter. Her brother, Zorig, was one of Mongolia's leading democrats. He had been the prime mover of the pro-democracy movement from 1989, when he was a young political science lecturer. Partly as a result of his work, the entire politburo stepped down in April 1990, opening the way to peaceful elections two months later. In 1998, at the age of 35, he was stabbed to death by assassins who have never been found, a deed that shocked the nation. A bronze statue of this studious, gentle, determined, idealistic figure now presides over a crossroads in central Ulaanbaatar. If Den Barsbolt gives his creation a title, it should be 'The Lost Leader', for Zorig has the aura of a Mongolian Kennedy. Yet not all is lost, because his ideals live on in his sister, now a member of parliament, and in the foundation she established in his memory to promote democracy, transparency, human rights and high moral standards in a political climate of increasing corruption.[1]

Oyun is a remarkable woman in her own right, a scientist with a Ph.D. in geology from Cambridge, proficiency in four languages (Mongolian, Russian, Czech and English) and her own political party. Her huge office, with its view over Ulaanbaatar's main square, the three research assistants, the discreet warble of mobile phones, the austere short-cropped hair, the smart business suit, the incisive manner, the readiness to focus all her attention on my questions – all speak of power, status, smart management and a formidable intelligence. This was a lady prepared to deploy every weapon – looks, education, background – in the service of her ideals. I think we shall all hear more of Oyun, and in my view the more the better.

When I went to see her, I passed a group protesting against a draft law – the poster read 'Protect Our Holy Land!' – that would allow the private ownership of land. This has become necessary in the capital and a few other cities, where people need a legal base to buy and sell individual plots rather than staking claims like squatters. In Ulaanbaatar, where half the population still live in *gers* on the fringes of the city, there are no records of who lives where or any guaranteed rights, and thus no taxation and no services. But the law would also apply in the countryside, where land has always been held in common. The implications of acquiring individual rights over common ground are potentially revolutionary; one dramatic scenario sees huge tracts being bought up by land-lords and then sold off to foreigners, namely the much-feared Chinese. Oyun was among those arguing for debate and caution – to little effect, because the law was passed the next day: suspiciously fast I thought, with long-term effects that can only be guessed at.

This is what Oyun had to say on the subject of Mongolia's number one symbol.

[1] See www.owc.org.mn/zorig_foundation

'These are turbulent times, and people need something to hang on to. Before, people had little, but enough. And now? Look around: what do ordinary Mongolians see? The social fabric torn apart, street children, corruption. People do not see the real fruits of democratic change yet. Democracy is supposed to empower people, but we have seen an increase in poverty and unemployment, and an increasing gap between rich and poor, so a lot of people are *less* powerful, more threatened economically, than they were under communism. Half the population have to struggle to survive. They see the nation threatened by poverty, by weakness. So they look to Genghis and that part of their history as a symbol of strength.

'Genghis's strength lay not just in conquest, but in the idea of just administration rooted in a written legal system (yes, brutal conquest co-exists with an idea of justice in Mongolian minds, because they enjoyed the benefits). There has been no strong rule of law here in the last ten years, not since the introduction of the multi-party system, after seventy years of one-party rule. With pluralism, disagreement is natural. But here there is no notion of a loyal opposition. They – especially the older people – can't take this political fighting. They think Mongolians are fighting each other, dividing the country. My personal opinion is that if you asked Mongolians what they feel, many would say: Since we were once strong, why can't we be again? Shouldn't we have a strong presidential role, a sort of modern version of Genghis Khan? Not that there is any dream of empire, but at least the rule of law.

'Is there an answer? Well, some press for industrialization, western-style development. They say we have to urbanize, *get connected*' – here she gave an ironic laugh at a term degraded by over-use. 'There's a project to build a two-thousand-kilometre east–west highway, the Millennium Road, right across Mongolia. But all this would be to rival other industrialized nations, and court failure. Our countryside would be under threat, our towns polluted, and our industries owned by outsiders.

'There is another way. We need to capitalize on our strength, which lies outside our towns, and under our feet. I believe our competitive advantage lies in three things: our countryside, our nomadic ways and our resources. Genghis knew the strength of the first two – the beauty and purity of our pastures and mountains and deserts, our freedom to wander and raise our animals. What we should be doing is looking back to the rural economy from which we came originally, looking back to look forward. And in this Genghis as a symbol is perfectly valid.

'This does not mean no development. We are a rich country. The Gobi used to be on the edge of an ocean, and as a geologist I know you get interesting things at the edge of an ocean. Just recently, we discovered huge new deposits of copper and gold. Our problem is that we have no infra-structure. But we have high-value resources, rare and expensive minerals that demand very little infrastructure, which could be exploited without damaging the countryside with factories and roads.

'We need economic strength – from our livestock, from wilderness tourism, from our resources – to guarantee our political existence. Yes, this is a serious matter. I was in the Foreign Correspondents' Club in Beijing two months ago, and one young journalist actually said to me, "We have very confused feelings about Mongolia, because Mongolia is part of China!" '

Ah, China: the bogey-man, the spectral giant, where Genghis is the symbol of past strength, and possibly of future assertiveness. I recalled the hints I had seen and heard sug-gesting China's attitude to its historical limits, and the developments that underlie it. Tibet forcibly sucked back into the fold. Mongolia snatched away by the Russians before the Revolution, the theft confirmed after the Revolution, and then reconfirmed by a plebiscite agreed by the defeated and corrupt nationalists, never by the communists. So, in the eyes of those with a sense of history and of what China should be, there is a wrong to be righted; a 'righting' which, if it ever comes to pass, will be done in the name, naturally, of Genghis Khan, because it was his heirs who reunited old China, and thus he, as the founder of a Chinese dynasty, who reasserted the roots of new China, the China now remodelled by the communists in almost-final form. The Communist Party has adopted some of the ways of capitalism, but is still the centralized power, showing no signs of letting go of the reins – or of its opinions about what regions are 'really' Chinese.

There are deep currents at work here, a powerful undertow, hardly noticed at the surface, where individual lives and passing policies ripple and fade.

A century ago the British geohistorian Sir Halford Mackinder started an intellectual fad for what he called 'the Heartland', by which he meant inland Asia. 'He who rules the Heartland,' he wrote, 'commands the world.' Well, not quite. But let's reduce this over-dramatic notion, replacing 'the world' by 'Eurasia'. Then it captures something significant – not a literal truth, because no-one has actually ruled all Eurasia, but a powerful historical tendency that was expressed in its purest form by Genghis and his immediate heirs. Afterwards, technology, in particular gunpowder, made nomadic armies obsolete, and the torch passed to settled cultures, which also contested the Heartland. China, Russia and Japan have all regarded Mongolia, the heart of the Heartland, as strategically crucial, so that the struggle for dominance here has persisted over the centuries. China dominated from 1379 to 1911; then Russia rose, China failed and Mongolia, nominally independent, fell into the Russian fold; but since 1990 Russia has failed, and China is resurgent. Today, the concept of military domination from a geographical heartland is undermined by air power; America can attack Afghanistan from Central Asia, Iraq from the Persian Gulf. But this is not just about warfare; it is about slow change, expressions of *cultural* dominance, with armies in the background, behind the shift of people and the intrusion of corporations.

Where does this leave Mongolia and the legacy of Genghis? Either in a peculiarly dominant position, and/or in a peculiarly dangerous one; and in any event at a turning-point, when the nation, the creation of Genghis, must rethink its nature and its role in the world. Today's version of the Heartland theory is a wider theory of geopolitics, which sees recent history and the immediate future based on rival civilizations. In a popular and powerful statement of this theory, Samuel Huntington argues that there are nine players in the contest of civilizations.[2] The United States is the core of an expanding western empire, of which western Europe is (at present) a part; Islam is another; China a third; Orthodoxy (i.e. Russia) a fourth; the others are Latin America, Africa, Hinduism, Buddhism and Japan. Two of the nine – the West and Islam – have already clashed. It is as well to take seriously the pressure from another, which consists of one-quarter of humanity, namely China. If empires seek to expand, then so do civilizations, with inevitable clashes at their interfaces. Look, for example, at Russia in Inner Asia and China in Inner Asia. In the words of a Russian defence minister, Pavel Grachev, quoted by Huntington: 'The Chinese are in the process of making a peaceful conquest of the Russian Far East.' In addition, Huntington continues, 'China's developing relations with the former Soviet republics of Central Asia may exacerbate relations with Russia. Chinese expansion could also become military if China decided that it should attempt to reclaim Mongolia.'

[2] Samuel P. Huntington, *The Clash of Civilizations and the Remaking of World Order*.

At present, this is all mere theory for armchair geostrategists in the West. But it is a lot less theoretical inside China, where there is a feeling that China is still not quite China, that the 'real' China was the empire as it was under Genghis's heirs, that Genghis is to be admired as the only Chinese ruler to invade Europe *and win*. And not theoretical at all when you sense the visceral antipathy of Mongolians towards the rulers from whom they escaped less than a century ago, and whose businessmen constantly seek opportunities in their former colony.

It may all come to nothing. Or change may be managed with mutual respect and benefit. But half of Genghis's heartland, the half that lies south of the Gobi, has been absorbed already, and its traditional way of life turned into designer chic and tourist fare. It is not beyond the bounds of possibility that the other half will follow. There would be no need for war. The pressure of commerce and slow colonization would be enough. It would be a strange irony if the farmer and urbanite were to take over the remaining heartland of the pastoral nomads; for if they do, it will be in the name of Genghis Khan, the man who made Mongolia part of China. And if Mongols resist this pressure, then they too will do it in the name of Genghis, the man who made China part of Mongolia.

There is a greater irony in all this, an astonishing one, particularly for westerners used to seeing Genghis as destroyer. Whatever the nature of the clash of these two civilizations, its resolution may also be achieved in the name of Genghis, because he is not only a symbol of politics and culture for two very different peoples; he is also a symbol of spirituality, of peace, of the unity of opposites.

In Mongolia there is a spiritual yearning that will not be answered by the current boom in Christian sects or even the rebirth of Buddhism. As Oyun pointed out: 'Religion is supposedly much freer, but although there is a huge religious revival, it is degraded. Take *ovoos*: once *khatags* [the lengths of blue silk that flutter from *ovoos*] were very rare, things to be venerated; in my grandparents' home we had only one or two; now you see them everywhere, and the *ovoos* are covered with rubbish. It makes religion seem superficial. People get the sense that the religious revival is not real.'

But there is a religion that may offer both guidance and authenticity. The Genghis Khan Mausoleum is the heart of this religion in the making, with a developing and (for some) effective set of beliefs. It exists on many levels, echoing the early days of Christianity, with its historical roots, its evolving rituals, its struggles for insight. Perhaps one day the Cult of Genghis Khan will have its breakaway heretics insisting that Genghis, as the Son of Heaven, was more divine than human, wrangling bitterly over how his dual nature should be balanced. For the sect is more than its ceremonies and its community of acolytes. It has genuine spiritual aspirations, formulated by its own theologian, Sharaldai, whose name I had heard at the Mausoleum. He is the author of a book, *Power of Eternal Heaven*, explaining the nature of Genghis's semi-divinity.

I caught up with Sharaldai in Ulaanbaatar, where he had come for a conference on Genghis Khan studies. Over our hotel tea, with the help of Erdene, the animal-husbandry expert, I tackled Sharaldai on the subject of Genghis's divinity, and instantly I was in a different sort of universe, away from ritual and conflicting myths, drawn into the realm of theology and philosophy. Sharaldai did not suffer me all that gladly. He is a Darkhat, with the cult in his blood over generations, and impatient with those, like me, who pretend to a little knowledge.

When I asked whether the Lord's Enclosure was ever associated with miracles, he became quite heated. My question implied a lowering of the purpose of the place. 'The worship of Genghis Khan is a way of connecting us to the Eternal Sky.'

'You mean he is an intermediary?' I was trying to find an equivalent from my own experience. Was the worship of Genghis comparable to Christian worship of, say, the statue of a saint? You direct your prayers to a statue; but the real object is the invisible spirit of the saint; and that is a gateway to God?

'Yes, there are three levels. Look—' He forced himself to be patient. 'The basic tenet of Eternal Heaven philosophy is that we on Earth are part of Eternal Heaven, our system of nine planets. People say we human beings are the highest level of a hierarchy of life. That may be so in terms of biology. But in terms of philosophy, we are a part of Eternal Heaven. To think of ourselves as the top of a hierarchy is to separate ourselves from Eternal Heaven. Our task is to reintegrate ourselves with creation. That's what people don't appreciate today.'

'So when one worships Genghis Khan, does one worship Eternal Heaven through Genghis?'

'It is so. Also you can worship Eternal Heaven directly. You see, there are three components: Eternal Heaven, the *power* of Eternal Heaven and *being subject to* the power of Eternal Heaven.'

This was getting complicated. I had always been baffled by the Trinity.

'Christians say that God is three in one: Father, Spirit, Son.'

'There are similarities. But Eternal Heaven has real power. You can feel it, you can see its effects. That is the difference. Genghis knew that all living things owe their power to Eternal Heaven, and he was able to use it to lead. You can see how we Mongols did this by looking at our three national sports, wrestling, horse racing and archery. A strong body, good horsemanship, accurate shooting. By these means, we conquered half the world.

'But to use power in such a way was not Eternal Heaven's

true purpose. In conquering, we saw that this was not the way to live, bringing suffering to others. What we learned was that the time had come to stop fighting, and live by talking. Now we use our sports to sharpen our mentality, not to fight, but to talk.'

What does this mean for today?

'We are in the process of discovering. I think there are many things we Mongols have not yet understood in *The Secret History*. Some words, some things are still unclear. If we can understand more, we can discover a philosophy that will help the world.'

He was warming to his theme, forgetting me, speaking to his fellow Mongol, Erdene.

'In the world today, there is no philosophy of life! There is science, but science only looks at the surface of things. Science makes nuclear weapons – a stupid weapon, which cannot be used because the user destroys himself! Leaders use nuclear weapons to spread fear, but the power of the weapon does not prevent people like Bin Laden from doing what they want. All of them have forgotten about the existence of the power of Eternal Heaven.'

This was the real purpose of the Mausoleum – to awaken not just Mongols but everyone to their place in the universe. 'It doesn't matter whether the objects are genuine or not. The real significance lies in the connection with the Eternal Sky. So in this sense, as I say in my book' – he pointed to the page for emphasis – '*Genghis Khan is a spirit for all of us*. We are created by Eternal Heaven. If we follow the way, then we shall all be eternal.'

It was an unlikely, extraordinary vision. If – I can hardly imagine it: a flow of priests through the Mausoleum spreading the Word to the outside world, the formation of study groups and peace institutes and pressure groups, all the attributes of a new faith – if Sharaldai's message spreads, there will be those who will teach that Genghis's life was the first faltering line on a graph, which strengthens and soars over eight centuries to these astonishing conclusions: that violence, whatever its initial success, must ultimately fail; and that all conflict should be resolved in peaceful discussion.

This is surely the oddest of all Genghis's transformations: in life, from a 'louse' on a mountain to world-conqueror; after death, to demi-god; and now to a spirit of universal harmony.

BIBLIOGRAPHY

A full bibliography of Genghis and related themes, including books and articles in all the different languages involved, would make a substantial volume. It does not exist. The best bibliographies are in Ratchnevsky (in the English edition, superbly edited by Thomas Haining) and Morgan (invaluable for his expertise in Islamic history). Major works are listed in Nordby. English readers should note the limitations. The two richest sources for Mongol studies are in Persian and Chinese. Very few historians, let alone English-speaking historians, read both, let alone the source material in a dozen other languages. We all depend on translations. Even then, some sources – in particular the Chinese *Yuan-shi* ('Yuan History') – are so opaque that they demand expert commentaries, which themselves have to be translated. The *Yuan-shi* and a prime source in Persian (Rashid ad-Din) are still not fully accessible to English-readers. For 20 years the only Mongol source, *The Secret History*, existed in two versions, one by Cleaves (written in an odd pseudo-biblical style), the other by Onon. Both will shortly be superseded by de Rachewiltz.

The following are the books, articles and chapters that were my main literary sources.

Allsen, Thomas T.: see Franke and Twitchett.

Arnold, Edward: *Geocryology*. London, 1979.

Barthold, W.: *Turkestan Down to the Mongol Invasion*. London, 1977.

Bawden, Charles: *The Mongol Chronicle Altan Tobci*. Wiesbaden, 1955.

Bawden, Charles: *The Modern History of Mongolia*. London, 1989.

Bazargur, Dambyn: *Chinggis Khaan Atlas*. Ulaanbaatar, 1996.

Bulag, Uradyn E.: *Nationalism and Hybridity in Mongolia*. Oxford, 1998.

Bulag, Uradyn E.: *The Mongols at China's Edge*. Lanham, Md, 2002.

Cavalli-Sforza, L. Luca: 'The Spread of Agriculture and Nomadic Pastoralism: Insights from Genetics, Linguistics and Archaeology', in *Origins and Spread of Agriculture and Pastoralism in Eurasia*. London, 1996.

Chambers, James: *The Devil's Horsemen: The Mongol Invasion of Europe*. London, 1979.

Cleaves, Francis Woodman: 'The Historicity of the Baljuna Covenant', *Harvard Journal of Asiatic Studies*, vol. 18, 1955.

Cleaves, Francis Woodman (trans.): *The Secret History of the Mongols*. Harvard, 1982.

Damdinsuren, Ts.: *Mongolin Nuuts Tovchoo* ('The Secret History of the Mongols'). Ulaanbaatar, 1990.

Dunnell, Ruth: 'The Hsi Hsia', in Franke and Twitchett.

Fletcher, Joseph F.: 'The Mongols: Ecological and Social Perspectives', in *Studies on Chinese and Islamic Inner Asia*. Aldershot, 1995.

Franke, Herbert and Denis Twitchett (eds): *The Cambridge History of China*, vol. 6: *Alien Regimes and Border States*, esp. Thomas T. Allsen's chapter, 'The Rise of the Mongolian Empire'. Cambridge, 1994.

Gernet, Jacques: *A History of Chinese Civilisation*, trans. J. R. Foster and Charles Hartman. Cambridge, 1982; 2nd edn 1996.

Grousset, René: *Conqueror of the World*. London, 1967.

Grousset, René: *The Empire of the Steppes*. New Brunswick, NJ, 1970.

Haenisch, Erich: 'Die Letzten Feldzüge Cinggis Han's und Sein Tod', *Asia Minor*, vol. 9, 1933.

Halperin, Charles: *Russia and the Golden Horde*. Bloomington, Ind., 1985.

Heissig, Walter: *A Lost Civilization*. London, 1966.

Heissig, Walter: *The Religions of Mongolia*. London, 1980.

Hung, William: 'The Transmission of the Book known as *The Secret History of the Mongols*', *Harvard Journal of Asiatic Studies*, vol. 14, 1951.

Huntington, Samuel P.: *The Clash of Civilizations and the Remaking of World Order*. New York and London, 1996.

Jackson, Peter (ed.): *The Mission of Friar William of Rubruck*. London, 1990.

Jagchid, Sechin and Paul Hyer: *Mongolia's Culture and Society*. Boulder, Co. and Folkestone, 1979.

Juvaini, Ata-Malik: *Genghis Khan: The History of the World-Conqueror*, trans. and ed. J. A. Boyle. Manchester, 1958; 2nd edn 1997.

Khazanov, Anatoly: *Nomads and the Outside World*. Cambridge, 1984.

Klopsteg, Paul E.: *Turkish Archery and the Composite Bow*. Manchester, 1987.

Lattimore, Owen: *Mongol Journeys*. London, 1941.

Lattimore, Owen: *Studies in Frontier History*. Oxford, 1962.

Li Chih-Ch'ang: *Travels of an Alchemist*, trans. Arthur Waley. London, 1931.

Liddell Hart, Basil: 'Jenghiz Khan and Sabutai', in *Great Captains Unveiled*. Edinburgh and London, 1927.

Martin, H. Desmond: *The Rise of Chingis Khan and his Conquest of North China*. Baltimore, 1950.

Metternich, Hilary Roe: *Mongolian Folktales*. Boulder, Co., 1996.

Mongolian Academy of Sciences and The Yomiuri Shimbun, Japan: *A Report on the Joint Investigation under the Mongolian and Japanese Gurvan Gol Historic Relic Probe Project, 1990–3*.

Morgan, David. *The Mongols*. Oxford, 1986.

Mote, F. W.: *Imperial China 900–1800*. Cambridge, Mass., 1999.

Nordby, Judith: *Mongolia*, World Bibliographical Series, no. 156. Oxford, Santa Barbara and Denver, 1993.

Onon, Urgunge (trans.): *The Secret History of the Mongols*. Leiden, 1990; new edn Richmond, 2001.

Peers, Chris (illus. Michael Perry): *Imperial Chinese Armies (2): 590–1260*. London, 1996.

Peers, Chris (illus. David Sque): *Medieval Chinese Armies, 1260–1520*. London, 1992.

Pegg, Carole: *Mongolian Music, Dance and Oral Narrative*. Washington DC, 2001.

Pelliot, Paul: *Notes on Marco Polo*. Paris, 1959.

Rachewiltz, Igor de: 'Searching for Genghis Qan', *Rivista degli Studi Orientali*, vol. 71 (1997), Rome.

Rachewiltz, Igor de: 'Where is Genghis Khan Buried? Myths, Deceptions and Reality', unpublished paper, 2002.

Rachewiltz, Igor de (trans. and ed.): *The Secret History of the Mongols: A Mongolian Epic Chronicle of the Thirteenth Century*, with a historical and philological commentary, 2 vols. Leiden, Boston and Cologne: Brill, 2004.

Rachewiltz, Igor de, et al. (eds): *In the Service of the Khan: Eminent Personalities of the Early Mongol–Yüan Period (1200–1300)*. Wiesbaden, 1993.

Rashid ad-Din: *The Successors of Genghis Khan*, trans. John Boyle. New York and London, 1971.

Ratchnevsky, Paul: *Genghis Khan: His Life and Legacy*, ed. Thomas Haining. Oxford, 1991.

Rihu Su: 'The Chinggis Khan Mausoleum and its Guardian Tribe', dissertation, University of Pennsylvania, 2000.

Ronay, Gabriel: *The Tartar Khan's Englishman*. London, 1978.

Rossabi, Morris: *Khubilai Khan: His Life and Times*. Berkeley, Los Angeles and London, 1988.

Saunders, J. J.: *A History of Medieval Islam*. London, 1965.

Saunders, J. J.: *The History of the Mongol Conquests*. London, 1971.

Saunders, J. J.: *Muslims and Mongols*. Canterbury, 1977.

Schubert, Johannes: *Ritt zum Burchan-chaldun*. Leipzig, 1963.

Sharaldai, Wu Zhanhai and Liu Yizheng: *Chengjisi Han Yanjiu Wenji 1949–1990* ('A Research Compilation on Genghis Khan, 1949–1990'). Hohhot, 1991.

Silverberg, Robert: *The Realm of Prester John*. New York and London, 1972.

Spuler, Bertold: *History of the Mongols based on Eastern and Western Accounts of the 13th and 14th Centuries*. London, 1972.

Ssanang Ssetsen: *Geschichte der Ost-Mongolen und Ihres Fürstentums*, trans. Isaac Schmidt. St Petersburg, 1829.

Strakosch-Grassmann, Gustav: *Der Einfall der Mongolen in Mitteleuropa in den Jahren 1241–2*. Innsbruck, 1893.

Turnbull, Stephen (illus. Wayne Reynolds): *Siege Weapons of the Far East, (1) 612–1300* and *(2) 960–1644*. London, 2001.

Waldron, Arthur: *The Great Wall of China*. Cambridge, 1997.

Williams, Peter and Michael Smith: *The Frozen Earth: Fundamentals of Geocryology*. Cambridge, 1989.

Xu Cheng and Yu Jun: 'Genghis Khan's Palace in the Liupan Shan and the Official Residence of An-shi Wang' (in Chinese). *Journal of Ningxia University*, vol. 3, 1993, Yinchuan.

Zerjal, Tatiana, et al.: 'The Genetic Legacy of the Mongols', *American Journal of Human Genetics*, vol. 72, March 2003.

INDEX